HORSE LOVERS' LIBRARY

An Expert's Guide to
HORSEBACK RIDING
for BEGINNERS

Louis Taylor

Formerly titled Ride American

Cover photograph

Diamond Chip

Michelle Corson — Owner & trainer

Published by
Melvin Powers
WILSHIRE BOOK COMPANY
12015 Sherman Road
No. Hollywood, California 91605
Telephone: (213) 875-1711 / (818) 983-1105

Printed by

HAL LEIGHTON PRINTING CO.
P.O. Box 1231
Beverly Hills, California 90213
Telephone: (213) 983-1105

LIBRARY OF CONGRESS CATALOG CARD NUMBER: 63-10624

ISBN 0-87980-229-4

Contents

Part I For the Beginner

Part II Variety in American Riding

Part III Selecting the Personal Mount

Part IV Selecting a Registered Horse

Part V Care of the Personal Mount

Part VI Equipment

Part VII Attaining Proficiency

List of plates

Preface

Horses, not readers, prompted this book.

Before tractors and trucks, the great draft horses of farm and city fascinated me as a child. Later I used Percherons in multiple hitches on the heavy horse-drawn equipment sold to farmers during the few years horses were still competing with tractors. I hunted with the Rockyfork Hounds, played enough polo to help get at least one university team on its feet, raised, showed, and dealt in three- and five-gaited, fine harness, and parade horses as well as hunters and stock horses. Before adopting Arizona as my state of residence, I managed one of Kentucky's largest Saddle Horse establishments and taught equitation in universities of Ohio. I have punched cattle in Arizona and Montana and judged horse shows from Sheridan, Wyoming, to Phoenix, Arizona. In short, I have seen most of the silly and gruesome things people do with horses.

When I come to "the Gate where Peter twirls the jangling keys in weariness and wrath" my earnest plea will be for forgiveness for my contribution to man's inhumanity to horse, for I have raised many horses and taught many people to ride. If this book helps diminish the agony humans cause equines, it will have served its purpose.

Acknowledgments

Potent but indirect aid in this work was given by James Ruiz, Ramon Ramirez, and George Miller, whose limitless patience and subtle skill when I started punching cattle in the Superstition country of Arizona saved my life more times than any of us knew. From Ramon (or Prieto, as he was called by his familiars) I learned the use of slack reins in work too fast for the kind of hands I grew up with. Prieto and George were both good men with a bozal; and Jim, a good man in any kind of stock work, taught me many of the virtues of bits I had never seen east of the Pecos.

Of the many friends whose labors assisted at the actual time of writing the book, Cynthia Rigden, excellent horsewoman and student of art, made some of the original sketches and helped with the plan of illustration. Leo Ryan also contributed some sketches; and all those not otherwise identified were done by Rosemary Taylor.

Don Carlson, journalist and photographic expert, gave unsparingly of his time in working over a mass of photographic material and much of the preliminary writing of the book. Annette Jarvis' typing and proofreading were invaluable. A list of the friends who helped with photographs would fill pages of this book. Clubs and breed associations too numerous to list were very kind in giving information and pictures.

My son, Louis, Jr., of Alamogordo, New Mexico, a good horseman wasted by becoming a systems engineer, served as model for some of the drawings.

Introduction

American riding today is composed of a greater variety of horsemanship than has ever before existed in one country at one time. It certainly includes the best of the old traditional "educated" or school riding. It also includes much that the Spaniards learned from the Moors and brought to our shores. Even the American Indian added a few tricks to our trade, after he finally discovered the horse could be ridden as well as eaten.

Yes, our horsemanship, like our language, is a blending of contributions from many lands. But there is a new, a unique quality our horsemanship has. This quality arises from a relationship between horse and man that is brand new.

The old traditional horsemanship that existed before royalty went out of style was based largely on a high degree of collection * and comprised a very formal, complicated, and difficult set of tricks or stunts that the horse was made to perform. As royalty declined in favor, hunting, jumping, and steeplechasing became more fashionable. An Italian cavalry officer discovered the "fluid balance" and the forward seat for jumping. This was all to the good, but old traditional love of form for form's sake led to some very ridiculous uses of this useful though very specialized way of riding.

The set-of-tricks way of riding created a relationship between man and horse in which the horse was a thing to be manipulated, like a machine. He was trained without regard for him as a living creature. The hunter-jumper-forward-seat school went to the opposite extreme and operated on the principle that the horse's "natural" way of doing things should not be interfered with by his rider, whose job was to stay on top, crouched like a monkey if need be, and ride the gaits that a few centuries ago were considered fit only for servants to ride or for pack animals to perform.

* See Glossary.

American riding has relegated the performance of tricks to the circus or specialty acts at horse shows and rodeos. American riding now includes the best of forward, or balanced, seat riding but confines it to the highly specialized fields where it is so useful—jumping and some classes in Western horse shows. The highly skilled modern American horseman is neither a martinet of the old school nor a horseman riding for the sake of the horse like the later school rider. Modern American riding calls for a relationship between horse and rider that is somewhat like that of partners in ballroom dancing. This relationship is most obvious in the two most intensely American fields of riding, the riding of the American Saddle Horse and Western riding. Riders of the American Saddle Horse speak continually of the "airiness" of the horses of their breed. The spontaneity of the great performers is their proudest boast, and yet the stars in the top show, the $10,000 Stake at Louisville, are performing entirely at artificial gaits, as artificial as are the movements in the dance. And they perform at racing speed much of the time in classes that have lasted longer than two hours.

The Western cutting horse knows as many tricks as did any manège horse, but he can perform with no bit in his mouth. His reins are always slack while he performs; and at his best he will do top work under a bare-heeled rider and with the bridle removed. On the trail, the Western horse also works with a slack rein, suiting the degree of collection to the terrain and the work to be done, yet he may carry a Spanish spade bit in his mouth. Ballroom dancers do not have to be locked in close embrace to perform well.

At first glance, American riding may seem very bewildering, contradictory, and complicated; but it is actually the easiest and most comfortable riding in the world. It is fluid and rhythmic, with a follow-through of all movements that makes it very graceful. It compares with traditional horsemanship much as the modern dance compares with traditional ballet, though the modern dance has already given rise to a body of literature and modern American riding has given birth to very few books. Many books about riding are published in America, but most of them are about traditional school riding or about one or another highly specialized kind of American riding.

Literally thousands of Americans today are riding, riding fine horses with fine equipment, in blissful ignorance of dressage (traditional school riding). The ignorance is not all one-sided, for the exponents of traditional riding seem entirely unaware that they are but a small minority of competent American horsemen. They continue to talk and write as if their highly specialized riding were the only highly skilled horsemanship in this country. They ignore two of the major American types of horses and the kinds of riding that are associated with them, the gaited horse and the Western horse. The kinds of riding associated with these horses constitute a very large part of American riding. It is a part of riding that has developed without much recognition. Only within the last quarter of a century have our institutions of higher learning in a few states, notably Kentucky, Ohio, and Missouri, included courses in riding the American Saddle Horse. Western riding, which is even more popular, more widespread than gaited horse riding, and at least as highly skilled, is even less blessed with academic attention, though the fame of Western riding has spread as far as Paris, where the Club Hippique du Lasso is thriving.

Even though it may lack any considerable body of literature and has only recently been recognized academically, American riding is no fledgling. The first book on American riding, and one of the best, *Patrocles and Penelope,* was written in 1885 by T. A. Dodge, the author of a book on the Civil War called by the *London Saturday Review,* "a more accurate outline than any other available record." Colonel Theodore Ayrault Dodge lost a leg in the war but not his ability on a horse or with the pen. The book is well illustrated by "instantaneous photographs" of the author putting his horse over various kinds of obstacles and performing the five gaits of the Saddle Horse. The gaits proper for an American Saddle Horse are very clearly and accurately described, though there is not a complete agreement with the names we now use to designate them. Colonel Dodge died before the term *five-gaited* was coined, but he uses the term *fine-gaited horse* for the animal capable of gaits suitable for saddle use as distinguished from the horse that can only walk, trot, and gallop. The Colonel's depiction of the relation between horse and rider and of the kinds of performance (including jumping) an American horse should be capable of are in accordance with American riding today.

Even the humorous attitude of the American rider toward British rigidity has a very familiar tone as Dodge quotes a contemporary comment on his saddle. (Because of his wooden leg, the Colonel rode a specially padded saddle.) "Naw man can weally wide in a saddle like that, ye know, not weally wide, ye know! Naw fawm, ye know! Wouldn't be tolewated in our school, ye know!"

Since 1885 American riding has improved greatly, but we have had no book on it as comprehensive as Colonel Dodge's *Patrocles and Penelope,* though we have many good books on specialized kinds of riding done in America. The present work will consider the variety of seats and kinds of riding that constitute American riding. It begins with instruction of the young horseman who has no experience and has just acquired a horse.

The writer realizes that in the method he uses he is running into a head-on collision with practically all other modern writers on equitation. It is thought by most writers today that the beginner should start out with the forward or balanced seat and hold every part of himself, from toes to eyebrows, in a prescribed manner. The reason for this sounds logical. It is to the effect that habits are formed early and therefore we should start by assuming the correct posture.

The author once held this very logical view. After years of teaching riding in Midwestern universities and subsequently teaching and observing riding in the West, he has reformed drastically. He has observed, first, that rigidity is the worst enemy of good riding and that rhythm is the most necessary companion to balance; second, that starting to ride in the logical way almost invariably causes rigidity, and that awareness of rhythm seems impossible to most riders when they are concentrating on an "unnatural" position with almost every part of their body.

By starting with what, for want of a better name, we call the "natural" or "basic" seat, we can have as much relaxation as we want and can concentrate on rhythm and balance. After we feel at home and are one with the horse while riding this primary seat, we can easily make such changes as are needed to become expert at any one of the very different specialized seats, each of which demands rhythm, balance, and a certain degree of relaxation.

Any rider who does not like this approach can easily skip the first chapters, turn to the discussion of the particular kind of riding he admires, and start from there.

We shall devote more attention to Western riding than to other kinds because more people are riding Western than ever before and because less writing has been done on this kind of horsemanship than on others. We shall consider the selection of the horse, especially of the horse to be owned by the rider who will keep only a horse or two. The writer will certainly not hide his own preferences, but he will present as objectively as is possible the special virtues and faults common to each breed. He does this so the young horseman wishing to own a purebred horse may choose from the breed best suited to his needs and taste and may avoid the disappointments that are perhaps too common among beginning horsemen of all ages.

The care of the personal mount and of his tack, the handling of the horse in a trailer, the shoeing of the horse, and common sense, courtesy, and safety to mount and man on the trail and in the field are subjects we shall also cover. Attention will be given to the problems of the young rider who is beginning to participate in small shows, and to those of the young rider who is furthering the training of his own mount.

The writer knows the importance to horsemen of shows and other competitions. He also knows that more riders are to be found on trails and in open country than are to be found in competitions. One book cannot answer all questions of the aspiring horseman, or give him all the instruction he needs. This one is intended to answer some of them and point the way to finding answers to others.

Part I

FOR

THE

BEGINNER

1

Getting ▨▨▨▨▨▨▨▨▨▨▨▨▨▨▨▨
acquainted ▨▨▨▨▨▨▨▨▨▨▨▨▨
with a horse ▨▨▨▨▨▨▨▨▨▨▨

Let us assume you have always wanted a horse. I always did. From as far back as I can remember, the shape, the color, the general form of a horse were satisfying to look at. Even toy horses were better than other toys. I had toy horses—all shapes and sizes of them. Whenever I could be with real horses I was happier than ever. I liked to watch a horse eat or just stand in the corral making slight movements with ear or tail, or maybe stamping a foot to scatter the flies pestering his ankles. I felt comfortable with horses, and I was delighted when I thought one was paying any attention to me. How I wanted one! A pony or a horse, it didn't matter.

So let us begin this book by assuming that you have always wanted a horse and now you have one! Even if you have had him for some time it won't be difficult to remember that first thrill of having a horse of your own. And if you do not yet have a horse, you are still in luck, for maybe you can learn a few things that will help you avoid some mistakes new owners often make. Maybe you can learn some things that will help you enjoy that horse even more when you do get him.

Now if you are going to be a lifelong horseman, you must always remember that you have a horse because you just plain like horses. Don't laugh at what I just said! Lots of people forget that. They get so excited at the idea of having a better horse than somebody else, at the idea of winning some kind of competition, that they lose all the fun they once found in just being with a good horse. The horse is no longer a friend, no longer really a part of them—just a machine for doing stunts. Not that stunts aren't fun. They are, especially on horseback. Later, after you are a real horseman, you can learn about all the stunts and the very special kinds of riding that call for special kinds of saddles—like hunting and jumping or fancy drill teamwork that call for the very latest American inventions in saddles and seats. Then, too, there will be the very special balanced Western seat for the cutting horse and the stock horse. These are all fascinating and you can learn about them without losing your enjoyment of horses.

Yes, some people do lose their enjoyment of horses, even lose all their friendship for them, by becoming specialists too soon. They may be pretty good specialists for a while, but pretty soon they ride only in competition. Then, finally, they don't even ride, don't even lay their hands on their own horses, or even have horses. They just talk about them.

This doesn't have to be the way of it. The real horseman—and there are lots of them, though not so many of them as of the other kind we just described—the real horseman first learns horses thoroughly. He learns how to communicate with them, how to "talk" (with movement, tone, and balance) so that a horse can understand, whether he is under saddle or in the corral. The real horseman learns thoroughly the basic things about riding—balance, rhythm, and timing, especially timing. Most important of all, he learns lessons so well that his horse can "talk" to him. Can you walk into the corral with your horse and tell how he is feeling? When you are riding, can he "talk" to you through the reins constantly, as you do to him? Are you so aware of the whole living creature, from the tip of his ears to the bottom of his heels, that you know what he is going to do before he does it? Do you anticipate his movements almost unconsciously as you did those of your partner at the dance when you won the prize waltz contest? If you can't say yes to these questions, you are not ready to specialize in your riding, unless you just want a brief fling at competitive riding and then care no more for horses.

Learn to be a real horseman, who can say yes to all our questions. Then you can star in any specialty and also go right on enjoying your horse.

We are assuming you now have your first horse. Let's assume a name for him, because it's going to be a little difficult to talk about him without one. Let's call him Juanito, for that's the name of my favorite horse.

The first thing to do is to get acquainted with your Juanito. If he has had several owners or has had one that was not particularly fond of horses, the chances are that Juanito will expect little consideration from you. All you will need to do is be careful that you do not suddenly pop up at either end of him and startle him. If you do so at one end, he will kick, unless he has had some very painful "conditioning." It is as natural and as involuntary for a horse to kick when startled from behind as it is for you to jerk your hand away when you touch something surprisingly hot. If the startling is at the front end, his reaction is to jerk back. This might be expensive, for halters cost money. Also, when a horse jerks back on a halter or rope, it hurts him. His immediate and involuntary reaction is to pull harder to get away from the pain. If the halter breaks, he soon sets up the habit of being a halter puller and will require some expert retraining.

If your first meeting with Juanito is in a corral, and he has grown accustomed to the bad manners of human beings from being owned by several, or one unthinking one, you can probably walk quietly right up to his shoulder without getting any sign of recognition from him. The shoulder is the proper place to approach. Walk close to it before putting out your hand. He may have learned that a hand poked out in space at him means trouble. When you shake hands with someone you do not stand four feet away and then stretch your hand out as far as you can reach to touch the friend's hand.

If Juanito stands still, touch him quietly, not nervously, on the shoulder. Move your hand over his withers and then around his neck, working it up toward his head. If he stands quietly while you stroke his neck a very little on the side away from you, you know he has not been abused in the corral, at least not at the time of haltering. Don't jerk your hand away and yell, "Whoopee. I can catch him." Move your hand quietly and step away from him, to return with a handful of grain, or to go about other business of your own.

If Juanito will not stand for you to put your hand over his withers you may not be behaving the way he has learned to expect.

If he turns his rump toward you as you approach and hurries to the other side of the corral, he may be used to being roped. This is unfortunate but not tragic. It may take quite a while to give him confidence that you will not throw a rope at him. I have a stocky little Quarter Horse that was my favorite trail horse before Juanito was old enough to climb mountains carrying a couple of hundred pounds on his back. This horse, Shorty by name, had a brilliant career as a bulldogging horse and a calf roper before he came to me. He had always been roped when caught up out of a corral. It took me several months to get him to stand while I walked up to his shoulder with a rope halter in my hand. I have had him several years now; and to save time I put my hand on his hip and work quietly up to his withers when I go to halter him in the corral. This, of course, would not be safe procedure if I did not thoroughly understand his "language" or if he did not have confidence in me.

If your Juanito is shy in the corral, do not dodge about and try to corner him. If you do so, you will be telling him you are dangerous, and he will do his best to avoid the danger.

The easiest thing to try first is a gunny sack feedbag. Almost any horse that has been roped in a corral is used to eating from such a feedbag. With two hands spread the headstall open and hold it out in front of you so that he can come up at right angles to you or slightly from your rear to get his head into it. When he has his nose in the feed, put the headstall over his ears and also a light rope; a clothesline will do, though of course you would not tie him up with it. Never stand directly in front of a horse when you are putting on or taking off a nosebag. He will shake the bag to get at the feed, especially about the time you are ready to take it off, and may give your midriff quite a punch with his nose. This may be no more than your carelessness deserves, but it will certainly make you jump or fall; and this will frighten the horse and make him silly about feedbags. As soon as the horse is finished with the little feed you have given him, you can take off the feedbag and lead him where you will with the light rope, which you can replace with halter or bridle. Of course you will leave the light rope on until you have the halter or bridle put on properly.

The horse that is shy in the corral should wear a halter or a light rope (one that will break easily if it gets caught) when loose in the corral. Soon a little feed in your hand will bring him to you, and you can quietly take hold of the rope or halter. Never grab at the halter or rope. If you do so, he will soon be afraid of your hand and will duck faster than your eye can follow.

If the feedbag method fails, competent help is your solution. It may take some time before you can communicate to your horse that the corral is not full of the dangers he has learned to associate with corrals. By quietness and patience two horsemen can convince him that no pain is going to follow being caught in the corral. Gradually the handful of grain will do the job. You need one caution here: don't fool your horse. Don't hold out your hand as if you had feed when you don't. When you learn to "talk horse," you can make a bargain with a horse and he will keep it without fail. It is up to you to prove to him you are equally trustworthy.

Horse Intelligence

Now, as much as you think of horses and as much as I love and respect them, there is one thing we must realize a horse cannot do: he cannot speak or "understand" English, or any other spoken language. Your voice, later on, will communicate a good deal to him. Some individual words will become signals for him, but don't expect him to understand the way a human does. This is not in agreement with the now popular notion that a horse has very limited "intelligence." His practical "intelligence" is a lot better than yours. Almost any honest cowboy can tell you that he has had his life saved by a horse who disobeyed in some crisis, proving that he knew more, saw or heard more, than his rider. Your horse can spot a deer that you can't see, hear, or smell. He can tell what a cow is going to do before you can even guess she is going to do anything at all, but the part of your brain that handles abstractions above a certain level, which includes speech as we use it, the horse does not have. No, the horse will never be able to invent devices for blowing up the world or to preach moral precepts. If that makes him inferior to man, then so be it.

Learning "Horse Talk"

Now to come back to your Juanito who is a little green in the corral. He doesn't turn away like a horse that has been roped. He just moves away so you can't get your hands on him readily. Don't try to sweet-talk him into your confidence and then lose your temper when this doesn't work. As I have taken some pains to point out, you aren't "getting through" to him when you use words. His language is movement—and a good many other things. If there are not too many other horses in the corral (and there should not be any at all if Juanito is a valuable animal) and if you have unlimited patience, there is one sure way of getting him to come up to you. Just stand or sit still long enough. Often I have been able to get a scared range-raised colt to come up to me by putting all my attention on some little object on the ground and examining it with my foot and stooping over it very attentively. This requires patience that makes Job look like a novice, but it works.

If Juanito is shy from inexperience, don't try to catch him the first day. Spend plenty of time with him in the corral. Gradually he will lose his fear. If you let him make the first advances and then make yours very carefully, you will reach the point where anything you do in the corral will be all right with him, including putting a rope around his neck.

If this method is too slow for your patience, then you will have to have the help of a good horseman—be sure he is a quiet and intelligent person—to get a halter on your horse. With a halter on Juanito you can catch him with feed in your hand and handle him in the corral until he has confidence in you and—more important— until you have learned to understand "horse language" enough to enable him to communicate with you. Lead him from his left side, walking even with his shoulder. Learn how to push against his shoulder with your elbow to get him to turn to the right and to pull him toward you to make a left turn. You can't do all this in one short lesson. Juanito may have been led by someone who thinks a horse should be pulled along like a mechanical toy on a string, with the man walking in front of the horse. If so, start around the corral in the manner he is accustomed to. Gradually you can shorten the lead shank. Finally you can walk beside his head, holding a very short shank. If Juanito is very quiet, a bit on the sluggish side, you can use a stick some three feet long. Of course if you touch him on the side nearest you, he will not go forward. He will just swing his hips away from you. However, if you can reach across his back and touch him with the stick on the right hip, he may get the idea and move forward so you can lead him by walking beside his shoulder.

Handling the Feet

Part of this job of getting acquainted with Juanito in the corral is the business of getting him to stand while you pick up his feet. After you and he have become fairly well acquainted by doing things in the corral together, you should be able to hold him with your left hand, with a foot of shank between your hand and the halter, while you pick up a front foot. Start with the left foot. Run your hand down his shoulder and down his leg until your fingers are around the big tendon between his knee and his ankle. Pull for-

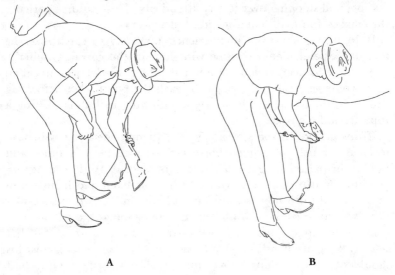

A   B

Fig. 1. Picking up horse's front foot. *A* With left hand pull cannon forward to get weight off front foot; *B* with right hand lift hoof toward horse's elbow.

ward until he raises his foot slightly. Then let go and pat Juanito on the shoulder. As soon as he will easily give to the pressure of your hand, you are ready to pick up his foot. The first time you try this, you should tie him to a safe fence or tree so both your hands are free. With your left hand put the usual pressure on the tendon to get the weight off his foot. Then with the right hand lift the foot up toward his elbow. (See Fig. 1.) When the foot is off the ground, keep both the pastern and knee bent. Do not try to pull any horse's foot straight forward off the ground until you are a professional or until you are communicating so well with the horse that he understands and trusts you perfectly. As long as you keep the leg doubled up, you can maintain control whether Juanito understands what you want or not, but you cannot hold a horse's foot off the ground in a forward position if he objects at all.

Grooming

Grooming your horse is as useful in getting acquainted with him before riding as is handling him on a lead shank. When you get ready to groom Juanito, "cross-tie" him if there is a convenient place in your corral or barn; that is, a place which provides a pair of solid anchors for ropes or chains. The anchors can be walls or trees or posts at least ten feet apart. Fasten a ring on the anchor at each side about the height of your horse's head. The rings should be large, so ropes will slip through them easily. Place Juanito between the anchors. Fasten a rope into each side of his halter with a snap. Tie the other ends of the rope to the anchor rings by a bowknot that you can untie easily by pulling it. The ropes should be just tight enough to keep him from putting his head to the ground when he stands with his head directly between the anchor rings. This will allow him a little freedom of movement but will not let him move more than a step or two either forward or back. If Juanito is of a fussy and nervous disposition, his first lessons on the cross-tie must be for only a few minutes, and you will have to keep one hand on his halter while you give a few strokes with a brush to his mane and neck. Gradually he will learn to stand on the cross-tie without twisting his hips around under it while you give him a thorough grooming, which will include picking up his feet and cleaning them out.

If a good place for a cross-tie is not available, you can get along very nicely by tying Juanito to almost anything solid that has no wire or other booby trap for him to put a foot into. If possible tie him about the height of his withers with a rope that is just long enough to let him put his head to the ground without any slack left over to put his foot through.

Establishing a Relationship

While you are grooming him you can learn how he "talks." Your Juanito may have been owned by someone who paid no attention to horse talk. If so, he will not be expressive at first. A dog never seems to give up the hope that his master will have sense enough to understand him. The dog's talk is so obvious that even the most insensitive human being cannot help but see it. A horse, on the other hand, will soon give up trying to communicate with a human being who does not respond. He is never as obvious in the movements he uses for communication as the dog. Little movements of ear or muzzle, sometimes very slight, may be all he uses; and he never wags his tail. However, if you learn horse talk about unimportant affairs while grooming or working about the corral, you will be on the road to communication with your horse when you start riding him. You will learn how much pressure it takes to make him move a step to one side or the other, how much to pull and when to pull on a halter shank to stop or turn him. You will also begin to learn the most difficult and endless part of the study of horse communication —timing. The horseman who knows the "how much" and "when" of each movement of his communication with his horse is ready for *haute école* work or almost any other difficult equestrian activity.

Later on, I shall talk about more advanced work on foot with your Juanito and about the first step in teaching him to be supple in his quarters so you can move his hindquarters as exactly and easily as you can his forehand. But this first groundwork will lay the foundation for all the rest of your horsemanship, give you an "eye," a "feel" for a horse. Many people who have grown up with horses and ridden more or less for years do not really see a horse. Such people are never aware of very much of the horse they are riding. They are the ones who tell you, "You can never trust a horse." They should say, "I can never trust a horse," for though a horse tells them what he is going to do, they are utterly oblivious of his telling.

I live close to a good private school that pays a good deal of attention to horsemanship. Some of the students own their own horses. A few weeks ago I looked out my window and saw a young man talking to two young ladies. He had evidently just dismounted from a very fine rope horse which I knew he had recently purchased. The young man's back was to the horse and he was engaged in what must have been a very interesting conversation with the young ladies. As I watched, I saw evidence that the horse had been trained by a horseman who knew horse talk. The horse grew weary of standing. He first very softly gave a little scrape of the ground with one forefoot. Then he shook his head. The young man was so interested in talking to the girls that he was utterly unaware of the horse. Finally, the horse nudged the talker's elbow with his nose. Whereupon, the young man, possibly to show before the ladies his masculinity and superiority over the beast, gave the horse's nose a terrific blow with his elbow. The startled animal jumped back; but he was so well trained that the minute he felt the rein taut, he moved up again.

Today I saw the same scene out my window, but with two exceptions. The horse no longer had the alert look or the apparent interest in human beings that he had had several weeks ago. Also, he wore a tie-down (a strap running from noseband to girth), which may have been evidence that the young man was so out of tune with his mount that he had been hit in the face by his horse's head a time or two.

This little story should tell you two things about your early experience with Juanito. First, if you want him to be machinelike in his later performance, do not encourage him to express himself. Have him whip-broken by a competent trainer (the whip-broken horse comes to you in corral or stall at the snap of your finger or other similar signal). Begin early to correct him, firmly but not in anger, if he wants to nudge your elbow. This will make sense to him and save him from later surprises. On the other hand, if you want a horse with spontaneity, respond to him when he talks. Even an aged horse that has never known human responsiveness will gradually begin to talk to a person who is always aware of him. A friend of mine says he would sooner ignore a good morning from a neighbor than fail to acknowledge his horse's greeting. Needless to say, my friend's horses are quite expressive.

Make up your mind what kind of relationship you want to establish with your Juanito and be sure you maintain it. He will do his best to do likewise if you give him half a chance to find out what it is you want.

Saddling

THE FLAT OR ENGLISH SADDLE

When you and Juanito have become acquainted and can talk and have some confidence in each other, it is time to think about riding. Certainly the first riding should be done with a saddle. (Bareback riding would teach you the bad habit of hanging on with the reins.

It is very useful in more advanced stages of learning balance, but should be done in an arena and without reins.) *For saddling, you should have Juanito on the cross-tie,* haltered of course (never cross-tie a bridled horse!).

Let us imagine at first that you are using a flat saddle, for that is the easiest kind to put on. If your saddle was properly put up the last time it was used, the stirrups were run up on the leathers as described in Chap. 18, and you will not have to do anything with them until your saddle is on your horse and ready for mounting. If the stirrups are not run up on the leathers properly, approach your saddle from its left side and pull the right stirrup across the seat of the saddle so that it hangs down on the side of the saddle toward you. If the girth is not already across the seat of the saddle and hanging down on your side of the saddle, make it do so now. (If the last person to use your saddle was extremely correct, he unfastened the girth from both sides of the saddle and laid it across the seat.)

Your flat saddle pad is a fitted one having straps with loops through which the saddle billets pass and hold the pad to the saddle, as detailed in Chap. 15. Pick saddle and pad up by running your left arm under the pad from the pommel end. Then quietly approach Juanito from his left side. If you are not very tall and Juanito is a full-sized horse, you will have to raise your saddle by taking hold of it with your left hand on the pommel and your right hand on the cantle, the raised back part, taking care to hold pad as well as saddle in each hand. Let the saddle down on his back quietly but don't dally. Overcaution or hesitancy on your part may well make Juanito think something horrible is about to happen. The saddle should be let down on the horse's back so that the front of the saddle comes just to the back edge of his shoulder blades. Then put your right hand firmly on the center of the seat of the saddle and wiggle it until it settles so that it is about the width of two of your fingers behind its original position. Most inexperienced horsemen put a saddle too far to the rear (as do the horsemen who bring gaited horses into the show ring). If your saddle wiggles too far back, do not slide it forward. This would ruffle the hair under it. Raise it up and place it at the edge of the shoulder blades again and repeat the settling process.

With your saddle properly placed, go around to the right side of your mount and see that all flaps and straps are hanging properly, not doubled up under the saddle, and that the pad is showing equally on both sides and at front and back of the saddle. If the girth has been detached on the right side, buckle it on that side. Pull the right stirrup from the seat of your saddle if it is still across the seat. See that the girth is hanging straight, not caught up by the saddle flap.

Now return to the left side of your horse. If the stirrup is hanging down, place it across the seat of your saddle so it will be out of your way while you fasten the girth. The girth should be about the width of your hand behind your horse's elbow. Fasten the saddle not too tightly at first and run two or three fingers of your hand under it just below the saddle flap. Then run your fingers down, straightening any wrinkles of skin under the girth.

On a round-backed horse with low withers, the inexperienced horseman is apt to pull a saddle to one side when he fastens the girth. If you have done so, don't try to push the saddle back in place without unfastening the girth.

Now take Juanito off the cross-tie and lead him a few steps. Then bring him back to the cross-tie and tighten up your saddle. Unless you are a very athletic person you are not apt to get a flat saddle too tight at this first tightening. If the saddle starts to turn when you mount, you do not have it tight enough. In such event, unbuckle the saddle and start over again.

THE STOCK (WESTERN) SADDLE

Now let us put a stock, or Western, saddle on Juanito, a stock saddle with a full rigging as detailed in Chap. 15. Your saddle blanket should be placed so that its front edge comes several inches ahead of the back of the shoulder blades. When you have finished saddling, there should be more blanket in front of the saddle than behind it. Most inexperienced riders place blankets too far to the rear. That is why I have in my tack room a good blanket or two that I have found on the trail used by winter visitors.

If your saddle blanket is a Navajo, the stripes should run across your horse's back; otherwise the withers will soon split it.

Be sure the blanket is free from wrinkles. Then go to the left side of your saddle as it hangs on the rack. Pull both cinches and the right stirrup across the seat of the saddle so they all hang down on your side. With your left hand holding the fork and your right hand holding the cantle, lift the saddle up and let it down on Juanito's back so that the front of the saddle comes just to the back edge of his shoulder blades. Settle it into position as I described for the flat saddle. Then go around to Juanito's right side and pull cinches and stirrup off the seat of the saddle and see that they are hanging clear and straight. Be sure the saddle strings are not caught up under the saddle and that you have not wrinkled the blanket in putting on the saddle.

Return to the left side and cinch up the front cinch. Remove wrinkles as I described for the flat saddle. The cinch should be a hand's width (of a small hand) behind the elbow. Next, be sure that the strap that holds the hind cinch to the front cinch is a good one and that it is short enough to keep the hind cinch hanging straight down. If the hind cinch can slip back, it will be a signal to buck. (Even for an inexperienced horseman it should not be necessary to say that a beginner should never put a hind cinch on a horse unless he has become used to one. If you are not sure that Juanito has been used with a full-rigged saddle, take the hind cinch off your saddle and put it out of sight!)

Now buckle the hind cinch. Have it just tight enough so that there is no daylight shining between it and your horse's belly—a little circulation of air will do no harm. Now untrack your horse, turn him around and bring him back to the cross-tie again. Then tighten up your front cinch. Tighten it just enough to keep the saddle from turning when you mount. With a good latigo strap, you can pull a saddle cruelly tight and develop a vice in any horse, to say nothing of cinch galls. The hind cinch needs no tightening now, but after you ride a few miles it is very wise to see that your hind cinch is tight enough to keep from catching a hind foot when a horse strikes at flies on his belly.

Bridling

To bridle Juanito, take him off the cross-tie and into a stall or corner of the corral where he will not be tempted to wander while you are learning to bridle him. You have your bridle held by the crown and reins in your left hand, which is the only way to pick up or carry a bridle. If your reins are not fastened at the ends, tie a knot in them for your present purpose. Stand at Juanito's left, just behind his head and close to him. With your right hand slip the reins over his head right behind his ears. Remove the halter. If Juanito starts to wander, you can control him by grasping the reins under his throttle. That's why you put them behind his ears instead of way back on his neck.

Now take the crown of the bridle in your right hand and bring the palm of your left hand up under the bit, but never use the left hand to raise the bit. With your right hand raise the bridle and bring it into position so that Juanito's nose is between the cheek pieces of the bridle and in the noseband, if your bridle has one. With your left hand you are now *guiding* the bit so that it comes between his lips and against his teeth, but you are not *lifting* the bit with your left hand.

If Juanito does not open his mouth, a finger or thumb put between his lips will probably get him to do so. (An all-wise Providence made the horse with a mouth that has no teeth where the bit goes.) If this does not work, the pressure of a thumbnail or fingernail on the bar of the mouth (the part the bit rests on) will prove effective. As the horse opens his mouth, your *right* hand should raise the bridle so the bit slips into place. Then you will slip the crownpiece over the ears and buckle the throatlatch. (See Fig. 2.) Buckle it about three holes looser than you think it should be. When a horse tucks his head in, he needs plenty of room in the throatlatch. Most greenhorns buckle the throatlatch so tight that the horse suffers when collected. They also do dreadful things with the curb chain or strap. You will find explanation of such things, as well as of adjustment of bridles, in Chap. 16.

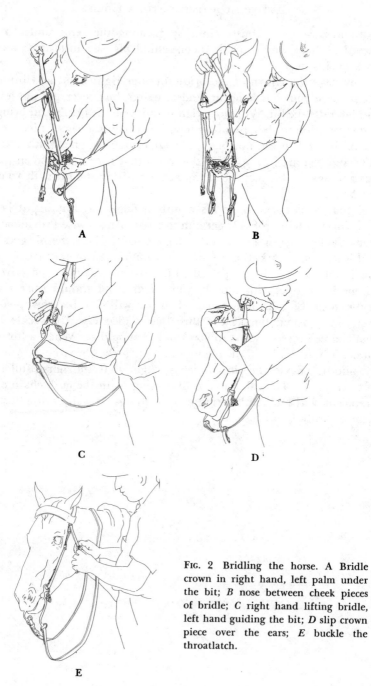

FIG. 2 Bridling the horse. A Bridle crown in right hand, left palm under the bit; B nose between cheek pieces of bridle; C right hand lifting bridle, left hand guiding the bit; D slip crown piece over the ears; E buckle the throatlatch.

2

Mounting ╾▰▰▰▰▰▰▰▰▰▰▰▰▰▰▰
and ╾▰▰▰▰▰▰▰▰▰▰▰▰▰▰▰▰▰
dismounting ╾▰▰▰▰▰▰▰▰▰▰▰▰

Mounting

Now that your horse is saddled and bridled, it is time to mount. The first thing to do is to put him in a corner of a corral or other place where he will not be tempted to move forward. Then gather your reins in your left hand right over the horn or pommel of the saddle or over Juanito's mane just in front of the saddle. In the hand that has gathered the reins, also take a good hold of the saddle or of the mane. Be sure when you take hold of the mane that you have plenty of hair. A little bit of mane in your hand will pull and hurt Juanito. With your right hand adjust the reins so they are even and so that you can just feel his mouth. The reins should not be tight enough to signal him to back up or so loose that you cannot put pressure on the reins instantly if he starts to move forward.

Now stand close to Juanito's left shoulder, facing his croup. Put your left foot in the left stirrup. You may help your foot by holding the stirrup in the right hand and turning the proper side of the stirrup toward your foot, but be sure to keep a firm hold on the front of the saddle or mane and of the reins. Never relax the hold of your left hand while you are trying to put your foot in the stirrup. If you cannot reach the stirrup when you are standing close to Juanito's shoulder, you may have to change your stance and stand

17

facing the middle of your saddle just opposite the middle of the horse. The height of the horse and the length of your leg will dictate how near you can come to standing close to Juanito's shoulder, the proper place when mounting.

When you have the ball of your left foot in the stirrup, put your right hand on the cantle of your saddle. Then spring from your right foot high enough to straighten the left leg while you are facing the rear of the saddle. When your left leg is straightened, remove your right hand from the back of the saddle. Put it on the front of the saddle and swing your right leg over your horse and sit down in the saddle, placing the ball of your right foot on the tread of the right stirrup. (See Fig. 3.) As you settle into your saddle, you will of course release the hold of your left hand on the horn or pommel of your saddle or on the mane, while at the same time keeping the reins in your left hand and not allowing them to slip through your fingers. While doing this be careful that you do not make such a sudden move with your left hand that you are signaling Juanito to move or to do something that he doesn't quite understand. If you have inadvertently done this and he moves forward, pull gently on your reins until he stands still. Stroke him quietly with your right hand and speak to him gently in a calm voice. Then put him back in the place where he was standing when you were mounting.

Checking Stirrups

When Juanito is again quiet and sure that you want him to stand still, the next thing to do is to check the length of your stirrups. To do this, keep your feet level with the ground; straighten your knees and hips so that you are standing straight in the stirrups. Then you should just clear the seat of your saddle by two inches. If you cannot do this, your stirrups are too long. If you clear the seat of the saddle by more than two inches, your stirrups are too short.

An alternate way to check the stirrups is to take your feet out of the stirrups and let your legs hang down as far as they can. When you are in this position the treads of the stirrups should just reach the bottom of your ankles. If you are sitting in the middle of your saddle, these two ways of checking stirrup length will do for both Eastern and Western saddles for the first seat that you will use when riding either kind of saddle.

This may seem strange to you if you have heard a good deal of

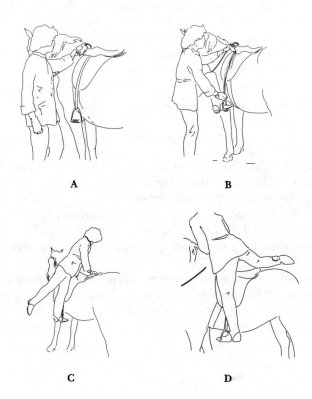

A

B

C

D

Fig. 4

Fig. 3. Prepare to mount. *A* Take a good hold of mane with bridle hand; *B* help foot with right hand if necessary, but keep firm hold of mane and reins with left hand. *C* Straighten left leg before starting to swing right leg over horse; *D* swing right leg clear of horse.

Fig. 4. In mounting stock saddle use same procedure as in Fig. 3, except that horn instead of mane may be held in same hand with reins.

talk about how hard it is to ride an Eastern saddle after riding Western or how hard it is to ride Western if you have been riding Eastern. The only important difference between the Eastern and Western saddle, as far as you are concerned at this stage of your riding career, is that the stirrups of the Eastern saddle are hung farther forward than are the stirrups of the Western saddle (unless you have a specially built saddle of either kind).

The Basic Seat

For your first riding, whether on a stock saddle or flat saddle, you will use what I like to call the natural or basic seat. All the other seats are merely variations or adaptations of this basic or natural seat. We shall later study carefully the ever-changing center of balance of the horse and find that each special seat is useful for special performance calling for special placing of the horse's center of gravity.

Now that your stirrups are properly adjusted, this is the way to assume a natural or basic seat. (See Fig. 5.) Place the balls of your

FIG. 5. Basic seat—Western. Position same as in flat saddle.

feet on the stirrup tread. Your heels should be no higher than your toes. In an Eastern saddle, your stirrup will be directly below your knee, with your stirrup leather vertical. In a stock, or Western, saddle the stirrups are hung a little farther back and your knees will be a little ahead of your feet. Your heels should be just forward from a point directly below the place where the weight is greatest in the saddle. The insides of your knees and the insides of your calves should be comfortably close to the saddle. (See Fig. 6.) If your knees and calves are in the right position and your toes are no higher than your heels, you do not need to worry about keeping your toes in or keeping your toes out. Your feet will naturally be in the right position. This is about forty-five degrees from parallel with your horse.

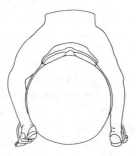

FIG. 6. Leg position. Right leg correct; left leg incorrect. Inside of right leg comfortably close to the saddle.

To keep the feet parallel with your horse's side, you can easily see, will mean cramping your ankles; and you cannot point your toes out if you keep the inside of your knees and calves comfortably close to the horse's side. The leg from hip to knee inclines forward at about a forty-five-degree angle. This will vary slightly with the relation of the size of horse to the size of rider, because the curve on the inside of the leg just below the knee must be in contact with the widest part of the horse's barrel just behind the shoulder, and the rider's hips should be over the middle of the saddle. Therefore, the tall rider on the small-barreled pony will have his thighs more nearly horizontal than will the short man on the big-barreled horse.

The position of the torso on the saddle and the position of the curve below the knee in relation to the horse's barrel are more important than the slope of the thigh. The position of the body weight on the saddle we shall discuss presently. The position of the curve below the inside of the knee must be correct for gripping, an important part of riding, often misused and usually overused, which we shall consider when you have ridden enough to use it without becoming stiff. Any rigidity or cramping of muscles, any discomfort of any kind at this stage of your riding, is an indication that you are doing something wrong. In this basic or natural seat you should sit flexibly erect. Your shoulders are directly above or slightly behind your hips. Your back is straight or slightly convex. The weight of your body is carried on the center of the seat of the saddle largely by the bony structure rather than the fleshy part of the buttocks. The upper part of the thighs carries some of the body weight, especially at movements faster than a slow uncollected walk.

Dismounting

Before starting out on your first ride, it is a very good idea to try to dismount. To dismount properly, do it this way: Gather your reins in your left hand as you did when mounting, get a good hold of the mane, or the front of the saddle, with the left hand as it holds the reins. Then put your right hand on the front of the saddle. Put your weight on your hands and on your left stirrup. (See Fig. 7.) Stand up in your left stirrup and swing your right leg across the rear of the horse and saddle. Then move your right hand to the back of the saddle. Put your weight on both hands and lift your left foot out of the stirrup. Then let both feet reach the ground at the same time. (See Fig. 8.) Then you may release the hold on the horse's mane and let the right reins slip free from your left hand, but be sure to retain the left reins and shorten them a little.

Now it is time to remount and start your first ride. Be sure Juanito is placed so that he will not want to start forward. Mount as you have already learned. This time you may come down in the deepest part of your saddle in the basic or natural seat. You are now ready to take hold of the reins and begin to talk to Juanito on the reins.

Picking Up the Reins

I will have a good deal to say later on in this book about the use of the double bridle. But let us assume that at this stage of your riding you are using a single bridle. Now take your reins in your right hand. Place your left hand in front of your right hand with the back of the hands toward the horse's ears and your fingers pointing toward the ground. Put the ring finger of your left hand between

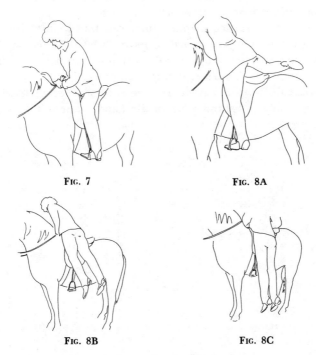

Fig. 7   Fig. 8A

Fig. 8B   Fig. 8C

Fig. 7. Prepare to dismount. Weight on hands and left stirrup.

Fig. 8. Dismount. *A* Swing leg across rear of horse; *B* put weight on both hands and take left foot out of stirrup; *C* both feet reach ground at same time.

the reins and let the ends of the reins come out between your fore-finger and thumb. (See Fig. 9.) Now is the time to learn how to lengthen or shorten the reins. (See Fig. 10.) You do this by holding your reins in your right hand well toward the ends of the reins and by slipping your left hand forward on the reins to shorten them or letting them slide back to lengthen. On this first ride your reins should be just long enough so that your left hand is a few inches above the front of your saddle and your reins are just tight enough so that you can feel Juanito's mouth. Your arms from shoulder to elbow should hang down comfortably, with your elbows just touch-ing your sides. (See Fig. 5, p. 20.) Your left arm from elbow to wrist should be approximately parallel with the ground. Your wrist should be flexibly bent so that most of your signals on the reins are made by flexing of the wrist and not by movements of the whole arm. Now you are ready to ride Juanito.

For your first practice in mounting, you put Juanito in a spot where he would not be tempted to move forward. This may mean that you will have to ask him to take a step or two backward before you can begin your first ride. If this is so, proceed this way:

Be sure your reins are even. If they are not, shorten the longer one by grasping it behind your bridle hand (your left hand) and

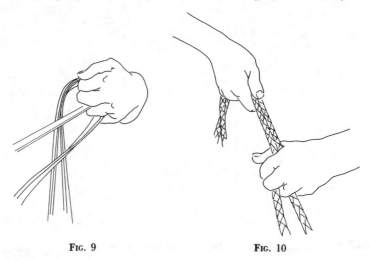

FIG. 9   FIG. 10

FIG. 9. Single rein in one hand. Ring finger between reins, end of reins come out between the forefinger and thumb.

FIG. 10. Shortening rein when riding with single bridle. Right hand *behind* bridle hand (left hand) pulls rein through bridle hand. Right hand should never touch rein between bridle hand and bridle.

pulling it through your bridle hand until it is even with the other rein. Never take hold of the reins for any purpose whatever with your right hand between your bridle hand and the horse's mouth. Now that your reins are even, pull them straight back without raising your bridle hand. If Juanito's neck is long and supple, he may at this point merely flex his neck. He may bring his chin in and give you much rein when you pull straight back. Your hand comes against your waist and cannot pull enough to signal Juanito to move his feet. If this is the case, shorten your reins by grasping them with the right hand behind the bridle hand and sliding the bridle hand forward on the reins. Then pull on the reins until Juanito takes a backward step. When he does so, immediately release your pull and pat him on the neck. We are, of course, assuming that Juanito is a well-mannered horse and more experienced than you are. This means that if you have followed directions he has performed satisfactorily.

3

The first ride

Now that you have Juanito backed out of his corner, it is time to start forward. Put just enough pressure on the reins so that you have a good feel of Juanito's mouth but not enough to signal him to back. At the same time take a little hold of him with the insides of your calves and knees. Then ask him to take a step toward one side. Do this, if he neckreins, by moving your bridle hand in the direction you want him to turn. Doing this should bring the pressure of your rein (your right one if you are turning left) to bear on the side of his neck at the roots of his mane and about one third of the length of his neck in front of the saddle. This neck signal should not be a jerk, but it should be definite and hard enough to get the response of a step toward the direction indicated. As soon as Juanito takes this first step, move your hand back to starting position and relax your leg muscles. This will probably result in Juanito's starting to walk in the direction he was facing before you asked him to take a step to the side. If it does not, if he immediately stands still as soon as your hand returns to center and your legs relax, he is very probably doing exactly what he thinks you have asked him to do by relaxing your leg muscles. Start all over again. Take the one step to the side and then back to the direction faced at the start, but do not relax your legs until Juanito is walking forward.

There is a great difference in horses in their response to the signal for impulsion (going ahead). The horse's natural disposition and the way he has been handled both influence the way he responds.

Very slight leg pressure will get almost too much response from some horses. Others require a touch or a quick series of very definite touches with the heel. Still others require a touch with spurs. It is best to start with the light touch and by experiment find out how much of a signal is required. Remember this: If you ever ride a horse that is accustomed to a very definite heel signal, don't lackadaisically move your heel a time or two toward his side and then complain, "He won't go." On such a horse, bring both heels into his sides smartly. Be sure it is your heels hitting his sides you hear, not just your legs flopping. If one heel tap doesn't get the response, continue your signals in rapid succession, with increasing intensity until you get it—not just one flop with the heels and then another flop. When you use heel signals of this kind, be sure before you start that you have the feel of your horse's mouth in your hand and that your reins are short enough so you can take hold of him if necessary. Above all, be sure that the kick with your heels is not transmitted through your body into a jerk with your hands, and that you *do not pull back or up on the reins as you kick.* The way to make almost any horse rear is to kick him and pull up on the reins at the same time.

Until you are well on the road to being a good horseman, always start Juanito by first turning a step to the side and then straightening out. You will soon learn how much you must signal him to go ahead. Never oversignal any horse. Remember it is the would-be horseman who complains, "My horse does so and so," or "My horse won't do so and so." The real horseman knows that what the horse does, unless he is free and out of sight, sound, and smell of human beings, is largely the result of human activity. When there is trouble under the saddle, look for the cause on top of the saddle, especially at the ends of the reins.

On your first ride you should begin to learn about two things—balance and rhythm. To your question, "Balance of what—horse or rider?" I answer, "Both." Certainly the goal of your learning is to make them one and the same thing. At the start, we shall have to talk about balance and rhythm as if they were two separate things. Actually, balance and rhythm cannot be separated, but we have to separate them when we study and talk about them.

One of the best horsemen I ever knew said to me, "All riding is a matter of balance."

I asked him, "Balance of what?"

He said, "Balance of impulsion against restraint."

I didn't like that very well when I first heard it, and I don't feel much affection for it yet; but I have never been able to observe anything in riding that contradicts it.

On this first ride on Juanito you will notice at once that his head has a rhythmic motion as he walks. That rhythm is his and his alone. Each gait a horse has, of course, has a different rhythm. But the rhythm at the walk, or any other gait, of one horse is distinct from that of any other horse in the world. When I was small there were no cars on the city streets—only horses and buggies. The streets were full of them as they are today of cars. My daddy was a doctor. In those days doctors went out to the homes of their patients to treat them. So Dad often came home long after I had gone to bed. One of my earliest recollections is that of waking up to the rhythm of Daisy's or Joe's or Dick's trot coming down Eighth Avenue toward our house bringing Dad home. Other horses might be trotting down Eighth Avenue at the same time. Certainly within almost any hour of the day or night many other horses traveled that block of the avenue; but to a kid who liked horses no two trots had the same rhythm, and I knew the sound of our horses as I knew the faces of members of the family.

Until you are as aware of the rhythm of your horse's gait as I was of Daisy's and Joe's, you will not be quite a horseman. You may be able to win prizes in equestrian competitions before that time, but you won't be quite a horseman.

You must not only hear but also feel the rhythm. Is your wrist at all times flexed enough and are your reins held just tight enough to let your fingers feel the rhythm of Juanito's mouth? The movement on the bit may be so slight that I could not see it if I were watching you, but your fingers should feel it and go with it. This is true whether you are just walking along or taking a five-foot fence— especially if you are taking a five-foot fence, as we shall learn later on. Sometimes, of course, you will ride many miles at a walk with your reins slack. That will be after you and Juanito know each other very well. Some people claim that Western riders are better than Eastern riders because in the West there is communication between horse and rider on a slack rein. This you will have to decide for yourself when you have ridden many kinds of horses trained in different ways.

If you are to be aware of rhythm, there must be no rigidity in any part of your body. At this early stage of riding do not try to force your heels lower than your toes, but do not stand tiptoe in your stirrups. Keep your feet level as you would if standing on the ground. If the inside of your knees touch your saddle and your legs are not tense, you need not worry about whether your toes are in or out.

Now try to find the most comfortable way to ride that walk of Juanito's. Pretty soon you will find that you are most comfortable ✕ with just a very slight pressure, a rhythmic pressure on the stirrups. Your ankles will flex in rhythm to Juanito's head movement. The variation of pressure on the stirrup will be very, very slight and the weight in the stirrup will be just about what your foot and leg would weigh. Now you can see one advantage of riding with the ball of your foot on the stirrup. Unfortunately, in some of the special seats you must learn later, you will have to ride with your foot home (instep of foot on stirrup) and your wrists straight. Then you will have to make up for the loss of flexion of ankles and wrists by doing other things that we shall consider when we get to them.

You will notice very shortly that though you are most comfortable when you feel that your leg muscles are relaxed and your legs hang so that the inside of knees and calves are just touching Juanito's sides, there is actually a very slight rhythm of movement from your flexing ankles to your hips, so slight that your legs still seem relaxed.

At your waist the flow of rhythm stops. From your waist up, your body moves steadily ahead at the speed of your horse's walk, with a slight swinging of your shoulders perhaps. As it is hard to tell which is the most important part of a three-legged stool, so it is hard to tell what is the most important part of your body in this business of balance. However, if there is one most important part it is your waist. Without a relaxed but flexing waist you will never be able to ride any gait well. Most certainly you will never be able to sit a trot, the test of the good waist—and of a lot of other things. Only the rider who lives on a horse ever learns to sit a trot perfectly. So true is this last statement that today there are few riders who can sit a trot, so few that even in Western classes in shows it is now "correct" to post a bit at the trot, a rhythmic rocking on the knees, which we shall consider carefully later. Certainly it is better to post than to beat your horse's kidneys because you cannot use your waist well enough to sit a trot properly.

The waist absorbs the difference between your rhythmic follow-ing of your horse from waist down and the steady progression of your body from the waist up. Later on, when you learn to jump, the bending at your waist will be a very important factor in main-taining the perfectly balanced seat that eliminates interference with your horse's movements and eliminates jolts to the rider. The time to start to learn the use of your waist is on your first ride, and you should learn more every ride thereafter.

To find out something about your waist, stiffen your waist mus-cles and let Juanito take three or four steps at a jog trot. Have your reins in hand so you can stop him at the end of a few steps. Now relax your waist. Lean back just a little, so that your shoulders are an inch or two farther to the rear than your hips. Let your back bow out just a little as you relax your waist. Now try a few steps at the jog trot with your waist completely relaxed. Now you don't have to be told that the relaxed rider takes less beating than the tense rider.

For many kinds of riding, for many of the things you will do on horseback when you become proficient, your body will be tense and your position will be very different from the natural one you are trying to learn now. In high jumping, for instance, your entire body will be like a set of fine steel springs and your feet and legs will be in positions that would be silly and painful on a pleasure ride. However, your present purpose is to *learn the basic matters of rhythm, balance, and natural seat* (dictated by the shapes of human and equine anatomy); and to become *aware of the "feel" of a horse,* both on the reins and through your entire body.

Your first ride should be taken at the walk. Some of the best rid-ing instructors America has had have insisted on thirty days at the walk before any other gait is attempted. The sensitivity and learning ability of riders and horses (don't forget that Juanito is learning how to understand you while you are learning to ride) varies so greatly that I can set no general limit on the amount of walking to be done before other gaits are tried. Certainly I still spend a great deal of time at the walk when I get a new horse. I may do little but ride him at a walk for several days until I get the feel of him. Of course many a greenhorn buys a horse, jumps on him immediately, and flails him with heels and rein until the poor beast bursts into a wild gallop. Not only should any rider get the feel of a new horse before riding off a walk, but also any beginning rider should con-fine his riding to the walk until he can stop, start, turn, increase or decrease speed at the walk, collect and extend his horse at the walk, and feel perfectly at ease in the saddle.

If I had to pass judgment on a rider's ability and could see him only as he rode one particular gait, I would ask that it be the walk. The rider who is one with his horse continually while it walks is very likely able to do anything else with his mount that the horse is capable of—and even a few things that the horse was never capable of before. Most inexperienced riders will stir a horse up and

FIG. 11. Sack of potatoes seat. No balance—no rapport between horse and rider—everything wrong.

make him look brisk at the walk for a few minutes if spectators ask to see the animal walk, but the rest of the time the horse might just as well be packing a sack of potatoes when he walks. (See Fig. 11.) The relationship between horse and inept rider at the walk is much like that of two dancers walking flat-footedly around the floor without regard for each other or for very much else, neither dancer leading and neither being led. With the skilled rider the communication line between horse and rider is never broken, even though the reins may be slack, as they are on Western horses walking on trail or range.

4

Walk, trot, ⬛⬛⬛⬛⬛⬛⬛⬛⬛⬛⬛⬛⬛⬛
gallop, ⬛⬛⬛⬛⬛⬛⬛⬛⬛⬛⬛⬛⬛⬛⬛
and canter ⬛⬛⬛⬛⬛⬛⬛⬛⬛⬛⬛⬛⬛

One of the first things you have learned on the first ride is the amount of impulsion (provided by leg pressure, heel pressure, whip, or a combination of all these) needed to get Juanito from a stand-still to a walk. You learned this by trying. In the same way you must learn about increasing and retarding speed at the walk, or maintaining a steady rate of speed. If you have patient friends who are more experienced riders than you, ask them to ride beside you at a walk. Let the friend walk his horse at a slow, steady rate and you try to keep right beside him, with your stirrup touching his. You will be surprised to see how difficult this is. When you can do this, let the friend vary his speed. See if you can keep right beside him no matter at what rate of speed his horse walks.

While doing this, you will learn some very important things about handling your reins. You will learn very early that if you hold your reins too near the ends, that is, too far from your horse's mouth, you will find when you want to pull on the reins to stop your horse that you have no room to pull back. You must pull up, which will make most horses very nervous, even if it doesn't make them rear. Keep your reins short enough so that when your horse brings his chin in you have some room left to control him. At the same time be sure that your reins are not so short that you cannot release pressure on them when necessary. Also, do not become so intent on your reins that you creep forward in your saddle or, worse still, lean forward. During your early riding, you should sit in the deepest part of your saddle and your shoulders should never get ahead of your hips. The sitting forward or crouching forward habit is very hard to break if acquired early and develops a stiffness that makes learning the proper forward seat very difficult.

While considering reins, remember that a good rider can hold his reins in two hands or in either hand. He can communicate with a horse easily with a double English bridle or with double reins of the West (hackamore and bit reins). While you are walking, try shifting the reins from one hand to the other. If you are holding your reins in your left hand with the ring finger separating them, the ends coming out between forefinger and thumb, shift hands this way: with the fingers of your right hand outstretched have right palm facing your body and fingers pointing down. Now put the ring finger of your right hand between the reins just ahead of the ring finger of your left hand. Then let your left hand slide back on the reins and pull them across the palm of your right hand so the thumb and forefinger of your right hand can close upon them.

To practice turning at the walk at this stage of your riding you do not need elaborate equipment. Trees not too close together, greasewood, or a scattering of chips will serve as targets among which you can weave in and out. Do not make your beginning targets too close together. Make your turns shorter as you progress. Do not keep at any stunt of this kind until you become tired and your horse sullen. Try a little downhill and uphill riding to be sure that you do not pull your horse when he is going uphill. Once on a fox hunt I saw a young lady who overestimated her own ability accidentally pull her horse over backward as it tried to scramble up an unexpected little hill at the beginning of a run. You should practice walking downhill to see how to keep your horse from increasing speed as he descends. Do not try steep or long hills until you are quite experienced. At this early stage of your riding, your horse's judgment is probably better than yours in deciding where it is safe to go. It will do no harm to defer to his judgment at this stage. Many a horse has developed the vice of refusing to go certain places or to leave stable or crowd. However, this vice is rarely the result of a timid rider's deference. It is usually the result of one of two things. One is the silly rider's habit of getting on his horse before the crowd he is riding with is ready to start and then riding his horse a short distance from the barn and back again time after time. Or the vice may result from the would-be he-man-with-hair-on-his-chest sort of rider who wants to show off by forcing a timid horse to go where it is afraid to go, forcing it repeatedly until it rebels. The timid horse, like the timid dog, is very dangerous when pushed beyond endurance.

Collection

The most difficult thing to learn at the walk is what is called variously *collection, pulling a horse together, getting his hocks under him,* and so on. It is the art of shifting the center of balance of your horse (with such side effects as shortening stride, increasing alertness, and heightening the attention of the horse). As the term *collection* is most widely used, I shall use it to indicate this art which you are about to learn.

As I have said, all riding is a matter of balance between impulsion and restraint. Very generally speaking, that is what collection is. No two horses are alike. Certainly no two of them can be collected in exactly the same way. The experienced and sensitive rider can tell a good deal about a new horse the instant he picks up the reins. He can frequently tell at once how much impulsion and how much restraint are going to be needed to collect the horse he is riding. The inexperienced rider must carefully feel his way. If he uses too much impulsion (application of leg, heel, spur, or whip), he will have to use too much restraint (pull on the reins) to keep his horse from a burst of speed. All this "too-muchness" may result in rearing, or even in pulling the horse over backward. On the other hand, the very placid horse may be the one that the green rider says won't collect, when in reality all the horse needs is a very definite and persistent pair of heels on his sides and a firm, definite hand on the reins. Furthermore, it is very important to realize that many horses, even many that have been ridden a long time, have never been taught to collect. Horses that have been raced, horses that have been used for hire, horses that have been used mostly in harness are quite apt to be impossible to collect. For many good reasons such horses have learned not to yield to the bit as does the horse that collects easily. The young horse that has not been taught what a bit is for by a kind and skilled horseman cannot readily be collected by the inexperienced rider, though if the rider is possessed of more than average human intelligence and good will, horse and rider can learn collection together.

Let us do a little more assuming about your Juanito. Let us assume that he has been given some education by a horseman of at least ordinary skill and so has been taught to yield to the bit when gentle pressure is applied and to shorten his stride and bring his hocks up under him when he is squeezed by his rider's calves. Now then, as you are riding along at a walk, try a short time, say from thirty seconds to one minute, to collect Juanito. You have already found out how much pull on the reins is needed to stop him. Now, for collection use just barely enough pull to stop him but at the same time, or even a fraction of a second before you pull, apply just as much impulsion as you ordinarily need to start him. Look at his head. See how it comes up just a little and how his neck flexes at the poll (the place where neck and head join). Feel how his step quickens and his stride shortens. If you are quite perceptive, you can feel that he is balancing with more of his weight on his hind feet than before he was collected. See how he mouths the bit as if he were saying, "Roger: o.k., what's up, I'm ready." If Juanito starts to break out of a walk and into a trot, you will of course increase rein pressure; and if he stops or slows down you will increase impulsion with your legs or heels.

Don't ask Juanito to walk very far this way the first time you collect. Keep him at it just long enough to let him realize he is doing something special. Then stop him. Speak approvingly to him and pat him gently or stroke him on the neck before you start again on your usual walk.

Not all horses will be as easy to collect as your Juanito. Some will collect only if a spur or whip is used for impulsion and for restraint a constant rhythmic pressure is kept up on the reins. Others will overcollect or rear unless the squeeze with the rider's calves is so slight as to be almost imperceptible and the pressure on the reins is equally subtle. Only by trial can you find out exactly how much impulsion you need to quicken your horse's stride and how much restraint you need to keep him from breaking into a faster gait. More than just enough may cause trouble. On the other hand, the inexperienced rider on the veteran mount may say, "He won't collect," when all that is needed is a continued and vigorous application of heels until the smart old horse realizes he really does have to go to work.

Do not think that you have learned to ride at a walk until, by practice and by gradually increasing your riding time at a collected walk, you can ride for an indefinite period at the walk either with collection or with communication on a slack rein at an extended (uncollected) walk. Of course you may have friends and advisors who insist that at this point you should begin using the aids (foot pressure and balance to signal the horse to move his hindquarters or to respond in other ways). You have, of course, used the aids already when you first started your horse and in a more complicated way when you collected him. You could now begin to learn to move your horse sideways, to guide him with legs and hands while he is walking backward, and to open a gate; but these refinements of your skill can be learned much more easily after you have been riding long enough to feel perfectly at home in the saddle. I have found from experience that at this point the beginning rider, having learned to walk, can best proceed to the trot and slow gallop, which latter gait can easily be followed by collection into the canter.

The First Trot

For your first lesson at the trot you should try only a minute or less at the gait, and you should keep your horse to a very slow trot, a mere jog. Before starting be sure that you are sitting well back in your saddle and that your body is leaning slightly back; that is, that your shoulders are behind your hips. This you had better do where you will have no spectators, or at least none that are critical of your riding; for the seat you are using is not the conventional one for the trot, not the one which you will use at the trot when you are a finished rider. It is, however, the only one that enables you to achieve the relaxed rhythm without which no rider ever looks anything but silly at the trot—a fact which is illustrated at most amateur horse shows and some professional ones. During your first try or two at the trot, there are two important things to remember: Be sure your body does not lean forward, and that your legs from the knees down do not get back into the horse's flanks except momentarily if it is necessary to touch him with your heels. At this stage of your trotting, your heels should never be further to the rear than your knees.

Now to get Juanito into that easy jog. Start him at the walk, the gait from which any horse, even a five-gaited one, should take each other gait. Let your horse do an extended walk until you and he are comfortably relaxed. Then collect him. Now decrease restraint; that is, slacken your reins a little by moving your hands forward (and be careful that you do not immediately break into a jog trot), increase impulsion by increasing leg pressure or, if that does not bring results, by a touch with your heel. If he starts out on a full, rapid trot, restrain him with your reins. Since you will be bobbing about on his back at this full trot, your hand will be so unsteady that any pull you exert will so resemble a jerk that Juanito will stop completely or at least come to a walk. Then you must start the process all over again. It is by such experimenting that you will discover the exact amount of impulsion and restraint that are necessary to keep Juanito at the rate of speed you want.

When you learn how to keep your horse at the very slow trot, you can begin to analyze your own movements. By experimentation you will discover that the instant you lean forward or get your feet back or stiffen your muscles, you bounce uncomfortably.

Increase gradually the time you spend trotting each day and continue at the slow trot for a proper period of time, say for at least fifteen rides. You will discover that you ride more easily if the pressure of your feet in the stirrups is slightly rhythmic and in rhythm with the hoofbeats of your horse. You will also notice that your abdominal muscles, though not tense, have a slight rhythmic contraction at the slow trot. The supple waist is the prime requisite for sitting the trot at any speed. If after a year or so of sitting the very slow trot you can gradually increase the speed until you can sit a trot at a fair rate of speed, you can begin to take pride in your seat. You will then find that your waist is so in rhythm with your horse that you do not need to lean back to keep from bouncing and that you can use your feet most effectively when the balls of your feet are directly under your knees. Practice at sitting the trot is beneficial to any rider, and the horseman never lives so long that it will not benefit his riding to practice sitting the trot now and then.

Posting

After you have ridden the slow trot long enough to become aware of the two-beat rhythm of the gait and have learned how to keep your horse at a fairly constant rate of speed, you may learn to post the trot. This way of riding the trot has not been in good favor in the West very long, but Western riders have long known that the trot is, next to the walk, the most useful gait a Western horse ordinarily has. And since we no longer have many riders who have grown up in the saddle and learned to sit a trot, it is now considered proper in the West to post; that is, alternate the weight of the rider from seat to stirrups in rhythm with the trot. Certainly this is better for you and the horse than a bad attempt to sit a moderately fast trot.

The first thing to do in learning to post is to have your horse stand perfectly still while you learn the movement. If Juanito is a bit fussy, have a friend stand at his head while you devote all your attention to your own movements, with your horse stationary. Be sure your stirrups are adjusted as I described in the discussion of mounting; that is, the leathers just long enough to reach your ankle joints when you sit with feet out of the stirrups and legs extended toward the ground as far as possible. It does not matter greatly whether you use a flat saddle or a stock saddle for learning to post. The stock saddle is a little easier for most beginning riders because the stirrups are hung farther back than are the stirrups on a flat saddle. This makes it a little easier to rise in the stirrups. It is a little difficult to sit far enough forward in some flat saddles to get the weight of the body directly over the stirrups. Sit with the balls of your feet in the stirrups and the weight of your body carried by the bony structure, not the fleshy part of the buttocks. This will necessitate leaning forward, with the shoulders a few inches farther forward than the hips. You should sit far enough forward in the saddle so that the weight of your body is directly over your stirrups, with stirrup leathers vertical (straight up and down).

Now, using your knee joints as a pivot, rock forward so that the entire weight of your body is carried by your stirrups. As you do this, your hip joints should not straighten. Your knees are the pivotal joints. The hip joints do not function. In other words, the angle formed by the upper leg and the lower part of your body does not change. It is only the angle at the knee joint that changes. Note that we are now considering the most elementary kind of posting and that later on you may learn useful variations of what you are now learning, if you learn this part of posting well.

With Juanito standing still, practice this rocking from seat to stirrups until you can do it in time to counting or to a whistled

tune in two-four time. This, of course, will take much more effort
than will posting a real trot after you have learned to do it, because
at the trot the horse's rhythmic movement provides the momentum
for your rise at every other hoofbeat. When you are able to rock
forward and back in a regular rhythm, you are ready to try posting
a real trot.

For the first few trials at posting, it is very helpful to have a
friend ride with you and lead Juanito while you are making your
first attempts to rise to his trot. This obviously guards against your
jerking on the reins because of the unsteadiness of your body during
these first efforts. However, assistance is not indispensable. Try
Juanito at the very slow trot at first. It takes much more effort on
your part to post a very slow trot than to post a moderately fast one,
but try the slow one until you can post without having the movements of your body translated into unsteadiness on the reins, As
soon as you can rise up and down on the slow trot and at the same
time keep your hand perfectly still on the reins, you can urge Juanito to go a little faster at the trot. You must, of course, at all
times keep your reins short enough so that if Juanito becomes dis-
turbed by the movements of your hands or body, you can slow him
down and quiet his fears. Do not try posting very long at a time at
first. Gradually lengthen the time from day to day.

If you are riding a stock saddle, it is no disgrace to keep your left
hand on the saddle horn for the first few days of posting. Continuation of this will of course spoil your balance and make you a lopsided poster; but, for the first few times, a hand on the horn may
enable you to keep your other hand, your bridle hand, steady on
the reins while you are learning to rise in your stirrups. The rhythm
of your rising and sitting should be exactly in time with the two-
beat rhythm of your horse's trot. If you are at all out of time you
will probably get a double bounce when you sit and have to use
unnecessary effort to rise. If you can keep in time with two-four
music on the dance floor, you can quickly learn to keep in time with
the trot of your horse. The height of your rise will depend on the
length of stride of your horse and on the amount of spring in his
movement. If you are in perfect time with your horse, his movement
will supply all the effort needed to raise your body from the saddle.
In other words, when you are in perfect time with your horse, you
should rise only as high as the stride of the horse sends you. Also,
you should note that you cannot be in time with your horse if there

is a moment of pause either at the height of your rise or at the moment you are seated. Your movement is like that of the rocking chair or the swinging hammock, continual movement.

On a horse with a short stride and little spring, the posting rider hardly leaves the saddle. On the long-gaited trotter with lots of spring and high action, the rider will rise very high, and will do so without effort. Posting, when properly done, makes riding any trot easy and requires little effort. A good rider on an alert and healthy horse can ride a trot many miles without fatigue. When you feel that you have completely mastered the art of posting, try this test. Take two silver dollars (if they are not plentiful, two cardboard disks the size of a dollar will do) and place each between one of your legs and the saddle at a point just below your knees. Take your feet out of the stirrups. Fold your arms across your chest, and let someone lead your horse at a brisk trot a quarter of a mile. If at the end of that quarter mile you still have the two dollars, you have passed the test. It is almost as easy for the good rider to post a trot without stirrups as with them, though it is considerably more fatiguing, because leg grip must replace stirrups.

When you have learned to post well, it is time to learn to collect your horse at the trot. It is also time to consider the diagonals, to learn to keep any rate of speed, and to learn to stop, start, and turn at the trot with facility.

Increasing Control

As in the walk, pacing yourself with another rider is the best way to learn to keep your horse at any given rate of speed. You should practice this. Don't ride a few feet or a few inches ahead of or behind your partner; ride *beside* him. The only way you can know you are doing this is to be sure your stirrup and that of your partner are touching most of the time. To anyone who has not done formation riding, my insistence on this point seems rather silly; but let the smiling one watch an inexperienced rider trying to ride beside a companion. He is usually a few feet or at least inches ahead or behind even when he thinks he is beside the other rider.

Before trying anything more difficult, you should be sure you can maintain any desired speed your horse is capable of and can do so (except at racing speed) either at the collected or extended trot.

Collection at the trot is obtained just as it is at the walk—by the use of impulsion and restraint at the same time. What must be learned about it is the amount of each that is needed to obtain collection at any given speed. The collected trot is rarely if ever asked for in Western show classes. There are many horsemen who would say that collection at the trot has no purpose in Western riding. However, unless you have the ability to collect your horse at the trot, you are not a horseman; and if your horse cannot be so collected, he is not a very versatile riding horse. Certainly the pleasure of riding demands that a horse be so responsive to his rider that he can be collected at any gait.

Learning to stop a trotting horse quickly and properly when occasion demands is very important, though the rider who habitually stops his horse suddenly is a show-off and will soon have a horse with crippled hind legs (he will probably not be horseman enough to know they are crippled). Another objectionable extreme in this matter of stopping (and also starting) is the pokey rider in company. The rider who needs formal notification from his companion when they are to increase or decrease speed is a very unpleasant riding companion. You should be able to increase or decrease speed and to stop and start easily. If you are hiking on foot (though why one who owns a good horse should do so is a puzzle) you walk, start, and stop easily with your companions. They do not have to give advance notice of a stop or an increase in speed. Certainly the horseman should have even greater facility in such matters than the hiker.

The quick stop is in reality a quick collection followed instantaneously by an increase of restraint and cessation of impulsion. In other words, you pick your horse up with reins and leg squeeze simultaneously and increase rein pressure until he stops; and as you increase the rein pressure, you quit squeezing with your legs. Of course, with the sluggish horse extreme pull may have to be used, and spurs may have to be substituted for leg squeeze. On the other hand, great caution must be used with the horse with a light (very sensitive) mouth and extreme responsiveness to leg squeeze. The beginning rider is quite prone to overdo in his first attempt. Gradually increase the quickness of your stop. Do not try to bring your horse to a sliding stop the first few times you try. A horse should stop straight, no matter how quickly he stops. If he does not, the chances are that pressure on the reins was not equal. If this is not the case, then one leg or heel must have been more active than the other.

Quick starting, a technique to be used only upon necessity, should begin with collection of the horse at a standstill. When he is well gathered together (well collected) restraint can be lessened (never "throw your reins away" for a quick start) and impulsion quickly increased.

5

Controlling ░░░░░░░░░░░░░░░░░░░░░░░░░░░░
the ░░░░░░░░░░░░░░░░░░░░░░░░░░░░░░░░░░░░
quarters ░░░░░░░░░░░░░░░░░░░░░░░░░░░░░░

As you increase your riding ability, you should become increasingly aware of what your horse is doing, especially with his hindquarters. Gradually you should become as able to move them sideways as you are able to turn his forehand (front end). At a standstill try moving your right leg to the rear while at the same time pulling just enough on the reins to keep your horse from moving ahead. If this does not cause him to move his hindquarters to the left, increase the pull on your right rein, neckreining him toward the left to keep him from turning to the right in response to the side pull; and at the same time use your right heel lightly to indicate you want him to move his hind feet to the side. If your horse has not been trained to respond to the use of the leg aid (that is what you have been using; so you can be proud like the gentleman in Molière's play when he discovered he had been speaking prose), you may have to dismount to show him what you mean. As you start by trying to move your horse's hindquarters to the left, you may well continue in the same direction when dismounted, though this will necessitate standing on your horse's right side while holding him, the incorrect side from which to lead a horse or handle him when on foot. Hold your reins close to the bit with your right hand. With your left hand placed where your heel would be if mounted, push Juanito's hindquarters a step or two to the left. Then stroke him and praise him.

Now do the same thing from the other side. If you repeat this for
a few days, you may be able to mount Juanito and move his hindquarters without difficulty. If not, ask a friend to·help you from the
ground. Remember, you are supposed to have at least as much intelligence as the horse and your first job is to communicate to him
what is wanted. If you get resistance from your horse, the chances
are that you have not made clear to him what you want. He may
become angry, just as you do, when confused. If he does, better
stop for today and start all over again tomorrow, going a little more
slowly and a little more clearly.

Diagonals in Posting

In learning to post you finally observed that one of the beats in
the two-beat gait, the trot, is accented and that it is easier to post if
you rise on the accented beat. A good many years ago, when the cavalry horse was an important part of our national defense, considerable
attention was given this matter of the diagonals of the trot. After
Robert E. Lee's surrender, all the United States cavalry was
mounted on horses with only three gaits. This meant that all march-
ing done at speed faster than a walk had to be done largely at the
trot. It was thought, by officials whose business it was to think about
such things, that long hours of posting the trot rising on the same
diagonal would lead to lopsided muscular development of both
horse and rider. Just what particular muscles would overdevelop
from rising at the trot on the diagonal of left fore and right hind
hoofbeat, for instance, was never determined, or at least never made
public. However, there was probably some basis in fact for the con-
tention; and good cavalry equitation dictated that the soldier should
rise for some time to one diagonal, say the left fore and right hind,
and then skip a beat and rise to the other diagonal, the right fore
and left hind, for an equal amount of time. Because, as you have
already discovered, the horse is more helpful to the rider on one
diagonal than on the other, some horsemen attempted with what
they claimed success to teach horses to change the accent of the beat
at the trot on signal. This they said they did by starting the horse
at the trot with his hindquarters carried slightly to one side of the
line of his progression. In other words, the horse was trotting with
his body slightly diagonal to the line of progression, as we have all
seen some puppies do. This twisting of the horse's body of course

is frequently seen in horse shows when force is needed to get a horse to take a requested lead on the canter, all of which we shall consider very shortly. To get a horse to carry his body at a diagonal, use the same technique that I directed you to use when you moved Juanito's hindquarters to one side. For example, if you want a horse to trot carrying his hindquarters to the left, you will use your right foot against his side just behind the girth, increase the pressure on the right rein slightly and keep him from turning right in response to that pull by neckreining him to the left slightly.

I do not recommend that you spend time on the diagonals unless or until you wish to participate in equitation classes judged by men who make a fetish of diagonals of the trot. Because I ride a horse with gaits suitable for a saddle animal, I can think of no less important, less enjoyable, or less rewarding way to spend time on horseback than in practicing the diagonals at the trot. It is necessary, perhaps, to know what is meant when horsemen of a particular school talk about the diagonals of the trot, and if you are ever faced with the necessity of riding on alternate diagonals at the trot, you now know what to do. Of course if you like the trot and spend a great amount of time posting, you should alternate diagonals.

Hindquarter Control in Turning

The ability to control your horse's hindquarters is a prerequisite in turning him at any speed faster than a slow walk, as is the ability to collect him. When turned sharply at any considerable speed, a horse may injure a foreleg (bow a tendon) unless he is collected as he turns. You should collect him at least a fraction of a second before you turn him. Also, the horse that turns by pivoting on his forequarters, whether or not collected, will injure his front legs. To prevent this latter danger always be ready to control your horse's hindquarters on a turn. If he has a tendency to move his hind legs to the right when turning left or out to the left when turning right, use your heel or leg behind the saddle on the side toward which he is moving his hindquarters. Many good teachers of equitation advise such use of leg aids on all turns. Some horses have a tendency to swing the hindquarters around the forehand on a quick turn, and it is necessary to use a spur vigorously to control their hindquarters. Such horses should never be ridden by inexperienced riders, or at least should never be ridden by amateurs on fast work of any kind.

Practice turning at the trot as you did turning at the walk. Such practice will improve your posting and your ability to control your horse's hindquarters. It will also improve your facility in collecting your horse. When you feel comfortable on the walk and the trot, can start, stop, turn, maintain any given rate of speed at these gaits, and can control your horse's hindquarters with reasonable dexterity, you are ready to learn to gallop, or, if your horse can canter without much help from you, to canter.

The Gallop

Almost any horse can be made to gallop from a collected walk by a sudden cessation of restraint and an equally sudden use of extreme impulsion. This is, a sudden slackening of the reins and a vigorous use of the heels will make almost any horse break into a gallop. Of course, the seasoned livery horse, resigned to abuse and knowing that most of the things riders do are utterly without meaning, will need spurs or whip instead of heels. It is at this point of putting a horse into a gallop that most of the so-called runaways or boltings occur on urban bridle paths and parks. The inexperienced rider after vigorous use of the heels gets his mount to gallop. The lurch of the break into a gallop disturbs the rider's balance and pitches him forward. His heels fly backward. His hands fly up. Frequently he yells for help. Everything he does is a signal to his horse to increase its speed. When he finally falls off, the newspaper reports that he was thrown from a bolting horse and uses the headline RUNAWAY IN THE PARK.

To put a horse properly into a gallop, start from a collected walk. In a suitable place for galloping, one that is not downhill and gives firm but not hard footing (good sod is best), increase impulsion by extra use of leg or heel pressure (depending upon the responsiveness of your mount). As your horse gathers himself in response to the leg aid, move your bridle hand forward to reduce restraint. If he does not gallop at once, do not continue use of leg or heel. Restrain him again on the reins and put him at a collected walk. Then try your signals again for the gallop. This time use your heels with more vigor. Be sure that you do not throw your reins away; that is, do not give so much slack on the reins that you cannot instantly reduce your horse's speed if he goes into the gallop at full speed. Be ready with your heels to keep him from slowing down to a trot until you want him to do so. At the same time use your reins to keep him galloping as slowly as he will gallop without dropping into a trot.

The Canter

This first try at the gallop was not a very dexterous affair, but if you repeat it a few times you can determine just how much impulsion it takes to start your horse into a gallop and how much you can slow him down without pulling him out of the gallop into the trot. You will make a delightful discovery if your Juanito has been well schooled on the canter, for when you slow down his gallop he will collect himself into a canter, which is actually a very collected and slow gallop, very pleasant to ride. Sit back on it. Move your feet as far forward as you can. Keep your shoulders well back, and enjoy that canter! There will be plenty of time to learn that heels-down-toes-in-shoulders-forward-chest-out forward seat for special purposes later, after you have learned to relax and get with the rhythm of the canter.

The Leads

If your Juanito has learned to canter beautifully, he will expect you to be able to tell him which lead to take if you start cantering on the straightaway. (When you turn him on the canter, he should always change leads of his own volition so that he is always leading with the foot on the inside of each turn.) To tell Juanito which lead you want, start out as always with a collected walk. Then, if you want a left lead, for example, use your right leg behind the saddle; pull his head slightly to the right, and at the same time neckrein him slightly to the left. Start him into the canter as you did into the gallop, by increasing the aid of your leg—the right one only, this time—and slightly decreasing the pull on your reins. Some horses are trained to take a given lead when the rider leans over the shoulder he wants his horse to lead with. By experiment you can find out whether Juanito has been so trained, but if he canters when you lean, straighten up and get back in your saddle immediately when he takes his first canter step or you will be bouncing along like a rubber ball and frighten him.

To make sure that Juanito has the lead you have asked for, look down over his shoulders. The shoulder on the side he is leading with comes up farther at each step than does the other one. If you are tall enough, or your horse is small enough, you can see his knee on the leading side as it comes forward. In the canter and gallop, two diagonal feet strike the ground at the same time. The other two have separate impacts with the ground. So if you are cantering on the left lead, your horse's hoofbeats will be in this order: right hind alone, right front and left hind together, then left front alone. It is the forefoot that is operating alone that you can sometimes see if you are very tall and on a small horse and look down over his shoulder as you are cantering. The forefoot that comes up higher than the other is the foot he is said to be leading with.

There is an error that a horse makes, not often, fortunately, that confuses the beginning rider. When making this mistake, the horse starts out with the leading foot asked for; but the impact of that foot is followed by the simultaneous impact of the two feet on the side opposite the leading foot. Then the hind foot on the same side as the leading foot makes its impact with the ground. This pseudo canter is easily detected because it is very uncomfortable and a horse will rarely hold it long. A horse that is prone to make such a mistake when doing fast work or working cattle on a downgrade is dangerous, for he may easily lose his footing.

It is very important to learn to distinguish instantly what lead your horse has. If you have difficulty, it is wise to get help for a little while daily from a competent horseman. Ask him to stand still and watch you as you put your horse into a canter and tell you which lead your horse has the moment he has a canter. Start the horse on his canter several times on each lead; watch his shoulder, and pay close attention to the feel of each lead. Continue this use of an assistant for a few days until you can tell at the first step of the canter which lead your horse has.

Along with learning about the leads, you will be learning the rhythm of the canter and learning to use your waist and ankles in rhythm with your horse's head movement. Also, you will find that you can increase the collection of your horse at the canter and slow him down in it without his dropping into a trot if you will keep a rhythmic pressure on the reins and some pressure with your legs and heels. This you should not do long at a time, but you can improve your horse's canter, probably, by collecting him and slowing him down now and then. Furthermore, you must learn to use your reins in rhythm with the canter and gallop before you can turn your horse and get him to change leads while galloping—a very useful accomplishment in American riding.

Do not try the turn and lead change at the gallop until you have ridden a great deal and have become thoroughly comfortable in the saddle and can do well and easily all that I have discussed thus far. Before you do any fast turning, you should graduate from the basic seat to the forward seat, which is discussed in Chap. 8. However, you can learn to turn and change leads at a gallop of reasonable speed while riding the basic seat, and it is a good way to become more aware of rhythm and balance.

To get Juanito to change leads by turning him at the gallop, have him collected and at a gallop on the left lead a little faster than a rapid canter. Your hands should be in perfect rhythm with his head movement. That is, each time his head rises at the gallop, your hand should tend to lift a trifle but not enough to make him toss his head and fight the bit. Be sure you do all this on firm but not hard ground and where there are no ground squirrel or gopher holes and no rocks. With your legs or heels you have Juanito well up against the bit. Now, as he comes up with his leading foot, lift him with your reins; turn him sharply to the right. As you do this, increase the application of your left leg or heel so that he will not flop his hindquarters out to the left as he turns. It will take several trials before you learn just how severely you must lift him to get him to shift leads, and how much quick impulsion you must give him with the left leg. With some horses, there is no tendency to flop the hindquarters to the side, so both of the rider's legs can be used to give impulsion to balance the lift of the reins.

At your first trial, if you are not successful, do not repeat your attempt too many times immediately. Your horse may become confused and irritated. Try again another day, and another, until you determine the exact balance of quickness, impulsion, restraint, and hindquarter control you must use to get results. Don't get irritated at your horse. What he does is in response to what you do. Keep experimenting until you learn what to do, but do not place your experiments too close together in time.

When you have become thoroughly at home on your horse and can do all the things I have discussed so far, you are ready to experiment with different seats, or to enter amateur competitions if you care to. Such things are discussed in other parts of this book in a way that I hope will be helpful to you.

Before you go on to group riding or more advanced riding of any kind there is one important warning I must give you. I have given it for so many years in vain that I had almost decided to omit it, but here it is for those few who may heed it: as you are learning to ride do not become so engrossed in your appearance that you forget what is the most important thing in the world to the really great horseman—the horse. It is possible to do an excellent job of riding and at the same time offend the conventions of form (watch a good polo game to see what I mean). Be more aware of your horse than of anything else, even your own appearance, and you'll learn to be a good horseman in spite of any faults in your form.

Learn the form of the particular kind or kinds of riding you want to do; learn so well that you can forget about it and put *all* your attention on your horse. You will not be riding him if you are thinking about where your own feet or arms are; you will be merely sitting on him and posing for spectators.

Certainly you are now ready to go on trail rides or otherwise participate in group riding, so the next chapter offers suggestions for your own safety and that of your horse. It also includes a few pointers that may make you a more welcome guest in riding groups.

6

Elementary ※※※※※※※※※※※※※※※※※※
courtesy ※※※※※※※※※※※※※※※※※※※
and safety ※※※※※※※※※※※※※※※※※

One of the few very basic facts that a beginning rider must learn very early if he is to be safe and happy in his riding is that the walk is the gait used most of the time by every good horseman. If you are a speed enthusiast, learn to be a jockey and confine your riding to the race track, or trade off your horse for a motorcycle. You may not be as safe by doing so but you will be less of a menace to horseflesh.

A good gallop is very exhilarating for both man and beast. So is a good fast trot or rack, but the good horseman indulges in them at proper times and places. Proper times are certainly not at the beginning of a ride or on the way home when within a mile or so of the stable. The proper place is where your horse's speed will not excite or disturb the mounts of others who may be riding with you or may merely be using the same trail or bridle path; and where the footing is firm but not hard, and free from rodent holes and rocks. If you live in the Southwest you need only one encounter with cholla cactus to learn that one does not run his horse in a cholla patch. (If you do pick up some cholla, do not try to remove the burrs without assistance. They will do no permanent harm and after the first panic of your horse, if he does panic, you can continue to ride him slowly to where an experienced horseman will help you soften up the burrs with water and then remove them, possibly with the aid of a twitch.)

51

One of the best and most charming horsemen of my childhood acquaintance, Dr. R. D. Bohannan, told me, "You can always tell how long a person has ridden by the rate at which he rides. If he has just started to ride and is scared of falling off, he walks all the time. If he has ridden just long anough to have a little confidence, he gallops most of the time to prove to folks he's a rider, or so he thinks. If you watch a seasoned horseman, you'll notice what a fine walk his horse has and how much the rider uses it and enjoys it."

Certainly anyone who is in possession of his faculties does not need to be told that a horse must always be slowed to a walk before he is allowed to set foot on a surfaced highway or other equally hard surface. No mentally competent rider will trot or canter (to say nothing of gallop) up to the graveled approach to a drive-in and fail to bring his horse to a walk before he sets foot on the gravel. However, I have seen more than one accident within the past few years in the town nearest my home, Scottsdale, Arizona, resulting from just this kind of moronic riding. When on the last occasion of seeing a horse brought down on the asphalt surface of the entrance to a local drive-in, I was much more concerned to see whether the horse was injured than I was about any injury to the young fool who had been riding him; and I was thought inhuman.

When crossing a highway, wait until it is clear of traffic and *walk your horse across*. Never try to hurry across, even at a slow trot, to avoid holding up traffic. Your chances of survival are better on an upright and walking horse than under one that has fallen on you on the pavement. I have seen a cowpony that was unbelievably sure-footed on mountain terrain slip and fall to his hocks and knees on an asphalt approach to a place of refreshment in town.

If you are riding in company, do not ride closer than the length of a horse to the horse ahead of you, but do not lag back farther than a length and a half when on the trail in a group. If you do wish to drop back, move out to the side of the trail so that the riders behind you can pass. Probably your horse, after seeing the others go ahead, will go on without further delay.

Never tie your horse with the bridle reins. Carry a rope halter for this purpose. Use a good cotton rope and tie your horse so that there is a distance of three feet between halter and knot. Be sure to tie the rope so that it will not slip toward the ground on the object to which it is tied. Never tie a horse closer to the ground than the height of the front of your saddle and never allow more than three feet of rope between halter and the object to which the horse is tied. Sometimes on picnics bushy trees are the only things available to tie to. If so, you will have to use a little longer rope than usual in order to get through the branches to the solid part of the tree or to take in enough of the branches to make a strong tie. In such a situation be sure that the rope is high enough and short enough to prevent your horse from putting a front foot over it. As he may scratch your saddle on the branches, you may remove it unless the weather is chilly and his back is very warm. Of course, if your horse is hot you will not tie him without walking him around until he cools off.

It is commonly thought that every beginning rider has to tear up a bridle and a halter and spoil at least one horse by making him a halter puller before the beginner learns to use care when he ties a horse. This is not necessarily so, but it has considerable basis in fact and should be a good warning.

Never water, feed, or stable a hot horse. Of course if you follow the horseman's rule of always walking the last mile home, you will rarely arrive at your own corral or stable with a hot horse. However, if you horse is particularly fussy and has not been out for many days, he may come in hot in spite of your care; and there are emergencies that interfere with cooling out on the ride. If you do bring your horse in hot, walk him around until he cools before you put him away. You do not have to lead him if you can ride him at a quiet, uncollected walk.

Now that you are aware of the rhythm of your horse's gait you can easily tell if he is lame; for, if he is, he will accent one beat at the trot very strongly and his head will bob on that beat. If he is very lame, from any but a very few causes, he will do the same at the walk. If your horse is lame, call a veterinarian at once. Do the same if he does not eat as usual or if he lies down and gets up repeatedly, looks at or kicks at his side. These latter signs, any of them, may mean that he has a belly ache. It may not be serious, but, if your horse is worth keeping, he is worth a veterinarian's fee. A very close friend of mine suffered the death of a beloved and valuable horse at the time this book was being written. He lost the horse because he wanted to wait and see if its stomachache was really serious. Any colic in a horse can be serious. There are as many causes for it in horses as in people. Some of the cures given by "practical" horse doctors may relieve some kinds of colic but will be quickly fatal to others. Most cases of colic are not serious, but a half-hour delay in calling a competent veterinarian may mean the difference between life and death in certain cases. Do not take a chance on losing your horse the way my good friend did.

Keep fresh, clean water before your horse at all times except when he comes in hot. Do not overfeed grain, and feed with regularity. Much more information is given on horse care later in this book, but the warnings I have given are very necessary at the outset of your career as a horseman.

Part II

VARIETY

IN

AMERICAN

RIDING

7

Rhythm
and
balance

Rhythm and *balance* are the magic words of riding. Rhythm is probably the more difficult one to communicate. One of the greatest players of jazz music America has produced was asked to define jazz. His answer was, "Man, if you have to ask what it is, you ain't never goin' to know!"

We shall consider rhythm and balance in more detail in later chapters, but in connection with the basic seat here are a few very vital matters: from head to toe all muscles act in rhythm with the movement of the horse. The freedom of movement the basic seat allows is very helpful in learning this. Even when we anticipate the horse, as in some signals for leads on green horses, we still keep with him while upsetting his balance slightly to get a desired result. One of the first obvious details of rhythm learned (often unconsciously) by the rider is that of the use of the legs, especially of the ankles, when cantering. The most obvious part of the rhythm is that of pressure in the stirrups. It varies exactly in rhythm to the up-and-down movement of the cantering horse's head—the same rhythm, of course, as that of the entire body of the horse, for the neck is the "balancer" of the horse.

The most difficult and most seldom learned detail of rhythm is the use of the waist in sitting the trot. That is why most good instructors of Western riding today either keep their pupils from using the trot except at very slow speed or instruct them to post.

While the ankles come into play at the trot somewhat as they do in the canter, the waist (also very important in the canter) is perhaps the most important part of the body. From the waist up, the body, when trotting, moves forward very steadily, progressing in a straight line. On the horse with a very high trot, the line will undulate a trifle. The rider's body from the waist down goes with the horse as exactly as if it grew out of the horse's backbone. The difference in these two movements is absorbed largely by the waist. The muscles of the rider's abdomen and those of the small of his back work in perfect rhythm with the movements of the horse. Sitting the trot should never be attempted until the rider has ridden so long in the basic seat, and later in whatever specialized seat he is using, that he can be perfectly relaxed. Any stiffening up or crouching forward will defeat all attempts at sitting the trot.

Relaxation

In achieving balance and rhythm the ability to relax is a prerequisite. Without it many a riding school does an excellent job of turning out pupils who in the show ring and under other special conditions have the *appearance* of excellence, but the excellence that makes riding a pleasure can be attained only by first using the basic seat at the walk and other slow and easy gaits—using it until the rider has lost all tendency to stiffen up whenever the horse makes some unexpected movement. Any discomfort is an indication of some failure to use the basic seat. This failure is often due to trying to increase speed before the rider has perfected basic posture, relaxation, balance, and rhythm at the slow walk. The rider should never allow the horse to do any gait that is persistently uncomfortable. The discomfort is rarely the horse's fault. More often it is the fault of the rider who has not mastered the basic seat and the fundamentals that go with it. When such mastery of the basics at the slow and easy gaits has been accomplished, the "hard gait" may be learned and become easy. Stiffness after riding is another sure indication of departure from basics.

The highly sensitive and timid rider (the kind that frequently makes the best horseman in the end) will do well to go against the advice of his more academic friends and ride sitting farther toward the cantle, the back part of the saddle, than normal, with feet a little farther forward and shoulders a little farther back than in the basic seat. This is rank heresy today when we have so recently discovered the usefulness of the forward seat. But it's easy enough to get forward after relaxation, balance, and rhythm have been achieved at the easy and slow gaits. On the first easy and very slow canter, the beginner will usually bounce like a rubber ball, but if he will lean back, way back, and shove his feet forward he will settle down in his saddle. The forward seat and the "balanced seat" can come along in due time.

In observing literally hundreds of his own and other riding pupils, the writer has seen a few spills on turf and tanbark when beginners were trying their first galloping or cantering. He has never seen one fall off backward. The spill results this way: Horse starts to canter. Rider's muscles all spasmodically tighten. Belly muscles beat back muscles, so body crouches forward. Calf and back-of-thigh muscles beat other leg muscles, so legs come back and heels drive into horse's flanks. Horse obeys with a burst of speed. Rider, now almost over horse's neck, loses all balance and tumbles over horse's shoulder.

Don't be afraid to lean back (you are probably sitting bolt upright when you think you are leaning back). Put your feet forward and relax when you begin to ride, if you have to fight stiffness.

There is the very sensible argument that some horses give quite a lurch when starting to go into a gait faster than a walk, and that a rider must lean forward to stay on top. Contrary to logic, unless the lurch is extreme, the leaning-back, relaxed green rider does not topple backward in such event; he just slides back a little in his saddle. Of course if the lurch is extreme, he comes a cropper; but on such a lurch he will come a cropper no matter how he sits. And the chances are he will go over his horse's shoulder, no matter how he leans. The remedy for such accidents is to ride a better horse or to ride so long at walk and jog with the basic seat that balance, rhythm and relaxation have been well established before he tries to canter. This may take months, but months riding a good horse at walk, slow gait, and jog are better than a few hours putting cold compresses on a bruised head, to say nothing of paying to have a spoiled horse reschooled.

8

Seats in ▨▨▨▨▨▨▨▨▨▨▨▨▨▨▨▨▨
American riding ▨▨▨▨▨▨▨▨▨▨▨▨

Early History

Our horses and our horsemanship have become unique through
much the same process as our language. The Hobbies and the Galloways brought over to America during the 1600's were all easy-
gaited animals. Trotting horses (boneshakers they were then called)
were practically unknown. Appropriately, the easy-gaited horses
were ridden with long stirrups, with the feet of the rider under the
horse's nose, as one exaggerating writer put it. As that century drew
near an end, the colonists had established roads and could use
wheeled vehicles. The little Hobbies and Galloways, and the Nar-
ragansetts and Canadians that had been developed in America from
them, were not suitable for pulling either carriages or plows. But in
a very few years enough new and more suitable blood had been
brought in from abroad to change the type of American horses. The
old easy gaits were soon in the minority. They were to be found
only in the then far Western frontiers—Kentucky, Tennessee, and
later Missouri. Riding styles changed, too, for gentlefolk drove on
wheels except in the back country; and it was only the young dan-
dies and sporting folk who rode. They did not seem to care if their
bones were shaken.

Furthermore, the colonists looked to England for standards of
taste and style. And since the English had earlier looked to the Con-
tinent in much the same way, the trotting, galloping Thoroughbred
became the height of fashion in America. Paul Revere probably

made his famous ride on a horse of the old foundation stock, but there may have been a drop or so of Thoroughbred blood in some of the officers' mounts during the Revolution.

All this meant changes in saddles and stirrup lengths, to say nothing of handling of reins. Most of the change was from England, but some of it came indirectly from France, where centuries later we were to get some of our jumping technique and the Saumur saddle.

As America moved west, the Texas cowboy was born. While the older and wiser Mexican cattlemen of the area called the new cowboy *vaquero*, he preferred his simplified American version of *buckaroo*.

From the Mexican the buckaroo learned as fast as he could how to use a *mecate* (rope) and called it, especially if there was a drop of Ireland in his veins, a McCarty. The cowboy took the Mexican saddle, which was of Spanish-Moorish descent, and, with true American inventiveness and disregard for tradition, worked it over into the ancestor of the modern stock saddle or Western saddle. The buckaroo also took the severe bits that the Mexican had derived from the Spanish, who got them from the Arabs and the Moors. He took the spurs. He caught from wild herds the descendant of Barbs, Arabians, and Andalusians, which he rode with a "bit that would stop a locomotive and spurs that would drive it through hell."

East and West met on horseback when early polo players found that the Texas pony was the best of all polo mounts. This superiority did not last long. The rules of the game changed, making the Thoroughbred the best of polo ponies. However, it did last long enough for the Texan to become interested in polo and to learn that the dude who rode the "postage stamp saddle" knew some things worth knowing. The difference between the old high Texas saddle and the modern rodeo saddle is evidence of this. During World War I, while American polo players were in combat, they learned much from the French and Italian cavalrymen. They brought home Saumur and Pariani saddles. For the first time, perhaps, nonracing horsemen began to learn what Tod Sloan, the American jockey, knew when he taught the English how to ride a race. (We had trouble beating the English until Sloan invented the monkey seat.)

American riding, born of the needs of the West and the frontier Midwest, was not replaced by the forward seat of France or Italy.

But what the boys brought back to ranch and farm from the war made us take a new look at our American riding. We began to see magazine articles and hear stable talk about the "balanced seat." Only in high jumping and very stiff hunting did we adopt the foreign seat. However, in Eastern Pleasure classes or Western horse shows we now see an Americanization of the European forward seat. Most schools of riding that use flat saddles teach a modification or Americanization of it.

What we have learned from this latest European influence is that the position and the balance of the rider affects or even limits the movement of the horse. Tod Sloan knew this and used his knowledge to beat the English, but it took a war to teach it to the rest of us.

Most good American horsemen now have and make use of that knowledge. Nevertheless, for certain purposes Western riders will not post a trot in a stock saddle without blushing. However, in Western riding, especially, we now use not the old Spanish methods or the English, French, or Italian; we have taken a little from all of them and added much that none of them have; we ride American.

Shortly after this century began, an Italian officer by the name of Caprilli made a remarkable discovery and gave one bit of very important advice to all horsemen competitive and athletic in their tastes. Like most important discoveries, Caprilli's seemed simple and obvious after he made it. It was the fact that a horse's balance, his center of gravity, is in a constant state of flux—a fact very much in line with all thinking about the physical world in this century. Caprilli's advice was that the chief aim in riding should be to avoid interfering with the horse's balance.

Caprilli's advice is all-important for the competitive rider and to be taken with a grain of salt by the horseman who rides neither to win a trophy nor to keep up with the Joneses. His discovery, however, emphasizes the fact that there is no one best seat. It has been amply demonstrated since those days that the horse's center of gravity ranges from somewhere over his withers to a point well behind his shoulders. It has also been demonstrated that the rider interferes least with the horse when the rider's weight is directly over the horse's center of gravity. For each specific purpose, a horse's center of gravity tends to be most of the time in a certain place. So, for each purpose, we need a slightly different kind of saddle and seat.

In noncompetitive riding, which means most of the riding done in America, it is fortunate that the horse's center of gravity tends to be located so that the rider can sit in greatest comfort and still not interfere with his horse. (Contrast this with the seat the rider of the race horse must assume.) In this book, we shall assume that this comfortable seat is the basic one and shall discuss all other seats as departures from or adaptations of this basic seat.

The Basic Seat

The good horseman can ride reasonably well on any kind of a horse that is fit for any use. We might except the bucking horse of the rodeo and the top race horse, though a good American rider should be able to weather the storm of a few modest bucks now and then, and he could ride the monkey seat of the race track, even if he could not boot home a winner.

Balance, as we have said, should be appropriate to the kind of riding done, but we might regard all balance in riding as a departure from a basic or normal seat. The more specialized the purpose, the farther we get away from the basic or normal seat and balance. Man o' War was ridden to glory with a monkey seat (rider over the withers, center of balance over the forelegs). Hell-to-set, one of the greatest bucking horses of all time, was ridden a very few times and then only after he was fifteen or sixteen years old (he was still throwing riders in the Garden when past twenty). Those few men who rode him used a seat we might call exactly the opposite of the monkey seat, the rider keeping his body well behind the middle of the saddle, and the center of balance over the loins.

American riding means use of the best seat for each purpose regardless of tradition. All kinds of expert riding, however, from the monkey seat to the forked-radish seat of the charro in a Western parade, have some of the common elements of the basic seat. Each special seat is a modification of the basic seat, the seat which most comfortably joins man and horse and enables them to move most nearly like one living body. The basic seat can be seen in much Greek sculpture. The frieze on the Parthenon shows it. (See Fig. 12.) Watch a polo player jogging or cantering onto the field and you will see it. The old fox hunter jogging to or from the hunt uses it, as does the cowboy on the trail. (See Fig. 5, p. 20.)

In this basic seat the body is erect; that is, the shoulders are directly above the hips. The back is straight or slightly convex (contrary to the riding school or "equitation seat"). The weight of the body is carried farther back in the saddle than in any other seat except the one used in showing gaited horses. The upper part of the thighs carry some of the body weight, especially at movements faster than a slow, uncollected walk.

FIG. 12. Riders on Parthenon frieze. Basic seat minus stirrups.

From hip to knee the leg inclines forward, approximately at a forty-five-degree angle with the body. The position of this upper portion of the leg depends on the size of rider and size of horse. A tall, long-legged rider on a small horse will ride with his thigh more nearly horizontal than perpendicular when riding the seat we are talking about. This is true because the curve on the inside of the rider's leg just below his knee should contact the horse at the thickest part of his body, just ahead of the girth, the part just behind the shoulder. This of course means that the short-legged rider on the good-sized horse will carry his upper leg more nearly perpendicular when riding this seat. The very short-legged rider on the very large horse will find this seat impossible (which does not mean that a short-legged rider cannot ride well on a large horse, though he may have to use excellence of balance to make up for slight difficulties in seat).

While we often read that it is the inside of the thigh that should contact the saddle in any seat, this is literally an impossibility if the rider sits down in his saddle. However, the contact, especially with the lower thigh, is made more nearly with the inside of the thigh than with the back of the thigh. If the back of the thigh makes the contact, the calf of the leg just below the knee will not contact the saddle at all, and the back of the calf, not the inside of it, will be the only part of the lower leg in contact with the horse. This will make the toes stick straight out away from the horse. With proper position of legs, the rider will not "grip the horse with his knees" as some fictional writers claim. He will not grip the horse at all when riding along casually. His muscles, all of them, are almost imperceptibly and unconsciously keeping in rhythm with the movements of the horse just as ballroom dancers keep in rhythm with each other. If the horse makes a sudden unexpected move, the legs grip the horse. Or, if the rider wishes the horse to make a sudden move, he will grip with his legs and seem to lift the horse with them in the desired direction.

The grip of the basic seat is not a knee grip; it is a grip with all the inner part of the leg from mid-calf to upper thigh. As the knee is just above the thickest part of the horse, a grip with knees *alone* would tend to force the rider up and off the horse. The good rider of the basic seat rides with legs relaxed but in the right position for gripping, and his stirrups are directly below his knee caps.

If proper contact is made with the horse from hips to the middle of the calf of the leg, the feet of the rider will satisfy any critic except the poor soul born to self-torture, who insists on riding, sometimes for hours, with his feet parallel to his horse's sides and his heels far below the balls of his feet. Though there are some purposes for which the heels should be well below the balls of the feet, in the seat we are now talking about the soles of the feet should be parallel with the ground. The leg position being as we have described it, the feet will be at about a forty-five-degree angle with the horse's sides. The beginner should have the balls of his feet on the stirrups, with any seat; the experienced rider using this seat may ride with his feet home (stirrups under the arch of the foot).

We have talked about this seat at such length and in such great detail because it is the basic seat from which others are deviations. As we have said, most old, experienced riders use it in relaxed moments; and it is to be seen in old Greek art as well as in Roman and early Italian art. This word of caution is needed by people who would study this seat in early Greek art. Some of the most expert horsemen the world has known (Xenophon, for instance) rode before saddles, or even horseshoes, were invented. The bareback seat they used varies from the seat with saddle and stirrups in two notable details. The feet were carried with the toes down and much farther forward than we carry them when using stirrups. Stirrups changed the position of the lower legs completely. (See Fig. 12.)

Except with the very large rider on the very small horse, the basic seat puts the center of balance of the rider directly over the center of balance of the horse when the horse is moving at an easy rate and not extremely collected. It is the seat for the beginner to use while he is learning the rhythm of his horse.

Pleasure Seats

After relaxation becomes a habit and some sense of balance and rhythm have been acquired, the rider is ready to learn the hack seat or "pleasure" seat, if he is to ride a flat saddle (the Western saddle we shall consider presently). (See Fig. 13.) In this seat the small of the back is slightly concave, the shoulders directly above or slightly ahead of the hips, and the seat well off the fleshy part of the buttocks with the body's weight carried by the "pinbones." This will put more weight upon the upper thighs than does the basic seat. From the seat of the "britches" to the middle of the calf, the leg is in contact with the horse. The nearer the contact is made with the inside of the leg, the better. This necessitates carrying the upper leg as described for the basic seat. The inside of the leg from the knee down to mid-calf will contact the horse. This is most easily done by carrying the feet a trifle farther to the rear than was seen in the basic seat.

Using this seat, it is important to sit in the middle of the saddle, not back on the cantle. This means that when the feet are properly placed the stirrup leathers are straight up and down. Except with the very tall rider on the very small horse, the stirrup leathers should be of such length that, when the legs are allowed to hang down as far as possible and the rider is sitting in the middle of his saddle, the bottom of the stirrups come to the bottom of the ankle bones. Another good test of length is to keep the feet level and stand straight up in the saddle. If the stirrups are the right length (for most riders), the rider will be clear of the saddle by about two inches.

The feet may be used best with stirrups carried under the balls of the feet; for when feet are home all ankle rhythm is lost.

The polo seat varies little more from the basic seat than does the hack or pleasure seat. In fast playing the polo player's back is apt to be quite convex rather than concave, and toes stick out. He rides

Fig. 13. Western pleasure. Same as Eastern hack or pleasure.

with his feet home and sometimes tends to ride "all over his sad- dle." The "correct" polo seat is the forward seat, which we shall presently talk about.

Contrary to popular belief, there is little essential difference be- tween the Eastern pleasure seat and the Western pleasure or trail seat. Many riders find it difficult to change from one to the other, but this is because of difference in saddle, not in seat. Most Western saddles are built up so that the seat slopes downward from fork to cantle (front to back). This makes it a little difficult for the novice to sit over the center of balance of his horse if the saddle is too long. However, as every kid who has ridden bareback knows, the movements of a horse tend to push the rider forward on the horse's back and the rider with balance and rhythm finds little difficulty in sitting in the middle of a Western saddle rather than with his back against the cantle.

These built-up saddles have a very good reason for being. In the old days a cowboy never knew when his horse might buck. The built-up seat helped the cowboy keep his seat. When riding a bucking horse in a rodeo the rider keeps back in the saddle. If he gets forward or leans forward, he has lost his day money, if not a good deal more.

The length of stirrup is the same for Western pleasure riding as for Eastern, though a shorter stirrup may be used without penalty in Eastern Pleasure classes.

While differences between the Eastern and Western pleasure riding *seats,* either for show ring classes or on trails, are slight or nonexistent, we must remember that Eastern and Western riding are vastly different. Horses are trained for very different responses, for very different use of reins, and for very different performance.

Dressage, Jockey, and Forward Seats

We have just considered two seats that are very similar to the basic seat we first talked about. Let us now consider some seats that vary considerably from the basic because they are used to get very special kinds of performance from the horse.

DRESSAGE SEAT

Of these very special seats, the dressage seat is least extreme. It differs from the basic seat only in the rigidity and straightness of the back and in placement of the feet. One or two American dressage riders have used a slightly shorter stirrup then we have considered for the basic. The feet in dressage riding are carried a little farther to the rear than in the basic seat. The heels are directly under the point where the body weight rests on the saddle.

JOCKEY SEAT

The seat that differs most widely from the basic is the monkey seat of the race rider. (See Fig. 14.) The horse straining every fiber for a brief dash of speed over a smooth track has most of his weight on his front legs, as his outstretched nose and neck attest. This means that his center of balance is practically over his front legs. So the rider uses a featherweight, diminutive saddle that sits well up on the withers. Then he shortens the stirrups, which are attached toward the front of the saddle, so that when he stands they carry all his weight directly over the withers. This gives him a very precarious

Fig. 14. Jockey seat or "monkey seat."

and uncomfortable seat but places all his weight over the horse's center of gravity.

It has been said that the forward seat used in hunting and jumping is midway between the monkey seat and a "natural" seat, whatever the latter may mean. This definition is more an indication of the loose use of the term "forward seat" than it is an accurate definition. The modern hunting and jumping seat that has now reached a high degree of efficiency in America has an interesting history. A slight knowledge of this history, part of which we have already considered, will help us understand the seat.

FORWARD SEAT

In 1900 the proper jumping seat dictated long stirrups and a backward inclination of the body when landing. It was quite correct to hang on to the horse's mouth for dear life because that was the only way Lord So-and-so could stay on top. At about this time Tod Sloan of Kokomo, Indiana, put into effect his brilliant idea that a horse could perform better if the weight on his back was placed over the withers. Almost at the same time, and certainly independently, Captain Federico Caprilli of Italy was voicing and practicing some very similar ideas about riding. His main idea was that the equilibrium of the horse changes with his speed, gait, and the kind of work he is doing; and it is the duty of the skilled rider to be constantly aware of and responsive to the equilibrium of his horse, riding always in a manner that will interfere as little as possible with his fluid equilibrium. Thus he went farther than did Tod Sloan in the general improvement of riding.

From Italy the new ideas spread to France. They were brought back to America by World War I veterans. In 1923 two American majors went to study at the Italian cavalry school, which was by that time quite in line with the ideas of Caprilli. Before the Russian Revolution, Lieutenant Rodzianko, a young Russian sportsman, studied in Italy. Upon his return home he found deaf ears, of course, among the old-line officers; but his writing made considerable impression on at least a few of the young and intelligent horsemen of his day. When the Revolution came, all men of cultivation were either killed or fled the country. Russia's loss was America's gain. Some of them came here, and more than one young Russian officer found Americans willing to pay for good riding instruction. A one-time captain of the First Hussars of the Russian Imperial Cavalry, V. S. Littauer, found, in his own words, "too good to be true" the fact that "Americans would pay $5 an hour for being shouted at." It is very fortunate for American horses and horsemen that he found this, for with his years of teaching and his half-dozen or more books he has advanced forward riding of amateurs in America far beyond that of any other country.

From Kokomo to Kiev and as far south as Sicily came the ingredients that went into the American forward seat. (See Fig. 15.)

In this seat the body leans forward until the weight is directly

over the stirrups. The shoulders are "open" and the back is straight
or slightly concave. The seat in the middle is so far forward that
"the crotch of the britches touches the pommel." Relatively little
weight is carried on the seat of the saddle and this is carried by the
bones of the pelvis, not by the buttocks. The upper leg's position in
relation to the body is much the same as that in the basic seat. Because of the position of the body, the knee, then, is farther forward
on the saddle and lower than in the basic seat. The stirrup leathers
are vertical, as in the basic seat. The foot is carried much farther

Fig. 15. Forward seat.

back than the knee. The heels are pushed as far as possible below
the ball of the foot so that all the weight of the rider seems to be
"pushed down into the heels." The feet are carried at about a
thirty-degree angle with the horse's sides. They are placed in the
stirrup so that the foot touches the inside bar of the stirrup and
more weight comes on the inside than on the outside of the foot.
The feet may be either home or with the ball of the foot on the
stirrup. (The latter gives more opportunity for use of the ankle in
rhythm with the horse, but the former gives more security.)

The position of the feet makes the calves hard, which, in turn,
makes them most effective for gripping. More weight is carried by
the feet in this seat than in most others, but the lower pelvis and
upper thighs should be snugly down on the saddle. Lower thighs,
inner surfaces of knees, and upper calves are relaxed but in close

contact with the horse during slow, quiet riding. During jumping or any other violent movement, these three parts of the leg grip the saddle.

Hands and arms are used uniquely in this seat. The elbows are of course carried in close to the sides, but they are carried a little ahead of the waist. From the elbow to the horse's mouth, arm, wrist, and reins form a straight line.

This seat gives the best of all opportunities for the fluid balance that goes *with* every movement of the horse. The hips, knees, and ankles give the rhythm a springy seat. It is a seat that seems very formidable to the Kentuckian who says, "For unrequited labor, nothing beats using a bucksaw or riding a three-gaited horse." However, the forward seat is extremely uncomfortable only for those who forget that the grip is relaxed in all but very energetic movements of the horse. Certainly it is not the seat to be used for casual pleasure riding on trail or bridle path. It is doubtful if many of the riders who developed and use this seat have ever ridden the uniquely American horse, bred and trained not solely for jumping or for speed over turf but for ease and delight of the rider for any distance over any terrain.

Balanced Western Seat

Though the forward seat was developed on flat saddles, changes in Western riding in recent years have made the forward seat extremely useful in the West, though when used on a stock saddle it is called the balanced seat, and some changes in the stock saddle of today have to be made in order to ride the balanced seat most effectively. (See Fig. 16.)

Early stock saddles, used in the days when wild stock was worked on half-broken horses, had high forks and cantles but the seat was flat. Today, when most of the people who buy high-priced stock saddles ride for comparatively short periods of time and then only for competitive purposes, stock saddles are of very different build. Lower cantles and forks as seen in the modern roping saddle, help in riding the balanced seat. However, the seat in most modern saddles is built up in front. This makes it very comfortable when the rider is riding slowly or waiting his turn in competition, but it also makes moving forward in the saddle to accommodate a shift in balance of the horse a very difficult matter.

It is obvious then that the ideal stock saddle for our present purpose must be specially made so that it will have the useful qualities of the low-down roper plus a flat seat—one that is not built up. In such a saddle, the rider can use the seat used on the Pariani or other forward-seat flat saddle. While he does not have the advantage of knee support given by the Pariani, so useful in jumping, he does have the fork of his saddle for thigh support when balance

Fig. 16. Balanced Western.

is far forward. This thigh support would be very awkward or even painful in jumping, but for the work of the stock horse it is very helpful at some moments.

When using the built-up seat for balanced riding in stock horse competition, the rider has to lean far forward to get his weight where it belongs when the horse's balance is forward, as in a quick start. Also, when a stock horse is executing a sliding stop, the rider using a built-up seat must lean far forward to keep his horse's haunches free from weight, though many a good stock horse learns to do such a feat in spite of a rider who leans back and puts all of his two hundred pounds over his mount's kidneys.

On the quick turns of the working stock horse, the rider using the built-up seat again has to lean forward to keep over the center of balance, but on such turns he finds the fork of his saddle very useful for a little thigh support.

It is obvious that stirrup leathers on the stock saddle have to be a little shorter for the balanced seat than for the basic seat, used for trail riding, and the stirrups must not be hung as far forward as they are on some of the specially built stock saddles of today.

Western Parade and Gaited Show Seats

At the opposite extreme from the forward seat are the Western parade seat and the show seat used with five- and three-gaited horses. (See Figs. 17, 18 and 19.) Let us consider the Western parade seat.

Fig. 17. Charro or Western parade seat.

Viewed from the side, it presents the rider in as near a vertical line as possible without forcing the legs to stick far out away from the sides of the horse. Head and body are erect, back straight. The rider sits well back against the cantle of the saddle. The leg from hip to knee may incline slightly forward, but not as much as in any other seat so far considered. The leg from the knee down is perpendicular. The heels are kept down and the feet as nearly parallel as is possible without cramping. The arms hang straight down from the shoulder to elbow. From elbow to wrist, the arms remain close to the body, with the wrist just high enough to clear well the horn of the saddle. The wrist should be flexed slightly at all times.

Fig. 18. Gaited and Walking Horse show seat.

This seat is used only at the walk and the parade trot, the only proper gaits for the parade horse. It shows off the rider as a fine, erect figure of a man, and by sitting back in the saddle and carrying his knees as far to the rear as possible the rider shows off the elegant front of his mount.

The seat for classes for American Saddle Horses (the three- and five-gaited classes) is nearer that of the parade seat than any other. (See Fig. 18.) It is designed for one purpose only—to show off the horse. It is uncomfortable and not too secure. The rider, on a saddle designed to stay nearer the croup of the horse than does any other saddle, sits as far to the rear as possible. He keeps his knees as far back as possible and rides with as long a stirrup as he can use and still just clear the saddle when standing in his stirrups. His body

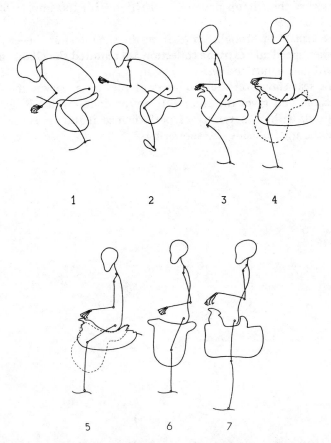

1   2   3   4

5   6   7

FIG. 19. Lines of thrust and balance in major seats of American riding: (1) jockey or monkey seat; (2) forward jumping seat; (3) balanced Western; (4) Western and Eastern pleasure; (5) basic seat; (6) gaited and Walking Horse show seat; (7) Charro or parade seat.

is erect at all times except when signaling his horse at the start of the canter. At the trot, his erect posture and long stirrups prevent posting, and the rigidity of his body prevents sitting the trot. He puts most of his weight in the stirrups when trotting and moves his body slightly in the same rhythm he would use if posting. In achieving what rhythm he can, he uses his ankles more than they are used in any other seat. At the canter, stirrup pressure is in rhythm with the horse's head. At the rack the horse's head is steady and the ankles vary the stirrup pressure in rhythm with the impact of the horse's forefeet.

The arms drop straight down from the shoulders at slower gaits, but when speed and extreme collection are required the elbows move forward and hands and wrists move upward.

This seat shows off the shoulders of the horse, makes the back look short and gives the rider full use of double reins in getting the speed, flash, and variety of performance required. It is not a seat to be used outside the show ring.

Part III

SELECTING

THE

PERSONAL

MOUNT

9

Factors in ~~~~~~~~~~~~~~~~~~~~~~~~~~~~~~~~
choosing a horse ~~~~~~~~~~~~~~~~~~~~~~

The "Safe" Horse for the Beginner

The man who says there is no such thing as a safe horse would be telling the truth if he would add two more words to his statement: *to me*. No horse is safe for such a person because no horse can communicate with him, though he may have ridden all his life. Therefore, no horse is predictable to him. The beginning rider is also unable to predict what a horse will do and is unable to communicate to the horse adequately. The beginner differs from our friend who says no horse is safe, however, because the beginner's condition may be temporary. This does not make it any less imperative that safety must be the prime consideration when he is buying his first horse. A first horse must have experience and judgment enough for both himself and his rider. He must be so wise in matters of conventional signals used by riders and conventional responses of trained horses that he can teach his new owner.

A wise and beautiful old son of San Juan, a veteran of the tanbark, was such a horse. I found him, by accident, in very bad condition and bought him for very little. After restoring him I gave him to a friend who used him to finish teaching a twelve-year-old girl to ride. The old horse was so wise that when the girl would signal him for any kind of performance with a conventional signal, such as a touch on the top of the neck for a trot, he would instantly do the requested thing, do it perfectly but never so fast or violently that he would upset his young rider. If she did not soon do her part properly, he would stop, and stand perfectly still as if to say, "Now let's start all over again." The young lady's biggest problem was learning about the leads of the canter. For some time the old horse would take the inside lead the moment his rider pulled his nose to the rail of the ring. But she could never remember which shoulder to lean over and sometimes would stiffen up and bounce horribly on the canter. Finally the old horse took charge of the situation. He was thoroughly cooperative but when his young rider made a mistake, he would stop, wait until she regained her composure and proper balance, and then start again to do whatever it was that he thought she was trying for; and he was usually right. In a few months the old horse was so successful in his teaching that the girl was showing him with some success in small local shows in pleasure classes. Before the season was out she showed him in open classes and won ribbons. This, of course, is an exceptional case; but it illustrates what I am talking about: The first horse must be wiser than the rider.

At the other extreme is the first horse that is a green young animal, well disposed, taught to neckrein moderately well, and to start and stop willingly. A friend of mine, whom I shall call Mr. Smith, bought such a horse recently. He did so because we have a mutual friend, Mr. Jones, who bought a green horse last year, learned to ride on it, and is now getting along famously with his horse—one of those exceptions that breed false optimism in the minds of wishful thinkers. Mr. Smith has just telephoned me about his problem. His originally well-disposed young horse a few days ago refused to cross a newly painted white line on the road. When my friend insisted, his mount reared and turned toward home. Any old horseman can finish this story. The young animal now rears and whirls habitually and my friend cannot ride it away from home. There are notable exceptions, but this is the usual story of the green rider with the green horse. The trouble is not always rearing and whirling and stable balking. It may be any one or more of a dozen bad habits or vices. The trouble may even be more serious if the rider is persistent, and result in serious injury to rider, horse, or both.

A first horse that is safe because he is dull and lifeless is no pleasure. Such an animal will soon discourage even the most ardent beginner. Furthermore, such a horse may not be as safe as he seems, for he certainly will not be able to move quickly out of harm's way.

The beginner can learn very little from the dull horse. The alternative is to buy a first horse that is wise, well-trained, and alert. This means considerable cost if the horse is in his prime. Fortunately the costly horse is not the only solution to this problem.

Cost

Cost is usually a very important item in plans for a purchase of a personal mount. Before deciding on how much to spend on a horse, it is a good idea to get in mind some basic facts about what it costs to produce a horse. A few horses are raised on Western ranges where feed costs are very low, but to make the horse raised on such ranges useful off the ranch requires rigorous and intensive training, so his cost may be greater than might be expected. In any event, good horses raised on open range are becoming very rare on the market. So let us consider the horse raised on the ranch or farm or on the city lot. The stud fee of a moderately good stallion is around $100. The feed for the mare during the time she is carrying and nursing the colt will be at least $100. Probably another $200 will go for the feed of the colt for the next three or four years. Then there is some labor cost and probably some veterinary expense. So at least $500 will go into the cost of getting the colt to usable age. If he is to have sufficient training to be safely ridden, more expense is involved. If he is to have training enough to keep from disgracing his rider in small shows, at least a year of training will go into him, which might double his cost.

Many years ago, William Belknap, one of Kentucky's wisest horsemen gave this advice: "If you have $900 to spend for a horse, figure on paying $200 for the horse and $700 for his training."

This may seem a discouraging picture to many young horsemen. However, luck may be on their side. Though it costs hundreds of dollars to produce a horse, many good horses are on the market at less than cost of production, for various reasons. Some people enjoy the business and knowingly raise horses at a loss. Others get enough use out of a horse before he is sold to justify his cost. Still others raise horses on farms or ranches that produce winners, and the winners pay the cost of the also-rans (at least that is what is hoped for). Then, too, the growing demand for registration papers makes it increasingly possible to buy an unregistered horse, especially if he is of unknown breeding, at a very reasonable price.

In view of all this, if you expect to buy a horse for less than the usual cost of producing a good young animal, make sure you know why the low-priced horse is priced low, and be prepared to make some compromises. Also, when buying a horse remember that the man who buys a diamond does not expect to be able to take that diamond into the market any time and get what he paid for it. Just so with a horse, or with an automobile. The man who buys a car, even a second-hand one, does not expect to go back to the dealer and get his full purchase price when he is ready to sell the car.

Of course a bargain is now and then found in surprising places, but many apparent bargains have been the cause of much sorrow. False bargains have driven many people out of the horse game. The best place to look for a horse is in the stable of a responsible dealer or in the corral of a reliable breeder. If the average buyer goes to an auction or answers an advertisement, he will do well to take with him, if he can, an experienced horseman. (Would that he could also take a good veterinarian!) I say, "if he can," because a reliable horseman is never eager to go on such an excursion. He knows that, at best, his judgment is only a guess and that it has been proved fallible on more than one occasion.

The reliable dealer will stand behind any statement he makes about a horse, because his reputation is what keeps him in business.

Before we consider horses suitable for special use and purebred or registered horses, valuable because of their breeding, let us consider the moderate-priced horse for the first personal mount. I have said that, to get a horse below cost, there must be compromise. The age of the horse is the safest place to make the first compromise. Many a good tune has been played on an old fiddle and many polo players will buy only aged mounts. (See Plate 1.)

As a personal mount for pleasure, the writer prefers the age of fifteen to the age of five. Joanna Jones was still winning championships in five-gaited classes at nineteen. Golddust Maid broke all trotting records at the age of eighteen. In the writer's stable is a grand old black gelding, long in the tooth and gray around the eyes. Plate 2 shows him as he looked in June of 1960, but by September, 1960 (Plate 3) he had become the best mount for a seven-year-old horseman in the country.

This horse is prompt, will stay up all day in any company and will put up for his young rider a show of reining, running, and sliding

PLATE 1. An eighteen-year-old gelding. Former show horse; now used for trail riding in roughest part of Zane Grey country. Rosemary D. Taylor up.

to a stop that delights onlookers. The old horse will never see thirty again and the condition of his teeth makes eating a slow process, but he is fat and sleek. His legs are clean as a colt's and he is a safe mount for his light load on any terrain. This is, of course, an exceptional case, but it illustrates the fact that years do not hurt a horse for personal use if he is sound and thrifty. Age does make a considerable difference in price, after a horse reaches what we might call "the age of discretion."

Soundness and Conformation

Regardless of age or pedigree, unsoundness should be avoided when selecting a personal mount. There is no such thing as an "almost sound" horse. If the buyer is not experienced, he should not buy a horse without a veterinary examination or an inspection by an experienced horseman whose integrity is absolute.

CAVEAT EMPTOR

The term *unsound* may be used to include impaired vision, faulty functioning of the respiratory system, or any ailment of the legs or feet that causes the horse pain when he travels. Most horsemen are aware of the importance of soundness of vision in the horse, and almost as many are aware of the importance of soundness of the respiratory system (largely because a horse unsound in the wind frequently makes unusual noise), but I have seen riders of considerable experience ride a horse that was lame in two feet and be utterly unaware of the distress of their mounts. Not only are unsound feet and legs painful to the horse, but also they are dangerous if the rider ever asks his horse to move quickly, especially over difficult terrain. Unsoundness of feet and legs is of so many varieties that a complete list would not fit in this book. The most common of them are joint lesions called variously spavins, sidebones, ringbones, splints (not always an unsoundness), and so on according to location and structure. I omit the superficial and general discussion of them that space in a book such as this might allow and also omit customary line drawings of them because I feel that in such matters, more than in most, a little knowledge is a dangerous thing. I have never seen a picture in a nontechnical book that would help a layman recognize a small spavin or an incipient sidebone, and I certainly do not want to give any young horseman false confidence that will lead to his buying an unsound horse. Unless the seller of the horse you buy is a man of absolute and proven integrity and a man of longstanding reputation for honesty in his community, do not buy any horse without an inspection by a veterinarian of your own choice.

Even if the horse is sound, his feet may have been pinched in at the heel by faulty shoeing and lack of care so that he may not go sound long. This is especially true of the Saddlebred horse that has been shown, or the cowpony that has been cowboy shod and used in the rocks. Unsoundness may be present any place from the shoes to the ears.

CONFORMATION

If a horse reaches the age of twelve or more, has had considerable use during his life and is sound and thrifty, the chances are that any defects he may have in conformation are not serious. However,

PLATE 2. José Viejo—June 30, 1960. Age thirty. Emaciated and deficient in dentures.

there are some matters of conformation that it is well to bear in mind when looking for a horse. First of all, his feet should be big enough to carry him. It is quite common now to hear horsemen who ride only in the show ring boast about "what tiny feet my Quarter Horse has." The writer has even heard working cowhands, who should know better, boast about the fact that a certain twelve-hundred-pound horse took a number 0 shoe.

It would be hard to think of any living tissue that takes a more severe pounding and strain than does a horse's foot. The bigger it is, the better—provided (and this is an important provision) that it is of the right shape. It should be larger at the shoe than at the coronet (top of hoof), concave in the sole, open at the heel and provided with a good, big flexible frog. When properly trimmed by a competent farrier the hoof should have an angle with the ground of from forty-five to fifty degrees, depending upon the slope of the pastern; and the heel should be well off the ground.

PLATE 3. José Viejo—September 1, 1960. Able to out-perform many young stock horses and a formidable contender in any Western Pleasure class.

The pastern should be strong and not extremely sloping or extremely upright. It should not be too short and stubby. The cannon bone should be short in proportion to the forearm and flat like a razor. The arm should not be too horizontal, and the longer the better, as in Plate 4.

The shoulder should be as sloping as possible, which makes the withers lie farther toward the rear than the elbows. The larger the girth the better, but the horse for saddle use should not be too wide, especially between the forelegs. The forelegs should not "come out of the same hole," however. They should not be stuck onto the body like wide-apart legs stuck onto a bench. This latter kind often gives the horse a rolling gait and also often goes with "paddling," a throwing out to the side of the forefeet as the horse trots. This is a bad defect and one that cannot be corrected with shoeing, as some optimists hope.

As any mechanic could tell, the shorter a horse's back, the

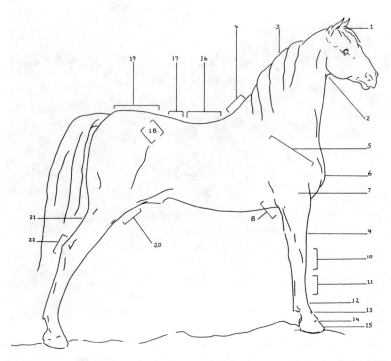

Fig. 20. Parts of the horse: (1) poll; (2) throat; (3) crest; (4) withers; (5) shoulder; (6) breast; (7) arm; (8) elbow; (9) forearm; (10) knee; (11) cannon; (12) fetlock joint (sometimes called pastern joint); (13) pastern; (14) coronet; (15) hoof; (16) back; (17) loin; (18) point of hip; (19) croup; (20) stifle; (21) gaskin; (22) hock.

stronger it is. It should be carried smoothly into the hips by good strong loins. The rib cage should be well sprung out, not tucked up in the flank. The old cattlemen said, "A horse ought to be able to carry his dinner with him." The hips should be long and not too sloping, though the slope of the hip is a debatable matter and perhaps the least important point we have mentioned. The tail should not be set too low on the horse's body, even if his hips may slope a bit. A plumb line dropped from the back point of a horse's hip should touch his hock and the back of his pastern. This means he is not cow-hocked or sickle-legged. His stifles should be well muscled and strong.

There is much disagreement on the proper length of a horse's neck in proportion to his body; however, this writer and most stu-

PLATE 4. Four-year-old Saddlebred, well proportioned for rider comfort and great endurance, illustrating desirable conformation for saddle use.

dents of the matter say they have observed that the longer the neck, all other matters being equal, the better the horse, provided he knows how to handle it. The writer has a stubby-necked mare on which he can carry a glass full of sacrificial wine on Sunday and never spill a drop, but this mare is the exception. Usually the short-necked horse has a short, stubby gait, is heavy in the forehand and not at all flexible. The neck should be fine and flexible where it joins the head at the poll. The nearer diamond-shaped the head is, the better. This means there is much brain room above the eyes. The horse should have a fine muzzle, but the jaws should be wide and strong where they join the neck. This means freedom from respiratory trouble and has the advantage of greater chewing power.

While the general requirements of conformation outlined and illustrated in Plate 4 are all matters of general agreement among horsemen, the horse without some fault in conformation is, if it exists, very rare indeed. Although no horse should be chosen as a personal mount if he is strikingly lacking in the qualifications we have set up, the young rider with limited budget may find a very satisfactory mount that is not perfect in all details. Many a horse that is a little rough in the hips has given excellent service. Many a cow-hocked horse has distinguished himself in competition. While the refinement of head that we have just outlined is desirable, I have seen some hammer-headed horses that were God's gift to deserving riders. However, the inexperienced had best stick fairly close to rules.

There are only two details that have been found to have a high correlation with endurance—size of girth and straightness of action. In the six-hundred-mile endurance ride that the Army used to conduct annually, these qualities were found in the winners. The girth or "heart girth" is of course the circumference of the horse right behind the withers. It must be large in proportion to the size of the horse. It should be so, not because of the great width of his body but because he has a deep body. That is, when viewed from the side, the distance from the backbone, right behind the withers, to the lowest point touched by the saddle girth is great in proportion to the size of the horse.

The action that endurance winners have makes the foot move at the trot as if it were part of the rim of an imaginary wheel. This means that the feet neither flop out to the side (called "paddling") nor turn inward (called "dishing") as they move forward and back. Paddling is a fault no shoeing can correct. In rare cases dishing can be lessened, though never completely corrected.

"Retired" Horses

Though the ex-show horse (either three-gaited or five-gaited) and the ex-race horse may measure up to all our requirements, the young horseman should certainly have very expert advice before choosing either. Both are apt to be or have been unsound (an old lameness may easily come back). Both have probably been painfully subjected to so much human cussedness that a pleasant relationship or even a safe one may be very difficult to establish. The old cowpony may have a disagreeable trick or two, but he has learned to "get along" with almost any kind of a rider. The ex-polo pony is in much the same class and probably will have a little better rein and be a little light in the forehand.

Temperament and Ability

If a horse is to be selected for pleasure, the most important consideration is temperament. Personality clashes are as frequent between rider and mount as between people. The dominant, aggressive male with a heavy, stubby fist needs a good stolid horse with a mouth that is not too light and responsive. The sensitive person with a good deal of tension needs a quickly responsive but not flighty horse, and so on. The wise rider should not buy any horse until he can try it out. Not only should he ride the prospective mount in company, alone and over different kinds of terrain; he should also wear a slicker (raincoat) while riding a short distance and try trailer loading. He should pick up each foot and tap it lightly to make sure the animal is easy to shoe or can be handled if a nail or stone lodges in a hoof on the trail. Even if the horse is safe and amenable during the tryout, if he is not responsive, he will be no fun. To many riders, including the writer, the horse that is a mere machine for transportation is not enjoyable. If the horse takes no pleasure in the ride neither does the rider, unless he is a show-off and the horse is a prancer.

Selecting the Cross-Country Horse

If the rider is more expert than the one I have just had in mind, he may want to hunt or show or compete in the endurance trail rides that are becoming popular throughout the Southwest and in some parts of the East.

Consider first the selection of a horse suitable for jumping and hunting at a moderate pace. Of course the most popular and fashionable hunters are Thoroughbred or part Thoroughbred, but good jumpers and hunters occasionally occur in all breeds. The outline of conformation we have given above is quite suitable for selection of the hunter. Here are some additional things to look for if hunting and jumping are anticipated. The horse should be at least fifteen and a half hands high but not long-legged. The length of his neck is very important, for the jumper uses his neck for balance. His bone should be especially good; that is, he should not be noticeably smaller just below the knee than just above the pastern. His girth must be large. If you have money enough to buy a horse already trained to jump, try him out. If he gets excited, don't be too optimistic and think you can quiet him down after you buy him. The chances are some rider's hands did not follow the horse's head over a jump. That meant that when he thrust his head out to land, his mouth was hurt, which meant his heels came down and knocked off a rail. Then the horse was whipped. This is the usual way of spoiling a jumper and he never gets over it. Better buy a green horse that has never jumped.

If the young rider will pick the right kind of green horse and has patience, respect, and feeling for a horse and half as much sense as the horse, he can be sure of owning a jumper and useful hunter. Almost any horse of the right conformation and reasonably good temperament can be taught to jump. He should be tried out as follows:

Get on him quietly. See if he will walk around the ring or on the trail with a slack rein without having hysterics. Then trot him, first with just enough hold on the rein to keep him to a slow trot; then give him impulsion by squeezing with the legs, or a touch with the heel if necessary. At the same time collect him with the reins. If he breaks into a canter, no matter. The thing to look for is fear of the bit, shown by undue head tossing or pulling. If his mouth has not been spoiled and if he responds easily to impulsion (without the latter response he cannot be taught to jump), walk him up to a low obstacle, one not higher than the diameter of a telephone pole. Walk him over it a time or two. Then trot him at it and over it, using mild signals of impulsion with leg or heel if he hesitates. The object is to see if he can easily be given impulsion and also to see if he can handle his feet. Do not expect a green horse to hop over an obstacle, even a very low one, like a finished hunter, but extreme awkwardness or lack of coordination will show up on a low obstacle. A wise horseman never asks the green horse to take any obstacle higher than a bale of hay lying on its side, and such an obstacle must be very long so that there is no temptation to dodge around to the side of it, or it must be extended with wings.

Any well-built horse that is not too easily excited, responds readily to signals of impulsion, and is not unduly awkward will easily learn to jump four feet. Of course if his action is marked by a defect such as paddling, he is not worth wasting time on. Also, if he tends to stargaze (carry his head high, with nose out) or if he is heavy in the forehand and will not give to the bit and increase weight on his quarters when asked, he is fit for neither jumping nor pleasure riding. However, the horse with fair length of neck, sloping shoulder, and reasonably fine head is rarely heavy in the forehand unless his mouth has been ruined. It is the short-necked, coarse-headed horse that is apt to be heavy in front. A last and most important caution for the young rider looking for a jumper or hunter is: Be sure he has feet big enough (of the right shape, of course) and bone heavy enough to stand the work expected.

Selecting for Park and Trail Riding

Let us consider next the selection of the horse for the rider who feels he will find most enjoyment in riding in parks and on country lanes, frequently with clubs or informal groups. The show-ring classes called "Eastern Pleasure" or "Road Hack" or "Park Hack" display the kind of horse he is looking for. However, a horse may win in such classes and still not be at all pleasant in everyday use. For most enjoyable use of the kind we are considering, temperament is the most important single consideration after soundness and reasonably good conformation have been found. Tests for temperament we have already suggested. Special attention should be paid to the pleasure horse's willingness to load into and ride in a trailer, both alone and with another horse. He should be a horse that will stand quietly overnight when tied to a tree and should be equally quiet when a slicker is donned by his rider.

Gaits of a Pleasure Horse

Show classes for the pleasure horse are limited to horses of three gaits—walk, trot, and canter, with now and then the requirement of a hand gallop. However, I feel that it is slightly ridiculous to use the word "pleasure" to describe a horse whose gaits are limited to three. Unless the owner will never ride longer than a brief hour in the park, a slow gait is a *must*. It does not matter greatly whether it be a fox trot, running walk, stepping pace, or amble, so long as it is a gait that is delightful and easy to ride and is done at from five to eight miles an hour. Of course the horse bred for perfection of this gait is the Tennessee Walking Horse, but many other horses have a very satisfactory slow gait.

The writer's choice of a pleasure mount is the five-gaited horse, seen in the highest development in the American Saddle Horse. In the five-gaiter we have not only all the utilitarian gaits but also the gait for moods of extreme exuberance, the rack. This gait gives the feel of riding on a magic carpet, swiftly and smoothly gliding through space above all worldly care. The five-gaited horse at his best is the horse for all moods and purposes, but he has many drawbacks. First of all, *good* American Saddle Horses are extremely expensive. Cheap, inferior ones are the most disagreeable horses to be found. They will mix their gaits; or, worse, they will pace, the most miserable gait a horse can have under the saddle, unless it is very slow or modified into a stepping pace.

For most riders who want a pleasure horse to use under flat saddle, the horse whose conformation, action, soundness, and temperament measure up to the requirements we have outlined will be most satisfactory if he has the three conventional gaits and a good slow-gait.

Sex

There is more disagreement among horsemen in their preference of sex of mounts than about any other equine matter unless it would be about what is the "best" kind of horse. Mark Twain once said that it is difference of opinion that makes horse trading.

PREFERENCE FOR GELDINGS

In the West, especially in the range country, geldings are almost the universal preference, though now and then we see a mare ridden by a calf roper in a rodeo.

When the West was young there was good reason for this. A mare when in season might attract a stallion from anywhere. A strange stallion will, of course, kill a gelding or other stallions if he can. In those early days of all open range and lots of wild horses, if a mare could not lure a mate to her, she might leave her own bunch and join a wild herd.

Today in the West the old aversion to riding mares persists, though the real grounds for it have disappeared. If you ask a cowboy or cattleman or posse rider why he prefers geldings, he may tell you that mares are dirty in stall or corral or that they are more nervous than geldings or that they are fighters in a corral. Though I have spent most, certainly the best, of my life with horses, I have observed little that will substantiate these claims. Certainly a mare that has some inflammation of uterus or ovaries will be nervous and irritable, but a chronically ill gelding may show some equally, though different, irritating traits of temperament.

It may be that if a statistical study could be made we would find mares slightly more quarrelsome in crowded corrals than geldings, though I have owned geldings that would fight and whip anything, even a stallion, turned in with them.

The young horseman selecting his first horse may well be alert to local prejudice; for if there is a strong feeling against mares in his area he will have difficulty selling a mare should he choose to do so. Also, in some areas the prejudice is so high, the belief in the quarrelsomeness of mares so strong, that posses and other riding groups the horseman may wish to join request members to be mounted on geldings. It is worth note that there is some inconsistency here, for a statistical study will show that, in competitive performance, mares have a slight edge on geldings; and competitive performance is usually an important part of posses and some other riding groups. This ability of mares to perform may be the reason polo players have a preference for them as strong as the cowboy's preference for geldings.

EXTRA VALUE OF MARES, IF PUREBRED

If there is no local prejudice against mares, the beginner may safely select either a mare or a gelding for his first mount, if it is not a purebred registered animal. Of course a registered mare has the advantage of being of some value as a brood mare in addition to her value as a riding animal. In case of injury, this often means that a mare still has value where the crippled gelding is a total liability. The unregistered mare, of course, is a liability when bred. The cost of raising a colt is more than an unregistered horse will bring, as I explained early in this book.

STALLIONS

The use of stallions for pleasure riding has until very recent years been extremely rare. A few show-offs and a very few horsemen who greatly prefer the temperament of a stallion to that of a mare or gelding were the only riders of stallions. Very, very seldom did a Western stockman ride a stallion. One of the notable exceptions to this was a man by the name of Casement who bred some of the finest horses in the West. If my memory is correct his operations continued into the present era. After the term Quarter Horse was invented, or revived, he became known as a breeder of Quarter Horses. His preference for the stallion as a working stock horse was so great that he wrote some splendid articles about it, published years ago in *Western Livestock Journal.*

This preference for the stallion, though rare, is very old. There is no record of gelding, or castrating, horses in California prior to the nineteenth century. Before that time "the caballeros preferred riding stallions to mares as more powerful and proud," according to J. Frank Dobie, dean of all careful scholars writing about the horse. The reverse of the coin is that (also according to Dobie) the venerable Bede, writing in England in the eighth century, stated that the bishops traveled afoot until A.D. 630. Then they were mounted but rode only mares as a token of humility.

Certainly stallions vary as widely in temperament as do mares and geldings, but there is an indefinable quality most of them have that endears them to those of us who prefer them. When used and fed as mares or geldings are used and fed, stallions tend in general to be a little less high strung or flighty than geldings or mares. Under such conditions they are less sensitive to pain and more courageous and responsive to a competent and kindly master than mares and geldings are.

J. Frank Dobie writes that Major John N. Merrill, U.S. Cavalry, retired, told him of having in his command in Persia about one thousand horses, all stallions. "Never having been used for service, they were, he said, not vicious," writes Dobie.

Of course, the widespread notion that stallions are nervous and hard to handle has some basis in fact. Stallions are frequently kept in very small quarters, fed well, and used only to show off to prospective customers. An equally well-bred mare or gelding so handled would be just as nervous and hard to manage. Also, if a stallion is not well trained early by a competent horseman, when a mare in season is near he will be as silly as the hoodlums down by the drugstore watching the pretty girls go by. He will not whistle, but he is not at a loss for expression.

Stallions must have well-built corrals, high enough and tight enough to keep the horse from hurting himself if teased by animals coming up on the outside of his corral. I use a heavy-gauge chain link fence six feet high.

On trail rides only well-mannered stallions, if any, are welcome. They must be securely tied, for, no matter how well mannered a stallion may be, it makes any good horseman nervous to see him carelessly tied. I use a five-eighth-inch cotton rope around the throat tied with a bowline knot (I don't trust a snap) and run through the halter ring. I make sure that what I tie to is solid and strong. A stout tree limb or several tough mesquite or ironwood limbs tied together are very good.

Today the use of good stallions under saddle is increasing rapidly. They are to be seen in parades, and on trail rides. However, when I am asked about the advisability of buying a stallion for riding, I answer negatively unless the inquirer is not mindful of expense. A taste for riding a stallion is easily cultivated; it is expensive and, I find, incurable. (See Plate 5.)

PLATE 5. Author on Arizona-bred four-year-old stallion, on lion hunt in Northern Arizona. *Photo by Rosemary D. Taylor.*

10

Special

requirements

For Horse Show Competition

If the horse looked for is to be shown at small shows in addition to his use as a pleasure mount, the requirements we have set up will serve as a good guide. The size of bone and of foot I have emphasized are not important in show rings today. Refinement of head and the head carriage that go with a good sloping shoulder will be very important. The hips should be level on top, with the tail set high. Of course to win in three- and five-gaited classes the horse must have a set tail. Before the purchase of a horse with a set tail, the buyer should ask to see the horse gingered to determine if he carries his tail to one side.

If the horse is to be shown, it is best to try him under the most exciting conditions that can be found to see that he has no tendency to "get behind the bit." Some horses trained for the show by cruel trainers impatient for a quick sale so torture a horse to gain extreme collection and high action that under unusual excitement the horse will not take any hold of the bit at all. In some instances, he will fly backward from a standstill.

In Eastern Pleasure classes out West three gaits are the rule. Extremely high action is frowned upon, though the action must be true, as we have already described. In the Midwest and East, most three-gaited horses are required to have very high action. Two of the many factors that go into the production of high action are the extremely long foot and the weighted shoe. Both of these can be used by experts without injury to the horse, as we shall explain later; however, if not expertly used, the long foot and weighted shoe can cause damage that can never be undone. When buying the horse that has been shown in classes calling for excessive action, the buyer should always consult competent and reliable experts. It should not be necessary to say that the horse that is shod for high action should never be ridden except in the ring until his shoes are changed and the length of his feet has been gradually reduced to normal over a period of several shoeings.

For Western Use

The Western pleasure and trail horse is not in general conformation, action, and temperament vastly different from the Eastern pleasure horse. The stock available to choose from is a little coarser and the temperament a little calmer. Because the saddles are heavier and the terrain a little harder to get over than in the East, strength in back, loins, stifles, and arms is necessary. When a Western horse is offered for sale, the buyer does not usually look closely at the refinement of head, length of neck, and animation as does the Eastern buyer. He will look for a good, short back, long, powerful hips, well-muscled stifles and arms, and a quick response to the rein. (See Plate 6.) One thing he will insist on that is not usually required in the East; that is the ability of the horse to work on a slack rein. The good Western trail and pleasure horse works on a slack rein and picks his own footing. No horse of this kind should be bought without the buyer's trying him out on mountain and desert trails to see that the horse is surefooted on rough terrain and able to avoid gopher holes on the desert.

All the matters of safety and docility discussed for the Eastern horse, such as trailer riding, carrying a slickered rider, and standing tied are of course required for the Western horse. In addition to all these, there are several other requirements of the Western trail horse. He should know how to eat out of a nosebag and should be quiet and able to take care of himself without picking a fight when turned into a corral with other horses. Many a newcomer to the West has to stay home from trail rides or borrow a horse because his horse will not get along in a corral overnight.

The Western horse must be unafraid of a rope. His owner may want to lead a pack horse. If the Western horse will "ground-tie," he is more valuable than a horse that will not. Hitching racks do not grow on the desert, so many Western horses are taught to stand when the reins are dropped to the ground. In regard to this a word of caution is necessary: Western reins, except for calf roping and other special work, are not joined together as are Eastern reins, so

PLATE 6. Red Gates, excellent Morgan conformation. Rider, Marjorie Hambly, top trail boss. *Used by permission of George Axt-Photography*

sometimes the newcomer ties reins together at the ends. If reins tied together (or otherwise fastened together) at the ends are dropped to the ground and the horse gets a hind foot caught in them, he is likely to tear his mouth, throw himself, tear up the bridle and get into further trouble. If you drop your reins to ground-tie your horse, be sure they are loose at the ends!

The good trail horse has "a good rein." He stops at a light pressure without raising his head high. At a standstill he will turn to right or left at a slight movement of the bridle hand to either side, and he will do so without moving his hind feet or at least not moving them more than a few inches. Also, when moving, he will turn with equal response. He turns by throwing more weight on his haunches and using them as a pivot. The Western horse that will not do so will bow a tendon in front when turning at work, to say nothing of the effect on his rider's disposition. At a canter or gallop, the Western horse changes leads instantly and smoothly when turned, a feat we shall explain in a later chapter. He must stop with his hind feet well under him and without putting his head very high. He must do all this without the use of a tie-down or martingale. No horse of any kind, except a polo pony (some of which make excellent personal mounts when retired), should be considered as a personal mount if he cannot be ridden without a tie-down.

The good trail horse is flexible in the quarters. That is, he will move his haunches to either side in response to heel pressure. If he has this ability, it is easy to move him sideways by applying heel or leg pressure on one side. Many a rodeo contestant's life has been saved by a hazer whose mount was responsive in this way. The trail horse must have this ability when opening a gate, when sidling up to another rider for assistance, and in many other situations.

While selection of a pleasure mount for trail riding and other noncompetitive uses leaves a rather wide choice of type and breed, the horseman who is selecting a mount for pleasure use and showing in Western Pleasure or any other Western classes is limited to very definite breeds and types. Western Pleasure classes have now and then been won by Arabs, Apaloosas, Morgans, Palominos, horses of mixed breeds, and Standard-breds. However, the ideal show conformation for Western pleasure horses and trail horses is the type claimed as ideal by most Quarter Horse breeders, though quite a range of types is to be found among registered Quarter Horses. If the buyer is prepared to spend enough money to buy a horse that will have a fair chance of winning, even in small shows, he will be wise to spend a little more and buy a registered horse. The horse will be much more salable if the owner ever wants to sell him, and the personal satisfaction of owning a registered horse may in itself be worth the difference in price between just a good horse and a registered one.

If the animal to be purchased has conformation, action, and temperament, is sound, and has the abilities we have outlined for the pleasure horse, an intelligent horseman may teach him to become a show horse. However, if the horse is to be shown soon after purchase, the buyer should be sure that he has all the basic abilities necessary at the time of purchase. Further than that, the prospective buyer should attend shows in his vicinity and make a study of the current fashions in requirements in pleasure horse and trail horse classes in local shows. Even in the older types of horse shows of the East requirements change from year to year, in spite of the valiant efforts of horse show associations. In the intermountain West there is even less standardization. Then, too, to increase our problem, the new owner may want to use his new horse in competitive events more specialized and more rigorous than pleasure horse classes, such as competitive trail rides or roping matches. These events should be studied carefully.

The general abilities needed in Western competition in addition to those we have explained for the pleasure mount are as follows:

He must be able to sidestep to either side (as if up to a gate), crossing both fore and hind legs in the same manner. He must do this without moving the least bit forward or backward. He must be able to go quietly through a gate while his mounted rider holds it by one hand. He must stop when through, without making his rider lose hold of the gate. Then he must quietly but quickly move backward or forward as the situation demands for his rider to fasten the gate. He must be able to back up through any kind of a course marked on the ground, turning at signal of leg and rein without excitement. He must have the ability to jump from a standing start into a full gallop and slide to a stop on his hind feet, making a perfect number eleven mark on the ground, and must do so on a light rein without throwing up his head. He must be able to "offset," which is a quarter turn, a rolling turn with weight on haunches, using hind feet as a pivot. He must also be able to spin; that is, complete several turns in either direction. Above all, he must do all this on a light rein and walk quietly the moment reins are slackened after a bit of fast work.

Of course the horse cannot do much of the work we have outlined unless his rider has the balance, seat, and hands to go with him. It is true that it takes two to tango, and it is truer that horse and man must be one if the kind of movements we have described are to be done correctly. This is a matter I shall consider in detail when I discuss riding the Western horse. If the rider is buying a top Western horse and has not perfected his own skill, he should require the horse to be ridden by a finished horseman under whom the horse can work without handicap. Then, too, he should require the horse under a skilled rider, other than the seller, to demonstrate his ability to work with a rope. While the calf-roping horse is a highly specialized and trained animal, the ordinary good Western horse should know what a rope is and be willing to stop with weight on his haunches when the rope is thrown and the rider shifts weight to dismount. It may be unreasonable to demand that any good Western horse be able to work a rope to keep a fighting calf prostrate, but at least he should stand after the rope is thrown and face his dismounted rider when he pulls on the rope, though it is entirely permissible for him to wear a foul rope at such work.

All the requirements for the ideal personal mount which we have just outlined are rarely if ever to be found in any one animal. They are the things to look for and to demand to have demonstrated by the prospective seller who claims to be offering a top horse for sale. The more the horse lacks in conformation, temperament, or training, the less he is worth. If he is not perfectly sound, the buyer should shun him like the plague. If he is not in good flesh, the buyer should be very wary. There are few booby traps more dangerous for the nonprofessional horseman than the hope that he can profit by buying a thin horse and fattening it. The coat should be bright, even if long because of the season of the year. The eye should be bright and the ears alert.

Part IV

SELECTING

A REGISTERED

HORSE

11

A discussion

of breeds

For almost any purpose a good horse can be found in any breed or among horses of mixed or unknown breeding; however, certain qualities are to be found more frequently in some breeds than others, and some faults are more frequent in some breeds than others. If the buyer is interested in the purchase of a purebred horse, he is fortunate if he likes a kind that is popular in his community. He will have a larger choice, will be more likely to find a reliable breeder or dealer who will stand behind a sale, and will have more classes in local shows to study and to compete in. There will be more congenial people to share his interests and more group activity he will enjoy among owners of the locally popular breed than among other horsemen.

For the horseman whose choice is not made on the basis of local tastes, some suggestions and warnings about the choice of a breed will be useful.

The Quarter Horse

A breed was defined by one of America's top authorities on horses as "a group of horses uniform in conformation and temperament, possessed of the ability to transmit their qualities uniformly to their progeny." Certainly there is more diversity in most breeds than this definition would suggest. There is of course diversity in the Quarter Horse, and it is the diversity in temperament that the beginning buyer should be most concerned with.

A registry for the Quarter Horse was established in the second quarter of this century. It contained no rigid requirements about blood lines. A horse could be registered if he passed inspection as being of any one of *three* types. (See Plates 7, 8, and 9.) Rules changed rapidly and are still changing. Fairly close up on the pedigree of any Quarter Horse you may find blood of several strains or breeds, each with its distinctive temperament.

PLATE 7. Three good Quarter Horses.

One of such strains with a very distinctive temperament and other qualities that are important in the breed is the Copperbottom. The history of this strain will help in understanding it and the breed of which it is such an important part.

The oldest Copperbottom I have been able to find an authoritative record of is the one on the list of the Foundation Sires of the first registry for Saddlebreds, set up in 1891 in Kentucky. As was the custom in those days, and for some time afterward, colts were often named after their sires; so there were written accounts of many Copperbottoms. The first mention of one I can find was a Canadian horse imported into Kentucky about 1812. He had all the gaits known to the Saddler and was called, as were all horses that did anything other than gallop and trot, a pacer. The Copperbottoms were in all probability some of the old English saddle stock, very different from Thoroughbreds, brought over to the colonies and Canada before the Thoroughbred was "invented." That early blood was strong. Its influence can be seen today. It is particularly important for its temperament. The temperamental virtues of the

PLATE. 8. Excellent Quarter Horse, rider using balanced Western seat, but with hand momentarily in very bad position.

American Saddle Horse, described elsewhere, are due to this blood. Copperbottoms were horses of unlimited fire and courage but amenable to restraint, if not abused, quick to learn and smart enough to work cattle or follow a furrow. If the buyer of a Quarter Horse to be used as a personal mount gets one with the old Copperbottom temperament, he will be fortunate.

In addition to Copperbottom blood in Quarter Horse pedigrees there is sometimes Morgan blood, with its distinctive temperament, which I discuss elsewhere in this book.

Many of the first entries in the Quarter Horse Registry were good working stock horses. They made excellent rodeo horses as well as

PLATE 9. Rider using Western pleasure seat on Quarter Horse. *Courtesy Arlene Goodheart, Scottsdale, Arizona.*

good personal mounts for other purposes. The popularity of the breed grew astonishingly. Race tracks for quarter racing sprang up almost overnight. Races mean money, and the breeders were not slow to plan their programs for producing winning racers. Since no breed will give speed as uniformly as the Thoroughbred, today it is possible to find Quarter Horses with little blood other than Thoroughbred. This means that before buying a Quarter Horse to use as a personal mount, the prospective purchaser should try out the horse for temperamental quality just as in the tryout I shall describe for the Thoroughbred.

As far as temperament is concerned, one big advantage of choosing a personal mount from the Quarter Horse breed is that there is a wide variety available. The buyer can readily find almost any kind he prefers. Most Quarter Horses have a good fast walk and can easily be taught to do a slow gait. The trot is usually short but easy to ride and most of these horses can quickly learn to do a very easy, slow canter. Of course the outstanding ability of the Quarter Horse, when properly educated, is his sudden responsive burst of speed and his uncanny maneuverability. He seems to have built-in "cow sense" and can tell what a cow is going to do even before she makes up her own mind. This same sense makes him a great horse for hunting. A Quarter Horse is often able to spot deer much farther than can his rider.

As a trail horse the Quarter Horse is apt to be very surefooted. He is rarely fussy in company, behaving as quietly then as when alone. His ribs are usually well sprung, so he can "carry his dinner with him" and look as good after a five-day trail ride as when he started.

One care the rider should have when choosing a Quarter Horse as a personal mount is about feet. The original horse of the Southwestern cow country almost invariably had good feet naturally, though many of them were ruined by careless and ignorant shoeing that contracted them and impaired the use of the lower joints. The Quarter Horse still usually has good feet, but there is a current fad among show fans for little feet. The writer has seen the feet of a good show specimen rasped down to take a shoe smaller than it should wear.

When I asked why he was ruining the horse's feet, the blacksmith, a competent one who knew the harm he was doing to the horse, replied, "The owner told me the judge of the last show said the horse was tied second because his feet were too big." The buyer should beware of a horse whose feet are not big enough to carry him. Especially he should beware of a horse that has been the victim of shoeing for any show purpose that may have injured the feet.

Very generally speaking, the racing type of Quarter Horse is not apt to be as pleasant a personal mount as those Quarter Horses that are of the "using" type which carry considerable blood of the old ranch stock, such as the RO's. The racing type resembles the Thoroughbred in build and looks more like a greyhound.

Conformation in the Quarter Horse breed is as varied as the temperament. However, the ideal of many Quarter Horse enthusiasts is a good one for the prospective buyer to have in mind. Let us consider it.

The ideal has a fairly short head which is not large in proportion to the size of his body. The eyes are wide apart and set about midway between poll and nose. The muzzle is firm and the jaw strong, with powerful cheeks for chewing roughage. The neck is flexible at the poll. The ideal Quarter Horse's neck is not as long as that of some other breeds. It has to be flexible and set on sloping, powerful shoulders.

While the natural head carriage of most Quarter Horses is satisfactory for a personal mount, many professional trainers of stock horses use chains behind the horse's ears, wire cable nosebands or other pain-causing devices to make the horse work with his head held low. A Quarter Horse that has had such training lacks the flexibility of neck desirable in a mount to be used for varied, noncompetitive purposes.

The ideal we are considering has long, powerful arms, short cannon bones, strong pasterns neither too long nor too sloping. His stifles should be large and his gaskins well muscled.

One outstanding characteristic of the horse we are considering is a tremendous heart girth. This means great depth of body. Width is not a defect as long as the inside of the juncture of front legs with body is a Gothic arch. There should not be any flat expanse of chest between the front legs.

The back should be strong, loins powerful, and hips long, powerful, and well muscled. The general appearance of this ideal is that of a compact, powerful animal, one that is well muscled but also flexible and quick.

The Apaloosa *

Three other breeds with registries originating in the West have ideals of conformation practically identical with the ideal Quarter

---

* As J. Frank Dobie says on page 44 of *The Mustangs* "The name has been spelled and pronounced Palousy, Apalousa, Apalucy, Appaluchi, etc." As the name obviously derives from the phrase "a Palouse horse" I shall, in this book, for the sake of consistency, and perhaps standardization, spell the word *Apaloosa*.

Horse conformation. These are the Apaloosa, the Palomino, and the Pinto. The Apaloosa was a favorite among the American Indian tribes most noted for their horsemanship, the Nez Percés and Palouse. A few horses of the strain and coloring known as Apaloosey or Apaloosa now and then got into shipments going to Eastern markets before the advent of tractors and automobiles. They were

PLATE 10. Apaloosa, Simcal's Snowy Rock of the Minidoka Stables. *Courtesy Bill and Neva Moore, Hansen, Idaho.*

always well thought of and had the reputation of being tough horses with good feet and bone. A very few years ago a registry for these horses was established. Their popularity since then has grown phenomenally. Apaloosa shows have sprung up in most Western and some Midwestern states. They abound in Florida.

One word of caution follows regarding the Apaloosa and other breeds emphasizing color. Any animal bred exclusively for one specific characteristic, whether of color or performance, is in some danger of losing other desirable qualities it may have. So the buyer of a horse of any breed emphasizing one very specific quality will do well to look carefully to see that it has all the other qualities he wants.

At the middle of this century the strikingly colored horses called Apaloosas were almost uniformly horses of excellent bone and feet. They looked as if they had started out to be of a solid color but a giant paintbrush full of paint of various hues had been shaken onto them, usually from the rear. They were of good size, a little larger and coarser of head than the ideal Quarter Horse. They were horses of excellent heart girth, which truly indicates their great endurance. They were rarely nervous or fidgety, but always had plenty of "heart" and impulsion. Their action was true and round, usually a little higher and longer than that of the Quarter Horse. Early in the century the writer owned a typical Apaloosa. She was a very satisfactory hunter, taking fearlessly any obstacle ordinarily encountered in a reasonably stiff hunting country. She was seemingly tireless in the buggy and could go all day at an eight- to ten-mile trot. On occasion she was pressed into service as the third horse on a grain binder and kept up her end of the job along with much larger horses, seemingly without distress.

The Apaloosa was the favorite war horse and buffalo horse of the Indians in the Palouse River country. It should be very easy to find among Apaloosas a horse that is or could become a choice Western pleasure horse, trail horse, rope horse, cutting horse, or horse for any other utilitarian purpose. Apaloosas are not the easiest of horses to teach lateral gaits, but their natural trot is brisk and square with plenty of spring, and their gallop is true and can be slowed down and collected into a good canter. Some Apaloosas are a trifle coarse, but it is easy to find those that are as near perfection as one can find in any other Western breed.

The Palomino

The Palomino presents a wider range of type than any other recognized breed. Certainly, one who likes horses of this golden color can find conformation that will measure up to that of Quarter Horse ideal. However, perhaps because of concentration on breeding for color in the early days of the breed, there are Palominos with round bone, long in the cannon bone and steep in the shoulder, to say nothing of coarseness in the head and some other undesirable qualities. The buyer must merely be sure that he chooses one that has not only the proper color for the breed but also has all the other qualities he wants. It is of course a mistake to buy a Palomino that does not have the correct golden color. His skin must be black, not freckled or "pumpkin color." His tail and mane must be white (beware of bleached manes and tails). White on face or lower legs is quite good, but body hair must be the color of newly minted gold or copper. The eyes must be dark, not the glass eye permissible

PLATE 11. Palomino. *Courtesy Louise Lee, Palo-Lee Stables*

in some other breeds. There is a slight general preference for dark-colored hoofs. The preference is based on an old notion that has some slight basis in fact. It is to the effect that dark hoofs are tougher than light-colored ones.

The breed contains such a wide range of types that the horseman who likes the color and is willing to spend the effort necessary to keep it looking attractive can find among Palominos the horse that will satisfy all his needs for a Western mount.

Pintos

Among Pintos or Paints we again have considerable range in type, not quite as wide a range as among Palominos. There is a rather prevalent type of Paint, once quite uniform among the many horses of the old 101 Ranch, a type illustrated by the horses seen in

PLATE 12. Excellent examples of Tobiano Pintos. Olmsted family up. *Courtesy Mr. Aaron G. Olmsted, chairman, Pinto Horse Association of America.*

the old Tom Mix movies. They are large-boned, good, big-footed horses with short backs, powerful haunches and necks that come up out of their shoulders in a proud arch. Their heads are well shaped and carry a good eye properly placed. The writer has known several of these horses. They were all of excellent disposition, kind, courageous, responsive, and tireless. The Paint is growing in popularity and his kind can be excellent Western mounts.

Mr. Aaron G. Olmsted, chairman of the board of directors of the Pinto Horse Association of America, Ellington, Connecticut, writes, "The Pinto is the only breed found throughout the world today.

Any country you go into the world over, you will find Pintos. A UCLA professor just back from Nepal and Mt. Everest has given me slides he took of Pintos over there for my collection."

It is gratifying to note that the Pinto Association allows no set tails on animals foaled after 1961.

The markings of the Pinto are clearly defined by the association as follows:

Pinto markings are divided into two patterns, Tobiano and Overo. These patterns are described: *Tobiano*—Clearly marked pattern. White as a base with black, brown, sorrel, or dun as the other color. Markings distinct and the colors usually divided half and half. Mane and tail the color of the region from which they stem. Legs white. Head dark or combined with star, strip, snip or blaze.

Overo—A colored horse, roan, dun, sorrel, bay, brown or black, with white extending upward and irregular in pattern. Mane and tail dark or mixed, head usually white or bald. Legs have a combination of both colors.

Pintos are also described as "piebalds," "skewbalds" or paints. However, "Piebalds" are black and white Pintos and "Skewbalds" are white and any other color BUT black Pintos.

The fact that the Pinto has been closely related to our American history and especially that written in the broad expanse of the West, clearly entitles him to a prominent place in our American Hall of Fame, as well as a permanent place in our affections. There is no need for the Pinto to establish himself. He has already done so.

Undoubtedly the Pinto originally drew attention through his color and to many this may still be his outstanding attraction. To the Indian brave, by nature attracted by the gaudy, the colorful Pinto undoubtedly proved an eyeful. However, though the Indian possibly selected his Pinto to indulge a fancy, he nevertheless made good use of him. In many of the most brilliant pages of Indian war history we read of exploits by Indian horsemen in many of which, doubtless Indian braves were carried into the thick of battle and often to victory on the backs of courageous horses, some of which were Pintos. Later, as civilization spread to the West, the early settlers frequently found it desirable and attractive to barter for the colorful Pinto horses. Still later the American cowboy adopted the vari-colored horse of the West, and "Old Paint" became both a fact and a legend. Countless reams of cowboy poetry and prose have been dedicated to the exploits and virtues of "Old Paint." Again, cowboy composers and cowboy tenors have carried tuneful legends to "Old Paint" to the ears of the entire world. Today, throughout the West, thousands of youngsters, mindful of their lineage and true to the traditions of the West, aspire to own and usually succeed in obtaining a Pinto horse or pony for their very own. At rodeos, in the multitude of sheriff's posses common throughout the West, in any large parade, and in fact at any gathering of horsemen, one may observe a generous sprinkling of Pinto horses.

The fact that the Pinto has persisted so long and that his popularity is on the increase is not a happenstance. Like any of the recognized and distinguished breeds, the Pinto horse has his proportion of undesirable in-

PLATE 13. Arabian stallion. *Courtesy Fay Cornish*

dividuals, but on the other hand he also has his proportion of outstanding individuals who possess performance, ability and physical quality and conformation comparable to the best of any breeds. Originally a product of the plains and probably of breeding not too selective, the early Pinto in many instances came in all sizes and shapes, but the fact that he survived against strong competition clearly indicates that he had utility as well as attractiveness and uniqueness. In rather recent years considerable breeding and quality have been injected into the Pinto horse through crosses with fine Thoroughbred, Arabian, American Saddle Horse, Standardbred, Morgan and other breeds. By adding this quality to the native stamina and ruggedness of the Pinto horse, the latter has taken on much refinement and has exhibited an aptitude and ability for many of the modern sporting requirements for fine horses. There have been a great many high class Pinto polo ponies. They too have established themselves in the hunting field, and many Masters of Fox Hounds have selected Pintos to ride in order that they in official capacity may be more readily distinguished in the hunting field. Many Pintos have made outstanding jumpers, and they too have entered to a lesser degree many of the sporting fields.

However, the stronghold of the Pinto is as a pleasure horse for the average American rider who is not seeking to win fame or fortune but merely desires a fine equine companion with whom he can explore the mysteries and observe the beauties of Nature. In other words, a horse that he can make a pal. The Pinto is ideal for this purpose, and it seems more than likely that he will continue to enjoy popularity for this use.

The Pinto horse has a background as colorful as any, and in the hearts of millions of Americans, past and present, "Old Paint" has cut a niche all his own and in which he can never be replaced.

Arabians

The Arabian horse, if his blood comes exclusively from the six families descending from the mares of the Prophet, is called "Asil" and he will give pause to any horseman or any lover of beauty. Prejudices are strong about the Arabian. Those who love and use him will not have and will hardly look at any other. When the writer unwittingly asked Linda Lightington what breed the horse was that she rode one hundred miles in sixteen hours, she almost gasped, "Why, an Arabian, of course!"

Certainly Linda's achievement was great and she has a right to her opinion; but Pittsburgh lawyer McCready, who made such a good showing in the Six-hundred-mile Endurance Ride many years ago on a horse of another breed, would have been equally sure that his breed could well be expected to be the one to win an endurance ride. Many horsemen who have slight acquaintance with Arabians, though they cannot help admiring their beauty, have very derogatory things to say about them.

Certainly there is no one best breed of horse. The Arabian will not be a pleasant mount for all people, but any young horseman who has any interest in Arabians will be wise to make a study of them before he buys his next horse. But let us look at the negative side of the subject briefly. The Arab is small, the smallest of the recognized breeds except ponies. Though the Selby Stud, home of one of the greatest sires of the breed in America, showed five-gaited Arabians in major shows in Ohio and neighboring states, the Arabian does not learn to do the lateral gaits easily. He will not stand abuse. If it is true (and the writer feels it is) that to get along with a horse the rider must be at least half as intelligent as the horse, then not too many riders are qualified to ride an Arabian.

The Arabian will never be the most popular horse among rodeo contestants, for he will not take rough treatment in which he can see no point. He will not do for the man who hires work done on horseback, for he is too valuable to be entrusted to careless help and will not put up with the abuse of the ignorant. The man who wants a gaited horse for the trail or the man who wants a large horse must look elsewhere. Nevertheless, we repeat that the man who thinks there is a possibility he might like an Arabian will do well to study him. This is easy to do, for the national association of Arabian breeders has much dependable literature that can be procured by contacting any Arabian breeder. Also, such old authorities as Wilfrid Scawen Blunt, the Victorian poet, and his wife Anne wrote books about the Arabian horse after devoting years to the study in Arabia. These and other equally reliable books are available at good public libraries. The national association has a motion picture of Arabian horses in all kinds of work and play, which can be borrowed by service clubs and other interested groups. It can be obtained from any prominent Arabian breeder.

To the writer, the greatest appeal of the Arabian horse is his responsiveness to his owner. He will, in fact, teach a kindly and attentive owner to be a horseman. When ridden with comfortable equipment, if he has been taught the rudiments of reining and response to the other aids, the Arab will usually be a safe mount for a very inexperienced rider. Such a rider can learn from his horse or with such a horse the rudiments of more advanced equitation, such as jumping and various movements required in the show ring.

The Arabian is usually possessed of good feet and legs. His back is almost invariably short, his loins strong, his shoulders oblique and his head fine, with large eyes placed low in the head. His movements are all "willowy" with a follow-through to each one. Though his gait is usually limited to the walk, trot, and gallop or canter, he is very comfortable on each of them. Under some riders, Arabians are prone to become excited in company; but the writer has seen many riders of little experience on relatively green Arabians get along on trail rides without the slightest excitement or trouble—a plain case of the rider having at least half as much intelligence as the horse.

The story goes that an Irishman was once asked by an Englishman, "Pat, if you couldn't be an Irishman, what would you rather be?"

"Faith, an' I'd rather be dead," was the instant reply.

The writer is not quite so prejudiced; for if he could not have a horse of his favorite breed he would prefer an Arabian. However, he is quick to warn all readers that the Arabian is certainly not a satisfactory horse for all horsemen. In fact, for some, he would be the worst of all possible mounts.

Morgans

The Morgan, the horse that pounded the city streets pulling doctors' buggies, plowed fields for small farmers, and won harness races when the writer was a lad, is still a very distinctive part of America. Though the history of the breed is stormy and it is now many years since Justin Morgan put his stamp on it, some of the old characteristics still prevail. On a recent trail ride comprising nearly a hundred mounts, the writer on sight recognized a half-dozen Morgans, or so he thought. On inquiry, he found he was right about five of them. The sixth was of unknown breeding, but there must have been a Morgan in somebody's woodpile.

Morgan horse conformation fulfills the general requirements of conformation I have listed earlier. The Morgan frequently satisfies the eye of the Quarter Horse fan, but is apt to have a little heavier bone than the Quarter Horse and a much more imposing front. He frequently has a well-arched crest, with head carried a little higher than the Quarter Horse's. His head is fine but with a very strong jaw.

The temperamental quality most distinctive in the Morgan might be called vigor. If a Morgan horse ever tires, which is doubtful, certainly nobody knows it. The writer has known several and owned some that were hard to keep from jogging or prancing. In self-defense he taught the ones he owned to do a slow gait, not a very easy thing to do in some instances. In addition to his extremely rugged constitution, the Morgan's temperament appeals to many horsemen.

Those who find it congenial will have no other horse. He is extremely versatile in all fields requiring not more than three gaits. Many Morgans make satisfactory hunters; others, parade horses. On the trail they are tireless. Many cattle ranchers use them, especially in the Northwest. They give good account of themselves in Eastern

PLATE 14. Marjory Hambly on Red Gates. This shows the conformation and powerful stride of the Morgan. *Courtesy George Axt-Photography, Covina, California.*

and Western Pleasure classes in horse shows. A few have made creditable showing in five-gaited classes in small shows but they are usually difficult to teach to rack and do not have the length of neck which is such a desirable feature in the gaited show horse. Furthermore, they do not take kindly to some of the uncomfortable practices of the show horse trainers. In fact, no Morgan will tolerate being put upon, and most of them will react violently to pain.

Thoroughbreds

The Thoroughbred breed includes one of the widest ranges of type of any breed; though, like the Arabian and Morgan, almost

PLATE 15. Cynthia Rigden on her Thoroughbred Mare, Lady Mary. *Used by permission of Jane Carter, Prescott, Arizona*

any member of the breed can be recognized as of his breed, and could never be mistaken for a horse of another kind. Within the breed, horses can be found that will exemplify all the requirements of conformation we have listed. Any size desired for saddle use can be found among them.

Because he has been bred for centuries for speed alone, and more recently for speed on a smooth track while carrying only token weight, his gait is long and low. However, Thoroughbreds can be found that are sure-footed over the most difficult terrain. It is difficult to teach them lateral gaits, but their natural gaits are usually not extremely uncomfortable.

Because the Thoroughbred has been bred to run and to exert himself beyond the usual limits of horseflesh, or flesh of any other kind, for that matter, his temperament does not usually please the nonracing rider.

If one looks long enough, he can find a Thoroughbred that can be restrained and taught to perform in almost any desired way. However, for centuries the Thoroughbred has been bred for one very specific goal—to win races. He has been used for hunting and some other purposes, but the one thing that brings the big money for the breed is the race track. All else may be willingly sacrificed for that. Love of tradition, and perhaps some other factors, kept many of the original qualities (such as beauty and bone) of the breed alive for a long time in Europe; but the American Thoroughbred breeders, many of them at least, seem to have been perfectly willing to disregard temperament as well as beauty and bone, and to concentrate all their attention on the quick dash of speed over the especially prepared track under token weight.

As a result of all this, many if not most Thoroughbreds have a very special kind of disposition. Such animals may seem kindly and well disposed when ridden very quietly, but as soon as they exert themselves, as soon as the hair begins to turn a bit on the neck (from perspiration), they resist restraint violently. Such horses can be taught only one thing—to run fast.

All this does not mean that a beginning horseman who is attracted to Thoroughbreds because they are the popular breed in his locality or because he admires their appearance should look to another breed or type for a personal mount. It merely means that he should look among Thoroughbreds long enough to be sure he is getting a Thoroughbred that can be something more than a race horse. Especially, any horse he is seriously considering should be mounted near the stable or corral where he is kept, then ridden away from home for a mile or so. The last part of the mile should be at a rate that will bring a bit of sweat out on the horse's neck, or at least increase his respiration. He should be allowed to start toward home on a good trot or slow gallop. Then the rider should ask the horse to walk. If he will walk fairly quietly back to his home stable or corral, he is not one of the silly kind and probably he can be taught to be a good mount, if he is not one already.

The man who can find among Thoroughbreds a horse with a teachable and pleasant temperament will have a horse that is always ready to give that extra ounce of energy, a horse that will not get heavy in the forehand when the trail is long or fail to rise over the jump when the going is heavy. The "heart" of the Thoroughbred is his most glorious characteristic. He has unlimited courage. A typical Thoroughbred (a term a trifle dangerous to use) does not know how to quit. If his rider asks, the horse will perform at top speed or with top energy output of any other kind, until he literally drops to the ground.

There is hardly an unsoundness known to horseflesh that cannot be found among Thoroughbreds, though Thoroughbred bone is stronger for its size than that of any other breed, with the exception of the Arab. To list all needed warnings about soundness when buying a Thoroughbred would fill a book, and then the advice given could be followed only by an experienced horseman. Certainly the horseman who so admires the beauty and great power and speed of the Thoroughbred that he wants to own one should get the advice of a good veterinarian before purchasing. Also, he will do well to avoid one that has been raced, for not only may such a horse have been fired or nerved, but also he is very likely to become uncontrollable for all but an experienced rider when in company.

This is not written as a condemnation of the blood horse. Neither this writer nor any other could dim his glory, but our purpose is to help the young or not-too-experienced horseman avoid tragedy. The writer, like most other horsemen of any considerable experience, recalls glorious days in the field atop a seventeen-hand, straight-bred, fearless hunter that made light of obstacles and miles. It is his hope that many young horsemen will live to have similar experiences.

The Standard-bred

The Standard-bred, the horse bred for use in harness, is very popular in some areas. (See Plate 16.) Many of them that cannot trot or pace fast enough to sell for use on the track can be bought at very reasonable prices. If their conformation and temperament fulfill the requirements we have listed, they may enable the buyer to have a very good mount at a very reasonable price. Most of such horses available have not had much training under saddle, so the purchaser

PLATE 16. One of the fastest harness horses in America today showing the Standard-bred's excellent conformation for saddle use.

must plan on training his horse or having it trained (which may add considerably to the cost). If the Standard-bred being considered has the right conformation and temperament, he should be ridden to see if he is, or has some promise of being, flexible in the neck. Rigidity is the fault most apt to make the Standard-bred unsuitable for saddle purposes. Also, careful attention should be given to his action to see that he does not dish or paddle. Unsoundness in the harness race horse is not quite the curse that it is in runners, but a veterinarian should pass on any horse to be purchased. Like the running horse, the Standard-bred that has been raced is apt to give trouble in company and should be tried out carefully.

The Standard-bred is much more apt to have a quiet disposition than is the Thoroughbred. He usually can learn any gait and is easier to teach collection and reining than the Thoroughbred unless he has been made rigid by a great deal of training in harness. One of California's most enthusiastic trail riders, a gray-haired matron, rides a Standard-bred mare she has trained herself. No one has a pleasanter ride than this lady. She has taught her mare all the saddle gaits and has given her a good rein. The mare is faultless in company and can help her rider open and shut any gate.

This little Standard-bred mare illustrates what is perhaps the most important of all the many qualities of the breed that recommend it for consideration as a personal mount. Her temperament is perfect for her use. This breed was for many generations as much a part of American family life as the car is today. True enough, the driving horse (for that is what the Standard-bred was) did not live as intimately with the American family as did the Arabian horse with Bedouin tribes, so his disposition is not as cozy as the Arabian's. However, he had to become just as good at knowing how to "get along" with his people as the Arabian did. Better, perhaps, for the Bedouins spent more of their lives at becoming good horsemen than did Americans. The driving horse often had to have sense enough for both himself and his owner in many dangerous situations. He had to have "go" enough in him to pound the city streets or gravel roads all day without stopping, or to stand tied to a post from eight o'clock in the morning until quitting time, when his owner would come out of office or store for a quick dash home.

Yes, those old buggy horses were smart, sometimes too smart. A lot of them could untie any knot a man could tie, and open any gate. One, who finally met death from eating frosted clover, would open the gate into the clover field and close it after himself so that the other stock would not get in and draw attention to his delinquency.

The Standard-bred's temperament makes him always interesting, always an individual. He has, of course, been bred to go, to go fast and long. So he is sometimes a little fussy at restraint, though rarely as uncontrollable as the other American racing breed frequently is. He usually pays attention to his rider and is very quick to learn anything within his power to do.

The American Saddle Horse

No breed has demonstrated greater ability to excel in a great variety of fields than has the American Saddle Horse. The writer has explained this at length elsewhere (see *The Horse America Made,*

PLATE 17. Five-gaited American Saddle Horse. Winner of $10,000 stake at Louisville. *Used by permission of American Saddle Horse Breeders Association*

Harper & Brothers, 1961). He is confident that he can find within the breed an animal for any specific purpose and that a properly chosen American Saddle Horse can hold his own in any competitive field that does not require registration in the registry of another breed. He has cited examples of authentic achievements of American Saddle Horses in all such fields.

Furthermore, this horse's movement and the variety of his gaits put the riding of a good American Saddlebred in a class by itself as a delightful experience. It is possibly, in the pleasure it affords, closer to modern dance than to other horseback riding. Certainly other kinds of riding are too "athletic" to suit the taste of some devotees of the gaited horse. Yet some of the movements of the Saddler are so fast and exhilarating that to the rider who can handle the Saddle Horse, riding any other kind of a horse, even at racing speed, is a monotonous and tame business.

The disposition of the Saddler also makes him particularly useful as a personal mount. The less a buyer knows, the more he is likely to be looking for a horse that "looks wild but is perfectly safe." Surprisingly often one finds such a horse among Saddlers. Like the Thoroughbred and the Arab, the Saddler is alert and lively. However, even the most vivacious Saddlers are amenable to intelligent restraint. I have known individuals of the breed forced by inclement weather or some other necessity to remain in a box stall for several weeks. When those individuals were ridden after such prolonged confinement, there was no bucking or other resistance to control. Under proper treatment the Saddler is always amenable and pleasant to handle. Rarely is he a "jigger" (a horse that will not walk but insists on doing a jog or "jig" trot even at very slow speed).

Saddlers are as a rule fond of people. My own four-year-old will leave grain or anything else and come to the gate of his corral the instant he hears my hand on the latch of the corral gate.

However, there are many disadvantages in the American Saddle Horse as a breed from which to choose a personal mount. Not only are good ones very expensive; there is also the great difficulty of finding a good one that has not been headed for the show ring and given training and hoof treatment that must be undone before the horse is suitable for a personal mount. But the horseman who has somehow or other got a hint of the experience of riding a good Saddlebred whose abilities have all been developed will be apt to want one. To a rider whose hands are as skilled as his horse's mouth, a ride on a great Saddler defies description. We might say that the Saddler's performance is to that of other breeds as the performance of a symphony is to any other kind of music—not necessarily better, but certainly different. There is a follow-through to every natural movement of the Saddler that gives the rider the illusion of riding on air. When he learns to jump, the Saddlebred's movements are like those of a deer, each movement flowing into the next.

All this sounds very enticing, perhaps, but two things should be remembered: (1) the Saddler one looks for as a personal mount is hard to find and expensive; (2) also, it takes more and probably subtler training to ride a five-gaited horse *well* than for any other kind of riding. Few riding schools offer good training in this kind of riding. The cost would be too great in money, time, and patience before the student could achieve any degree of proficiency.

Let us now consider some of the faults to avoid when choosing an American Saddle Horse. Every breed has culls. American Saddle Horses are no exception. The faults the culls most frequently possess are lack of heart girth; light bone, cut away below the knee; tails ruined by faulty surgery; feet ruined by lack of care during show season; and ruined mouths. The culls of the breed also display various results of faulty training or riding, such as mixing gaits, getting behind or ahead of the bit, hysteria, and other faults common to all breeds. Good representatives of the breed are high priced. If the prospective buyer is offered an animal at a low price, he should look well for the reason.

When choosing an American Saddle Horse, the buyer should look for the temperament and the details of conformation and action we have listed for personal mounts of all breeds. In addition, he should be sure that the American Saddle Horse has a tail that grows high on level hips. The neck must be long and supple, carried high from sloping shoulders. It is true that some great representatives of the breed have been invincible both in five-gaited rings and as parade horses in spite of necks that were not all that the heart desires in length. But it is wise to choose a horse that has this distinctive quality of the breed and does not have to overcome any handicaps. If the horse is to be shown at all in the special classes designed for him (three- or five-gaited and fine harness classes), he should have a properly set tail. For the owner of a small stable especially, tail setting is an expensive and gruesome business. It is wise to pay a little more for a horse and let the producer take the chances and bear the expense and grief. The action must be true, which means free from paddling or dishing. If the horse is to be shown, action must be high and fast. Especially it must be uniform; that is, as high and snappy behind as it is in front. Front action can be induced by artificial means, but God must lay a good foundation for hind action.

The bars of the mouth should be examined to see that they have not been crushed or that the edges have not been bruised during training to get high action or specific gaits. (The bars of the mouth are the parts of the mouth that the bits rest on.)

While the American Saddle Horse is willing to put up with more man-caused misery than horses of other breeds and will often in kind hands regain confidence lost during brutal treatment, it is wise to observe the horse in the stall to see if he has been kept so stirred up for display purposes that he has lost all confidence in man and is head-shy and difficult to approach.

As the saddle used in gaited show rings puts much strain on the loins, it sometimes does permanent damage even to the unusually strong loins of good American Saddle Horses. The careful observer will detect this trouble if he gets an opportunity to see the horse when he is first mounted after being brought out of a stall or off the cross-tie. If his loins are uncomfortable, he will switch his tail as much as it is possible for a set tail to switch and may even squirm from side to side with his quarters unless punished severely with spur and whip and taken off immediately at a rapid gait.

If the horse considered is five-gaited, the buyer should listen carefully to the animal's rack. It should be a true four-beat rhythm, with the intervals following hoofbeats all perfectly equal. Any tendency toward syncopation of rhythm means that the rider is attempting to simulate a rack with a broken pace, usually necessitated by some discomfort in the feet of the horse. If the horse will not trot instantly on signal, the buyer should be wary of him, for he is apt to mix his gaits under any but expert hands.

The Tennessee Walker

The Tennessee Walking Horse is closely related in blood to the Saddlebred we have just discussed. He is frequently of coarser build and less likely to display lack of bone and heart girth than the Saddler. His temperament is less high strung. Length of neck in this breed is less extreme than in the Saddle Horse. There is even more danger of permanent damage to the feet by show treatment than in the five-gaited horse. The cause of this (the use of chains and other devices to induce high action) is well explained in a series of articles published in *Sports Illustrated* early in 1960 under the title "The Torture Must End" by Alice Higgins.

This horse gives the easiest ride of all breeds. Its temperament is so amenable that even some of the top show specimens can be

PLATE 18. Tennessee Walking Horse mare. Marjorie Hambly up. *Courtesy George Axt-Photography, Covina, California*

ridden by inexperienced riders. Though most good representatives of the breed are over fifteen hands and weigh well over a thousand pounds, they are easy keepers. To the surprise of many old cattlemen who condemn all gaits but a jog and a gallop, the Walker is usually sure-footed in the roughest country, adapting his gait to the terrain. The writer has observed that on trail rides the owners of good Tennessee Walking Horses come in from the longest ride with less fatigue than do the riders of any other breed of horse. He has never seen a Walking Horse that fretted in company or caused his rider the least difficulty in management. The Walker can be ridden comfortably in any kind of saddle and with any kind of seat except the extreme forward seat.

There are few faults common to this breed except injury to feet from show training and one fault resulting from improper riding and training. This is the tendency to pace instead of doing the true four-beat running walk, which has the same rhythm as the rack, though it is a very different gait. Originally the true Walker always had one foot in contact with the ground when doing his most distinctive gait, but modern show requirements have changed this to gain speed. In addition to his flat-footed walk and running walk, the Tennessee Horse has a delightfully easy, slow canter. He should be able and willing to slide from one gait to the other smoothly at the will of his rider.

Many show specimens look awkward and probably are uncomfortable. The awkwardness and discomfort are the result of extreme training and conditioning for show. The show horse, if not crippled, can have his feet properly shod and return to his usual graceful and comfortable gaits.

Part V

CARE

OF THE

PERSONAL

MOUNT

12

Stabling %%%%%%%%%%%%%%%%%%%%%%%%%%%%%%%%%%%%%%
and %%
care %%%

The Boarding Stable

The man who rides to hunt or who rides largely for social enjoyment or for competition may find a good boarding stable a great convenience and the most satisfactory place to keep his horse. Many stables have a range of rates depending upon the kind of care given the horse. If the owner takes care of his own equipment, grooms his own horse and does not require a box stall, the rates are frequently not a great deal higher than the cost of keeping a horse at home.

When choosing a stable, the appearance of the other horses kept at the stable is significant. Watch the boarding horses as they are approached by stable help. If most horses instantly tense up at the approach of a groom, I would be reluctant to put my horse in the stable.

Riding area or trails adjacent to the stable are important. Also, for the horseman whose chief interest is in competition, the riding ring belonging to the stable is to be considered. Is it large enough to provide for practice of the kind of competitive riding which interests you? Is the footing free from rocks, reasonably level and sufficiently firm to allow proper performance but not so hard as to cripple a horse? Many a good horse's feet have been permanently ruined by a very little work on a track or ring that was too hard.

It is important to make certain before taking a horse to a boarding stable that the ring will be available for all boarders.

Safety factors are even more important in a boarding stable than in a private one. The evidence of careless disposal of baling wire, nails driven in walls where horses may injure themselves, gates or doors left open and swinging in the wind—all such things are warning signals.

A boarding stable is an excellent place to pick up any kind of infection. It is well to investigate the incidence of influenza in the stable, especially in the winter. Infection may not be evident during some seasons of the year, but local veterinarians can, and sometimes will, give information about such matters. Influenza vaccines are not always 100 percent insurance against infection, for there are many varieties of the ailment. Of course the wise horseman, especially if his horse is liable to exposure, will follow his veterinarian's advice about vaccination against the locally current variety or varieties.

Foot fungi are to be guarded against. Dry, clean stalls or corrals are the most important safeguards.

In the arid parts of the Southwest, manure in the corrals is not a menace to feet if it is kept scattered and dry, though it may increase danger of internal parasites if eaten.

If examination of the boarding stable shows it to be a safe place to leave an animal, it may be the ideal place for some horsemen to keep a horse. It does away with all worry about what to do with the mount when the family goes on vacation or when the rider is too busy to attend to the horse. Also, it may be a good place to learn, if the horseman is good at listening, gathering a diversity of views, and then sifting the good from the bad.

The Private Stable

There are at least two general kinds of horsemen who will have little interest in boarding stables and will want to keep their horses as close to their own living quarters as possible.

The first kind is the horseman who has very limited means, such as my very good friend who celebrated his fifteenth birthday last week with an all-day ride in the McDowell Mountains, at the edge of the little desert valley we inhabit. This young horseman has a newspaper route and manages to keep his horse on the proceeds from it.

The other kind of horseman (the two classes are certainly not mutually exclusive) is the one who finds close rapport with his mount the chief source of pleasure in riding.

In the more temperate parts of the country, very simple quarters will provide comfort for a horse. The fence or the walls that confine and protect him should be strong enough so they will withstand any strain he will put on them if he rubs an itchy tail, gives a playful kick, or paws with impatience at mealtime. Mangers must be provided, for prolonged feeding on the ground is not a safe practice. Mangers should be large enough and so shaped that feed will not be thrown out and so that they can be easily cleaned.

The footing or floor must be free of rocks, reasonably level and well drained. It must not be slippery or hard. One of the greatest necessities and one often neglected is shade. While a horse may voluntarily spend much time in the sun and even lie down fully exposed in mid-afternoon, he will suffer greatly if he does not have a spot of shade available. If a horse is properly fed, he can tolerate a great deal of cold. In Kentucky and Ohio horses thrive through the winter with no more shelter than a windbreak or an open shed provides. Cold rain and snow do not seem to hurt them; however, a wet snow or freezing rain will do harm if there is no shelter. The most important single requirement is a constant supply of clean water.

A garage can be readily converted into a stable and can be made luxurious if a bit of the back yard can be converted into a corral. However, plenty of ventilation must be provided. An open shed is much better for a horse than a tightly closed stall. Any gates or doors should be made so that the horse will not stick a foot through a narrow place and get it caught. It should be remembered when building anything for a horse that if a horse's head is caught, tied, or otherwise fastened so he cannot elevate it, he will panic and fight until dead, unless he is a very unusual horse indeed. Many a sucking colt has put its head through a gate, raised it up until caught by a diagonal brace, then pulled back until death caused it to drop its head and thereby free itself from the gate.

Also, it should be remembered that any stick, spike, or water faucet in a stall or corral on which a halter will catch may cause a horse to panic. The least costly result of such an accident will be a plumber's bill, a broken halter, and a horse with the vice of halter pulling.

The horse can be comfortable in most parts of America in a corral with a simple ramada or roof to afford shade and some protection from hail or freezing rain. A corral one hundred by twenty feet is better than a square one of equal area because exercise is easier in it. It should be at least four feet high and free from barbed wire. Woven wire will do if the mesh is small enough in the lower two feet so that a horse's forefoot will not go through it. Most horses will panic and tear a foot if it is caught in a fence.

Four longitudinal two-by-sixes make a good corral, if the upright posts are not more than ten feet apart and stout enough and set deep and solid. Wooden corrals should be painted with creosote so horses will not chew them. The ideal wooden corral is made of heavy poles; the ideal metal one is made of chain link fencing. In constructing chain link fence, the owner should be sure that there are no holes or spaces below the bottom of the chain link fence. If a horse does not paw and get his foot caught under the fence, he'll be sure to roll close enough to it to get a foot under it and do great damage to himself.

If more than one horse is kept in a small corral, especially if hind feet are shod and horses are well fed, the corral should be divided and horses kept in separate pens.

All gates must be provided with devices to hold them open. Many a tragedy has resulted from gates blowing or swinging shut at the wrong time. Dutch-style doors, the kind that can be opened only at the top if desired, are especially dangerous when opened and not fastened open.

An old-timer in the back country had a saying, "Every boy has to founder one horse before he learns to shut the feed bin." Founder, or laminitis, is an affliction that ruins the feet. If it is diagnosed and properly treated in its earliest stages, the victim is sometimes fit for limited use afterward. Founder has many known causes, such as too rapid cooling of a hot horse, and some unknown ones, or at least the cause sometimes baffles diagnosis. One of the common causes of founder is gorging on grain. Because of this, one of the most important parts of preparing living quarters for a horse is provision for grain storage, even if only one bag is kept on hand at a time. Grain must be fastened up with a horse-proof fastener immediately after each feeding. A stout garbage can will do if hasps or other devices are put on it to keep the lid on securely if the can is upset. Such a can serves a second function very necessary in any grain-storage device—it will keep grain dry. Moisture will create mold in grain. Some kinds of mold are quickly fatal to horses and only a highly trained specialist can tell what particular kind of mold is growing in a grain barrel at a given time. Furthermore, any moldy feed is very bad stuff to give a horse.

The larger the quantity of feed bought at the proper time, the more economically a horse can be kept. This is especially true of hay. However, hay storage requires so much room that the city dweller of limited means has to pay the price of buying a few bales at a time.

In arid parts of the Southwest, several tons of hay can be stored outside if covered with canvas. The canvas must be securely weighted down on all sides to prevent the wind from removing it. However, even in the driest part of Arizona, the bottom tier of bales will be lost to mold unless a base for the haystack is made to keep it a few inches off the ground. Old automobile tires, car stakes, railroad ties, or other such material can be used.

Feed and Water

"The eye of the master fatteneth his cattle."

Cleanliness, regularity, and *good judgment* are the watchwords of good feeding practice. Cleanliness is an attitude of mind rather than a set of directions to be followed. Irregular feeding is always costly and often dangerous. Any change in amount or variety of feeding should be gradual. Animals should be fed at the same times every day. Most horses are fed twice daily. This is the minimal number of daily feedings health will allow. However, if the horseman is more concerned with quick improvement of his horse's condition or with economical use of feed than he is with saving himself labor, he will feed several times a day, dividing the total daily amount of feed in small portions accordingly.

The greatest danger in feeding by the inexperienced is that of overfeeding grain. An underfed horse is usually (though not always) sluggish. Prolonged underfeeding will of course be very evident in the general appearance of the horse. Although many a starved horse has been rejuvenated to be as useful as ever, the horse that has been damaged by overfeeding may never completely recover. All this does not invalidate the old saying, "Fat is the best color a horse can have." Keep your horse fat, if you use him regularly. If he works every day, the more meat you put on him the better. The wise exhibitor knows that it is the last fifteen pounds he puts on his horse that wins the ribbons. However, this excellent condition cannot be achieved by overfeeding. I repeat, overfeeding grain is dangerous.

Amount of feed to be given depends upon the build and digestion of the horse being fed, upon the amount and kind of work he does, and, to a lesser degree, upon the climate he is in, the shelter he has, and the number of times a day he is fed. Standard recommendations for a thousand-pound horse vary from three quarts of oats a day to four gallons or more a day. Hay recommendations vary as widely.

The owner with a new horse will do well if he starts with a one-pound coffee can not quite full of grain at each feeding. He can increase this gradually, watching the condition and performance of his horse. If the amount reaches double the starting ration for a thousand-pound horse on moderate work in mild weather, advice of an experienced horseman should be obtained before increasing the amount of grain any more.

A horse may have all the good, clean hay he will eat. He should not be given so much that he leaves some and tosses it out to be trampled underfoot. However, if only a poor quality of hay is provided, the horse that is not starved will leave the coarse and unpalatable parts of the hay. These should be removed from the manger before each feeding.

Variety of feeds used may depend in large part upon the kind produced in the area where a horse is kept. To some extent the individual characteristics of the horse will dictate variety. An old horse whose teeth are not as good as they once were will need special feed.

If I could choose feed for my own thousand-pound horse without thought of cost or available supply, I would give him all the bright, clean mixed timothy and alsike clover hay he would clean up. I would be sure the hay had been cut at the proper time so that the clover blooms were plentiful and that it was approximately one-third clover. The timothy should be bright and in good head. Then I would feed a two-pound coffee can of good commercial horse feed, which always contains an ample supply of bran and mineral supplements. If I worked my horse fairly hard I would increase the grain by one-half. I would also keep available to him a block of mineral and vitamin supplement. Whenever I could give my horse some good green grazing I would do so, but I would not dump a great quantity of grass cuttings in his manger to give him colic. Grass cuttings, if fresh and cool and free from the deadly oleander leaves are good feed if a horse is used to eating fresh grass. However, local veterinarians tell me that the liberal feeding of grass cuttings to horses starved for green feed is the greatest cause of colic in my area in the summertime.

I would hold my horse out to graze whenever possible and give him a few handfuls of cool, fresh grass cuttings when I could. I would watch his manure, especially in winter when no nibbling at green grass is possible; if it became hard and dry I would add bran, half a one-pound coffee can full, to his grain ration. Or I might soak a tablespoonful of whole flaxseed, obtainable at any drugstore, overnight in a cupful of water and add that to his morning grain once or twice a week.

Living as I do in an area where no timothy and clover hay is available, I use the common local hay, which is alfalfa. I am always very careful about starting to feed alfalfa to a horse not used to it. I start him with a very small amount and supplement it for roughage with clean, threshed barley or wheat straw. (Probably the straw I get is what is cut in the field after the heads have been harvested.)

The grain I feed now is what I included above in my ideal ration, a good commercial horse feed; and a vitamin and mineral block is also available to my horse at all times. He gets almost as much good alfalfa as he will clean up and I keep clean straw in his stall. He drops his manure in his little corral. I keep it scattered and dry and have it removed every few months. Water is kept in a thirty-gallon drum, which I clean out frequently.

Feeding practices can be varied to suit individual needs. The information I have just given can be a suggestive basis for planning your individual feed program, which will vary from mine.

Feeding the Aging Horse

That "many a good tune has been played on an old fiddle" is a fact many horsemen are just becoming aware of. Your first horse may very well be one of advanced years. If he is a good one you will want to keep him a long time. This you can do if you care for him properly.

Only in recent years has the older horse really come into his own. Within the past year I have heard three captains of prominent Western polo teams say they preferred, when buying ponies, to purchase animals from nine to twelve years old and that they had played ponies much older than that. Today there is frequent reference to Golddust Maid, whose trotting record has never been surpassed, if we take into account track, harness, and shoeing. Diomed, whose blood is responsible for many of the greatest Thoroughbreds and Quarter Horses of past and present, made some of his greatest contributions in his late twenties and early thirties. A few years ago Charles Whitlow won a team-roping contest in Phoenix, Arizona, riding a little Palomino horse twenty-seven years of age.

Many remarkable old horses seem to get along without any special feeding. Some of them, if their teeth have been regularly checked by a veterinarian, retain good dental equipment until death. However, most horses have some tooth trouble by teen age or later. Some that have not been watched for parasites during their earlier years have some intestinal weakness. All such conditions require special care in feeding. As with the young horse, frequent feed in small quantities is the ideal procedure; but it is rarely convenient. At least twice-a-day feeding of a good ration in regular amounts will suffice. The elderly horse's manure should be observed daily. If it becomes dry and is not soft enough to be easily disintegrated at the touch of a stick or fork tine, more bran should be added to the ration. Alfalfa is better than any other hay for the elderly horse. If his teeth are poor, he will eat readily only the leaves and smaller stems, leaving the coarse stalks. These should always be removed before fresh feed is given. They can be put under him for bedding. If alfalfa is very dry it can be sprinkled very lightly, but thoroughly wet alfalfa is almost sure to cause colic. No hay of any kind should be left in the manger for more than one feeding.

If the horse's teeth are not good, grain (which should be good commercial horse feed such as Omolene or other similar brand) may be fed wet. If it is fed too sloppy, the manure will be too loose and formless. A mineral and vitamin supplement block should always be available.

As a concrete example of feeding the elderly horse, I give the case of José Viejo. (See Plates 2 and 3, pp. 84, 85.)

José, whose age was estimated by veterinarians to be approximately thirty, came into the hands of his six-year-old owner when the old horse had running sores over backbone and hip bones. He had been in a rocky corral where younger horses fought him away from his feed, and he was much thinner than shown in the pictures, the first of which was taken after his sores had been healed.

José's teeth are very poor. Even now, three years after his recovery, he can eat only the leafy part of alfalfa, though he can outperform many a young cowpony under saddle and he has made an excellent horseman of his young owner.

José was put in a comfortable separate corral with shade and water and was fed good leafy alfalfa dry, of which he could use very little at first. He was given a good commercial horse feed, less than a one-pound coffee can full at first. He was also given Bermuda grass pellets, fortunately available in his area. The grain and the pellets were mixed and fed wet—amount of pellets was about double that of grain. His manure was watched very carefully, and by replacing a little of the commercial grain with barley looseness was corrected. When the manure was definitely formed, the barley was no longer used. If the manure became well formed and dry, a little extra bran was used.

At the end of six weeks the old horse's ration had been increased until he was getting at each feeding a two-pound coffee can full of horse feed (grain), two cans of Bermuda grass pellets, and all the dry, leafy alfalfa he wanted to pick over. What alfalfa he didn't eat was taken out of his manger and given to one of my younger horses.

Had I not known José's history I would have suspected he had internal parasites. However, I knew that, in spite of the wretched care he had been given, he had been regularly wormed for the past few years. Furthermore, he was so emaciated when he fell into the hands of his present owner, my nephew, that he could not have withstood worming.

For the past three years his coat has been so glossy and he has been so lively and in such good condition that we have not bothered to worm him. The only veterinary attention he has had is annual inoculation against sleeping sickness.

I do not advise anyone (and would not do so myself) to buy a thin old horse with the hope of rejuvenating him. The case of José is unusual. All his life he has been an unusual horse. That is why we took him in. However, his case is a concrete example of what can be done with an old horse by using sanitation, regularity, and common sense.

Grooming and Shoeing

There is an old saying "There are oats in the curry comb." Curry combs have changed greatly since that saying was first uttered, for rubber has replaced metal as a material for making them. But the fact that a regularly groomed horse will keep fat and healthy on less feed than one not groomed is just as true today as it was before rubber was invented. However, the busy horseman who provides his horse with a good place to roll, and keeps the place dry, can spend very little time with the curry comb if he is not too particular about his horse's appearance.

The ideal way to care for a horse's coat is to go through the following procedure at least once a day:

With a rubber curry comb start at the hocks and with a back-and-forth motion stir every hair, finishing at the ears. The curry comb is not to be used below hocks or knees nor on the head. A body brush, which is a leather-backed brush with fairly short bristles, is then used vigorously, starting at the base of the ears and brushing with the hair, taking out all loose dirt. Then use a Turkish towel or piece of linen salt sack and rub the entire horse vigorously with a circular motion, shaking the towel clean frequently. This will remove much dirt that the brush did not get. Finish with a light brushing *with* the hair and then use the towel or rub rag *with* the hair to give a final gloss. Use of the bare hand stroking with the hair after the grooming will add luster.

The rub rag or towel should be used to clean lower legs (body brush can sometimes help here, too), face, ears, under side of the tail, and the dock.

Of course, the horseman who grooms his horse thoroughly each day and soaps his gear after each ride will have an outfit which will not be excelled in appearance. However, not all horsemen have time enough for such care. Those who do not have time should remember that a saddle should never be put on until the horse's back is thoroughly cleaned. Also, if a horse sweats, he should be curried as soon as the sweat dries. If not, he will rub and destroy mane and tail, or even make a raw place or two.

Handling the Feet

Never stand directly in front of or behind a foot when picking it up. To pick up a left forefoot, place the palm of the left hand flat against the inside of the cannon bone (the part of the leg between pastern and knee) with fingers pointing to the rear. Close fingers around back of leg. Squeeze and pull forward. As soon as the knee bends and weight is off the leg, take hold of the pastern, with the right hand just above the hoof, and bend leg up as far as it will go comfortably. (See Fig. 1, p. 8.)

As long as you keep the leg doubled up in this way the horse cannot exert any force to put the leg down.

To pick up a right forefoot, the duties of the hands are opposite from those described above. The right hand pulls the cannon bone forward and the left hand doubles up the foot.

To pick up a hind foot the cannon bone is pulled forward as with the forefoot. As soon as weight is off the leg, the foot is doubled up, raised, and then moved to the rear until you can slide a knee under it for support. (See Fig. 21.)

It is wise for the beginning horseman to watch his horseshoer carefully when he picks up his horse's feet. If the smith is not too rushed he may allow the novice to pick up a foot or two under instruction.

Every horseman, no matter how busy, had better take a look at the bottom of his horse's feet regularly. Sometimes a nail picked up on a ride can be detected and pulled before it goes deep enough to do damage. Certainly, shoes should be watched and be reset or replaced as soon as the hoof grows too long or starts to grow out over the shoe at the heel.

The inexperienced horseman must have a good horseshoer, one that "fits the shoe to the foot, not the foot to the shoe." The good smith keeps the angle of the foot the same as the angle of the pastern, so that from a side view the front of the pastern and hoof is a straight line from pastern joint to shoe. He will keep the foot short enough so that there is plenty of pressure on the frog but not so short that the sole is thin and bruises easily. A good smith will not pare frog or bars and will not touch the outside of a healthy hoof with a rasp above the nail clinches. If a horse's feet are hard and dry, he may recommend leather pads packed with tar and oakum, and he will recommend lanolin and oil dressing for the out-side walls.

In event of any lameness or hoof damage, a good veterinarian should be immediately consulted before the advice of shoer or any-one else is taken.

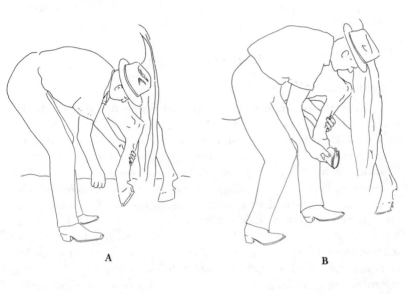

A

B

FIG. 21. Picking up horse's left hind foot. *A* To pick up hind foot pull cannon forward; *B* hind foot doubled up; *C* slide your knee under horse's foot for support.

C

In dry climates many horses lose their usefulness each year because feet become dry and hard, the interior parts of the foot are bruised or damaged by faulty circulation, and the horse goes permanently lame.

Clean water or sterile mud help prevent this condition, but a mere wetting of a corral may cause worse damage because various kinds of foot fungi grow in wet manure.

Matters of Health

COMMON ILLS

A list of ills common to horses is frightening but many a back-yard horse never has a sick day. In fact, if statistics were available they would probably show the horse as one of the hardiest of animals. Nevertheless, the wise horseman watches for any unusual behavior in his horse. The first symptoms of sleeping sickness, for instance, is difficulty in getting a horse to collect or give quickly to the bit. Sluggish hind action is the first sign of azoturia, the result, often fatal, of moving the horse faster than a walk before he has a chance to warm up. This occurs usually with a horse highly fed and regularly worked but rested for a day or two. For this reason it used to be called *Monday morning stiffs.*

Any biting or kicking at the belly or quickly repeated lying down and getting up may mean abdominal pain, called colic. Any other unusual behavior should be noted, and if persistent a veterinarian should be called.

Many a horse that could easily have been saved has died because a veterinarian was called an hour too late, or because the horse was allowed to hurt himself while waiting for the veterinarian to arrive. With some ailments, most notably azoturia, the horse must be stopped the instant symptoms appear. The horse with colic must be kept walking if possible, for death may occur from rupture of stomach or intestine if a horse throws himself violently on the ground. Sharp objects should be removed from the corral or the horse removed to an unobstructed place where the ground is soft.

The horse in pain is not in his right mind and is unpredictable, according to Dr. W. O. Kester, well-known veterinarian and regular contributor to *Horse Lover's Magazine.* The doctor reminds us that a horse speaks only through actions, which may be just as well, because if he spoke his first words would probably be, "Why did you get me into this mess in the first place?"

If the horse suffering from colic does go down, in spite of efforts to keep him walking, keeping him down may prevent him from injuring himself by jumping up and violently throwing himself again. Of course fruitless and faulty attempts to hold him down may do more damage than the colic. Horses' eyes have been gouged and faces bruised by a pile-up of humanity on their heads. One person can hold a horse down by putting one knee on the neck just behind the crest, kneeling on the other knee on the ground just behind the crest, and keeping the animal's nose pointed straight up and his poll on the ground.

Perhaps the commonest cause of tragedy is the home remedy for colic. It usually entails drenching, that is, making the horse swallow liquid by elevating its head and pouring liquid into its mouth. Many old-timers could drench a horse without damage and they often cured colic. Many cases of colic will get well without any medication; however, my own veterinarian tells me he dreads a call to the local race track for a case of colic because when he arrives on the scene there is a good chance that his stethoscope will tell him that foreign body pneumonia has set in, caused by faulty drenching; and a valuable race horse is headed almost certainly for the soap factory.

TETANUS AND SLEEPING SICKNESS

One of the most dreaded ailments of the horse is tetanus, or lockjaw. It may be caused by a puncture wound so small that it is not noticed. For this reason it is wise to have preventive shots given a horse. At the present time this means two shots the first year and an annual booster shot given thereafter.

Another *must* in prevention throughout the United States is the inoculation for sleeping sickness. There are two varieties, the Western and Eastern types. The shots must be given annually and have to be given by a competent veterinarian, for they are intradermal injections.

PARASITES AND FLIES

The horse that is properly fed and sensibly handled but that still has a dull coat and is in poor condition may have internal parasites. Most, but not all, of them can be eliminated by adding to the feed according to directions a preparation put out by several of the reliable veterinary supply firms and sold in good feed stores. If this method does not work, a veterinarian must be employed.

In the Southwest in the summertime, and in some places the year around, an eye infection is carried by flies. A fly mask will usually prevent this. Most feed stores carry them. They are fringes of leather strings that hang from a browband. It is difficult to keep them on most horses unless a halter is worn and the fly mask securely tied to it. The eyes should be wiped clean with a clean cloth daily and a veterinarian consulted if infection starts.

13

Fitting the horse ▨▨▨▨▨▨▨▨▨▨▨▨▨▨
for ▨▨▨▨▨▨▨▨▨▨▨▨▨▨▨▨▨▨▨▨▨▨▨
special purposes ▨▨▨▨▨▨▨▨▨▨▨

If you and your horse get to working or playing so well together and your balance and awareness of the rhythm of your horse are so well developed that you would like to enter a local horse show or gymkhana or a competitive trail ride, your horse will need special fitting for the event.

General Requirements for a Horse Show

Styles of mane and tail fitting are very different for different classes in horse shows and requirements in each class vary some from the East coast to the West. Also, styles change from year to year. However, there is one respect in which all fitting is alike and that is the physical perfection of the horse. The tight, short, glossy coat, the alertness of eye and ear, and the last ounce of good, solid flesh a horse can be made to carry are all factors in any class of any show.

The wisest advice I was ever given about showing horses when I was a young man was the word of Basey Howell, one of Louisville's most beloved horsemen. He told me, "Son, never take a horse into a show ring until he is ready."

The time needed to fit a horse depends on the horse and on the condition he is in to start with. Certainly a month is too short a time in most instances and six months not unreasonable.

Regularity of feeding, constant supply of clean water, and regular exercise are the chief requirements for fitting. This last requirement does not mean that the horse should be bored by monotonous repetition of exactly the same performance the same number of times in the same ring every day. It does mean that he will not stand up in a stall for a day or two and then be given a hard workout.

The wise horseman will almost daily give the horse a little schooling in the kind of performance he expects in the ring, but with any horse but the Walker or Saddler he may go for a leisurely ride one day and give a couple of short workouts in the ring the next, cooling his horse out properly after each workout.

COOLING THE HOT HORSE

Each trainer has his own pet method of cooling, but these things must be done to prevent founder at the end of a workout if the horse has become hot and dripping with sweat:

Keep the horse moving quietly until completely cool, even while saddle or harness is being removed. A woolen cooler made of long-staple Australian wool and large enough to cover the horse completely from ears to tail should be thrown over him immediately. The saddle can be removed, under the blanket (cooler). While still moving, the horse can be rubbed, especially over loins and shoulders, with Turkish towels or linen rub rag. As the horse begins to dry, he can be given three or four swallows of water every five minutes or so. When cool and partially dry he can be put on a cross-tie and vigorously rubbed dry, preferably by two people working on opposite sides. When completely dry he can be turned into stall or corral to finish quenching his thirst and to eat good clean hay.

BANDAGES

Because the beginning horseman will see legs bandaged after workouts in many stables, a word about bandaging is in order here. Much damage can be done to any horse by bandaging his legs tightly with insufficient cotton under the bandage. If any bandage is used on legs it should be a derby bandage, an elastic woolen bandage about nine feet long; and it should be noted that when a woolen bandage is used wet on a crippled horse it should not be allowed to dry on the horse; for in doing so it shrinks.

There is much difference of opinion about the use of bandages on sound horses. Around race tracks in the United States much bandaging is done; much less, I am told, is done in Canada. Some show horse stables bandage; others do not. My own firm conviction is that the trainer who accustoms his horse to work gradually and never overworks him will have no need for bandages unless a horse is injured by accident, in which event bandaging should be done under a veterinarian's direction.

The circulation in a horse's legs and the fluid supplied inside the tendon sheaths constitute a marvelously complex mechanism. Any bandage will certainly interfere with the natural functioning of this mechanism, which operates violently when the horse is at top speed and subsides gradually when he rests.

The old horse that has had a bowed tendon (caused by tearing the lateral ligaments between knee and pastern) may need a bandage after work, though the beginner should consult his veterinarian about this. If such is the case, at least one full sheet of cotton sheeting, the kind used to make comforters, should be wrapped smoothly around the leg from hoof to knee. Then a derby bandage, snug but not too tight, should be applied, from hoof to knee. If the bandage stops above the pastern joint and well below the knee, swelling above and below it may result.

If a sound horse whose leg circulation has not already been ruined by bandaging is not overworked and is cooled out properly, he will need no bandages.

FEEDING

Putting the last winning ounce of hard flesh on a show horse is not merely a matter of increasing grain and regular exercise, but grain is a very important factor. Some horses can take more than others. Any increase in grain should be very gradual.

The old Fort Riley Cavalry School manual stated that oats can be safely fed to a thousand-pound horse up to sixteen pounds a day but adds that ten to twelve pounds is usually ample. I would be very cautious about feeding over ten to twelve pounds of a commercial feed, for no grain is quite as nearly fool-proof to feed as oats. The bulk of the hull of oats seems to aid digestion and prevent ills that attend heavy feeding of other grain. However, the old cavalry ration is a guide. Today I prefer good commercial feed to oats in my area because it is fortified with many vitamins and minerals that are lacking in the oats raised in some localities, especially in mine. Commercial feed is uniform and it contains enough bran to make it reasonably safe.

In addition to all the grain up to twelve pounds my horse could take without his manure smelling strong, I would feed him, in several small feeds a day, all the hay he would clean up. It would be the best and brightest hay the locality affords, though I would never feed barley hay because of the sores barley beards can make in a horse's mouth. I would be sure not to feed hay immediately after feeding grain. A horse's stomach is small. If it is full of grain and he eats hay eagerly, the grain will be pushed on out of the stomach without the small but important function of the stomach acting upon it.

Doctors and veterinarians both tell us that much money is annually wasted on consumption of unnecessary vitamins. Nevertheless, I would use in addition to a feed supplement block one of the many good mineral and vitamin preparations put out by standard manufacturers for addition to feed, following directions carefully. This might be a waste, but whenever I take a horse to a show I take him to win; and I will not spare a few dollars on vitamins even if the chances are that they are unnecessary. Another thing I have found very helpful is an ounce or so of wheat germ oil daily. One successful breeder tells me he gets the same result from vegetable oil at less expense. Of course no oil fed will produce a show ring coat unless somebody adds a great deal of elbow grease behind brushes and rub rags.

WASHING THE SHOW HORSE

Even to think of bathing a show horse was blasphemy in the Saddle Horse country where I grew up. It was thought perhaps rightly that soap and water destroyed the coat's natural oils which alone produced the gloss and bloom that win ribbons. A lady could with her white-gloved hand stroke the coat of a show horse to her heart's content and the glove would not show a speck of soil. This condition was obtained by plenty of grooming with brushes and rub rags that were kept constantly clean.

The manes and tails were never touched with brush or comb. With careful fingers the hair of mane and tail was straightened, so none was broken or pulled out. Legs and feet were washed frequently but not above knees and hocks.

All this was the custom long ago and far away, but it contains suggestion for today. Certainly nowadays, with color classes, such as those for Pintos and Apaloosas, mild soap or shampoo and water are very useful and the only way to keep fit those horses with lots of white coloring. Tails and manes in most classes today are pulled or trimmed or clipped, but for those few classes that require long manes and tails, the Kentucky show barn method is best. To stimulate growth, a well-shaken solution of kerosene and rain water, equal parts, was put on a small piece of cotton and rubbed into the roots of mane and tail hair occasionally. Certainly no coat dressing or other similar preparation should be put on coat or mane and tail, though in very dry climates a little good hair oil is useful on manes and tails, which should be shampooed in the same manner and with the same frequency as is the beauty contestant's hair.

POLISH AND TRIM

Just the day before or morning of the show hoofs should be washed, dried, and then covered with a light application of beeswax and shined to a brilliant polish. If there are rough spots, they can be smoothed with very fine sandpaper. It should be used as little as possible, for it removes the natural enamel of the hoof, which keeps the hoof from drying and becoming hard and brittle.

Long hair inside the ears, under the jaws, and on the pasterns can be shortened with hand clippers. Sometimes a nervous horse stands better to have this done with curved scissors that can be purchased at any saddlery store and some feed stores.

If the kind of class your horse is best fitted for requires trimming, cutting, or pulling of manes or tails, observe closely the horses in the best show stables in your neighborhood and copy their methods of cutting or pulling hair. If this is not possible, such current magazines as *Western Horseman, Horse Lover's Magazine,* or *Western Livestock Journal* carry illustrated articles on all types of show horses and advertisements with pictures of an even wider assortment. Always remember that styles change, and if you cut your horse's mane off it takes more than a year to grow a new one. For some classes in which clipped manes are proper, a good braiding job with rosettes will do very nicely, and the mane can be saved.

If your horse is a Palomino and you ever want to show him in an all-Palomino model class or any other class calling for a full, long tail, you will be very sorry if you have pulled it out or trimmed it for one class of another kind.

I have seen $500 worth of white hair pulled out of a tail in half an hour, for a Palomino's value can be reduced that much by trimming or pulling if he has a beautiful full tail.

Fitting the Saddler

Much heartache could be avoided if all horsemen realized the folly of amateur competition in open classes in large shows. Show ring awards are not closely correlated with monetary value but it is certainly not probable that a $1,000 or $1,500 horse mounted by an amateur can go into the ring and defeat a $15,000 or $20,000 horse ridden by a well-paid professional. The kind of tragic optimism I have in mind is seen perhaps more frequently in five- and three-gaited classes than elsewhere. Even if it were not more frequent it would be more tragic than other areas of showing because there is more danger of permanent damage to the gaited (five- or three-) horse by the kind of shoeing the show ring requires than for any other class of show. Furthermore, the Saddler can be ridden only in a well-prepared ring while he is being fitted and shown, for the length of feet he carries will cripple him if used outside the ring, though many an old Saddlebred puts up remarkable performance in spite of pain long after his joints are crippled. (There is one gallant old fellow in Arizona who wins barrel races, though his ankle joints are deformed and he must find work painful.)

In addition to the feet that must be grown on the Saddlebred to win in any but the most limited classes, his tail must be set and must be kept up in a set.

Since the kind of grooming, washing, and cooling-out I have described for fitting in general will apply to the Saddlebred, I shall consider here only the two items that are unique in his and the parade horse's fitting—cultivating and shoeing the long foot and caring for the set tail.

The first necessity is a good blacksmith. Under his guidance the hoof can be grown to the proper length and kept healthy. This is done by using rubber pads packed with oakum and tar. The pads provide frog pressure and keep the foot pliable. When the first set of shoes is reset, turn the original pads upside down, fitting them

up into the frog, and put a new set of pads over them. (
with extremely shelly feet this may be impossible, but I h
excellent results from this method.

As the hoof grows, it must be kept at the same angle as the pastern, neither steeper nor more sloping. This means that as a rule a little has to be taken off the toe now and then, for the toe grows faster than the heel. The length of foot to be used depends upon the strength of the horse's leg to travel with the handicap of unnatural feet and on the ability of the blacksmith to keep a live foot of extreme length.

The tail should be kept in the set at all times during show season and must be watched very carefully. If the sets slip and remain crooked for any length of time, trouble will result. Too tight wrapping or bandage or ties left on too long will ruin circulation. Horses have been known to slough the entire tail—a very painful affair —because of careless wrapping.

The owner of a Saddlebred who does not want the chore of fitting his horse for a gaited class can show him in an Eastern Pleasure class. Also, some of the nation's best jumpers have been American Saddle Horses. In any class where performance alone counts, the Saddlebred needs no favors. The only things needed are to get his feet down to normal length by very gradual changes (always keeping leather pads on him to prevent bruising) and to let him learn, under an intelligent and kindly rider, what is wanted of him. No matter what kind of competitive work he does, he will always give a delightful ride outside the show ring—if his feet are properly prepared.

Fitting the Tennessee Walker

The Tennessee Walking Horse is also a problem in growing feet for the show. They can usually be grown just like the Saddlebred's. In some instances the Walker is a greater problem than the Saddlebred, for there is the possibility that his coronet, the growing part of the hoof, the top, has been bruised by chains during training. If such is the case, it is difficult to grow a long, sound hoof. The best that can be done is to shim up the foot with pads as much as the smith can.

The tail of the Walker is a simpler problem than the Saddlebred's.

It is possible to buy for him an artificial tail which fastens on top of the real tail. It is partly held in place by strings that go down between the horse's hind legs and fasten to the girth. These tails are advertised in some of the Midwestern and Eastern show horse magazines. Any good Walking Horse stable can give information on them.

14

Care in travel,
at shows,
and on trail rides

Inoculation

Some thirty days before show time attention must be given to two matters that are important in participating in any kind of horse competition—inoculation and loading in a trailer.

The only safe way of attending to the first matter, inoculation, is to consult a competent, established veterinarian specializing in large animal practice. Ask him about the prevalence of shipping fever or other communicable diseases in your area and follow his advice about whether or not to inoculate.

Loading the Trailer-Wise Horse

The second matter, loading in a trailer, you may be able to attend to without professional aid. If your horse has been hauled in a trailer and handled sensibly (I advise no purchase of a horse not trailer-wise) all that is needed is a little practice on your part.

If your horse is not acquainted with your trailer, it is a very good idea, though not indispensable, to put it in his corral or as close beside it as possible, block it up solidly on all four corners and leave it for a few days. If it can be arranged to put some hay on the floor (with doors fastened open if the door is not the ramp), so much the better.

When you load a horse, always put grain in the manger. Have a good shank on the halter. Hold the halter rope not more than a foot from the halter. Walking beside your horse's shoulder, go steadily up to the trailer and into it, not stopping until your horse is eating grain out of the manger. Then, unless you have a helper who has quietly remained out of sight until now and can fasten the chain or gate behind the horse, secure the fastening behind your horse. Then, and only then, tie his head. Do not tie it so short that there is any pull down on it when he raises his head. After tying the head, leave the trailer quietly, by the escape door if any; if not, climb quietly out.

If your horse has not been loaded for some time, he may hesitate just as you step onto the trailer. Do not rush him; give him a few minutes to look things over. Above all, do *not* turn around and stare at him. In a few minutes, if you remain by his shoulder or head, facing the manger, he will probably step up in the trailer. If not, you can hold his halter shank a little shorter to keep him headed in the desired direction and get the helper, who has remained quietly out of the way until now, to urge him from the rear.

Teaching to Load

If you find by trying the method I have just explained that your horse is not trailer-wise, here is the way to teach him to go into a trailer.

Put the trailer in your corral. Block it up very firmly on all four corners so that there will be no movement when the horse's weight is on it. Give the horse feed only in the trailer. If he will venture no farther than the end gate or the rear of the trailer, feed him hay there and let him go without grain until he learns to go into the trailer and can eat out of the manger. Use good, leafy hay and feed it frequently if necessary, in amounts so small that he will not scatter it all around the corral. Any force or quick moves at this time will be fatal to your project. Plenty of time with this method will get the horse so well accustomed to the trailer that he will walk in and out of it as readily as he will walk in and out of his own stall or corral gate. The trailer must be watched continually to see that it remains solidly blocked up. If the horse rubs his tail on it and threatens to push it off the blocks, heavy posts may have to be set in the ground.

An Alternate Method

If sufficient time is not available for the method just described, two 5/8- or 3/4-inch cotton ropes at least 25 feet long should be purchased. After putting grain in the trailer manger, tie one rope securely to each side of the rear of the trailer a few inches higher than the point of the horse's shoulder. With a helper on the free end of each rope a wide lane can be made leading toward the trailer. The person the horse is most familiar with should lead him into the lane. When he hesitates he should not be forced at once; and, most important of all, the handler should not turn around and stare at him! The helpers on the ends of the long ropes can keep the horse from swinging out to the side. They can gradually move closer together. By gently swinging the long ropes, they can tap the horse and urge him forward, being careful to keep the ropes high enough at all times to prevent the horse from putting a foot over one and low enough to keep him from slipping under it. Sometimes, just as the horse gets to the end of the trailer and refuses to step on it, the handler can pick up a forefoot and place it on the trailer floor or end gate. I have seen skillful helpers using this method cross the long ropes behind the horse well above his stifles and boost him into the trailer. Usually patience and tapping with the ropes will do best.

The wise horseman will do almost anything to avoid a fight when first loading a horse. The best way to start a fight is to turn around, stare at the horse, and start tugging on the halter. Then a quick move to startle the horse from the rear will finish the job.

A really spoiled horse may yield only to an expert with a whip, but he must be an old, experienced expert, absolutely fearless and possessed of a perfect sense of timing; otherwise, any use of a whip will make a bad matter worse. In any event, there is always danger of injury when a whip is used in teaching a horse to load.

When the horse is in the trailer, with end gates fastened, and he has discovered the grain in the manger and tasted it, he can be tied. As we said earlier, his head should not be tied too close to the manger and there should be no down pull whatever on his head at any time. If more security is wanted, a cotton rope can be tied around the rear of his neck, where a work collar would go. Tie another rope to it and fasten the second rope to the side of the trailer a little lower than the center of the horse's ribs. The rope should be just tight enough to be snug when the horse is well forward and eating in his manger. This rope will prevent rearing and nervous weaving from side to side. In a one-horse trailer, two ropes can be used from the collar rope, one on each side. There is some problem in fastening the rear end of the ropes attached to the collar. The best way is to have holes made in the side of the trailer, pass the ropes through them, and then fasten them securely on the outside of the trailer. A nervous horse usually quiets down as soon as the trailer starts to move, so it is wise to have everything ready to roll the instant the horse is secured in the trailer.

Trailers

Trailers are of so many types that much common sense must be used by the horseman to adapt any instruction about their use to the particular type of trailer used.

The most horrible accidents I know of have been caused by one or more of three factors: Poor hitches, weak flooring, and too much speed combined with insufficient tire surface. No hitch less sturdy and carefully made than those used on heavy house trailers should ever be used for horses. Frequent inspection of flooring to detect weakness or decay must be made. The weight of trailer and horses should be determined and a competent tire expert should determine the amount of rubber needed.

Some of the most luxurious and expensive trailers, especially of Western manufacture, are so low that a full-sized horse with a good neck cannot stand comfortably in them. It is just as unreasonable to ask a horse to ride holding his head lower than natural as it would be to ask a man to stand for hours stooped over to avoid bumping his head. Saddling to prevent bruising of breast is not necessary if the driver is not careless and the horse has not been spoiled for trailer riding. I have seen more damage done to the appearance of hocks of show horses hauled in trailers than to any other part of the horse except the tails of horses carelessly handled. There seems to be no way to keep a nervous horse from damaging the appearance of the hock, but padding hung behind him and secured to prevent flopping will help. I have hauled many horses in a trailer carrying two horses separated by nothing more than a bar mid-rib high and have never had damaged feet; but if I were hauling a spoiled horse, I would want a good stout partition clear to the floor. There are foot and leg coverings for trailer hauling now available and advertised in such magazines as *Western Horseman* and *Horse Lover's Magazine*.

Hauling

There is considerable disagreement among horsemen about the length of time a horse can be hauled. Certainly horses differ in their ability to ride in a trailer, and trailers differ in comfort. No horseman with any feeling for horses uses a trailer without good springs under it, though the action of trailer springs has to be very limited for safety's sake. Some good horsemen recommend unloading for a half hour every six hours. My own practice with horses that are not afraid in a trailer is to haul for from four to six hours and then stop half an hour. If it is convenient I unload, water, and let the horses pick a little grass; if not, I offer water in the trailer and give a light noon feed of grain. I like to keep pelleted hay in the manger. It will blow less in the moving air and cause less coughing than baled hay.

Perhaps the most treacherous road hazard is hail. It is very frightening to some horses. I have heard of two horses becoming so frightened that they overturned a trailer even though the driver had pulled to the side of the road and stopped.

I hauled a much-loved and very high-strung three-year-old stallion from Prescott, Arizona, to Phoenix last summer in a trailer that is only partly covered. I ran into hail. As the young fellow started to dance, I found a place to pull off and unloaded him. He tried to crawl into my pockets but I managed to get him in the lee of a building, where we both huddled and shivered until the hail turned to rain. He went back into the trailer very calmly. It would have been much wiser (and more comfortable for us both) to stop before the hail storm broke.

Of course in cold weather and in going from hot desert to cool mountains, blankets should be used. No horse should be hauled in an open trailer without goggles. Trailer floors should be kept dry and not slippery. I use a jointed rubber matting, a commercial product made for the purpose and advertised in the horse journals.

Care at Show

Many good horses have failed at shows because of improper care or handling in the stall. Horses vary in temperament as widely as people, even more so perhaps, because they are not subjected to the standardizing influence of schools, newspapers, radio, and television. I have handled show horses that were as much at ease in a makeshift stall at a county fair as they were in their own stalls at home. They never missed a meal, even if feed was a little different from usual, and any clean water was a good drink. Others I have had would not drink until suffering and then only half enough. They would go off feed the minute they left home. Such horses sometimes suffer from diarrhea. They lose weight rapidly. Some of them become so nervous that they cannot perform properly. Others lose their liveliness and become listless.

To insure good health and vigor during the show season provision must be made to have conditions at the show as nearly like home as possible. As variety of feed available at shows is limited, the owner of a nervous horse had best take his own feed with him. It is rarely practical to take water from home, but a familiar bucket will help.

The story is told of a famous stallion, Richlieu King, so intensely inbred and high-strung that the only thing that would keep him calm away from home was the constant presence of the handler who had looked after him from colthood. At shows, the handler would sleep on a cot in Richlieu's box stall.

When the champion was along in years and the handler's hair was gray, the horse was sold to a man in Chicago. The Kentucky owner of Richlieu suggested it might be wise to send the handler along with the horse. The Chicago buyer said he would be glad to give employment to the old fellow but believed the constant companionship business was all folderol. On arrival at his new home, so the story goes, the horse was turned into a nice grassy paddock, alone. He became so excited that in a few minutes he had injured himself so seriously he had to be destroyed.

I cannot document this story, but I have heard it from many different people who claimed first-hand knowledge. Certainly it could be true in every detail. I have personally witnessed similar happenings, though less spectacular and involving less-famous horses.

The level-headed horse that is handled gently and sensibly at home will probably need no special care at the show. If he will stand tied quietly, he may even be safe in a tie stall if all box stalls at the show are taken. If he is put in a tie stall there must be a strong barrier between him and the horse next to him. Also two strong ropes should be tied behind him to prevent accidentally loose horses from molesting him. He should be tied at shoulder height or higher and just long enough to reach the bottom of the manger and the floor next to the manger.

Care should be taken to see that there is no chance that the horse will put a forefoot through a narrow space in the manger or partition and get it caught. Plenty of clean straw should be kept under him and fresh hay in small amounts should always be available to him. A bucket of water should be secured where the horse can reach it easily. In a tie stall it will probably be difficult to place the bucket where the horse won't throw hay in it, so the water should be replaced and the bucket rinsed out every time the horse is fed.

The owner of one or two horses who does not care to sleep at the show can usually arrange to have an eye kept on them by an owner who does stay with his horses, though I have more than once slept on an army cot in or beside a stall to be sure my horses fared well overnight at a show barn.

One thing the beginning showman should be cautioned against is continued fussing with his horse. Some horses enjoy continuous attention but most horses do better if they are allowed some time of quiet between cleanings and feedings. In many parts of the country there is opportunity to hold the horse out to grass at the show grounds. A half hour of such grazing is usually good, unless the horse has a tendency to scour from the excitement of the show. When leading a horse out to graze or for any other purpose at the show, always keep hold of the halter shank close to the halter, using your shoulder against the horse's shoulder to keep him off your feet. Always watch out for danger from other horses and keep at least one horse's length away from them.

Care on the Trail Ride

Trail horses like show horses (they can be the same horses at different times) vary in temperament and physical requirements. Their peculiarities must be taken into account when plans for their care are made.

In addition to a cooler of long-staple wool and a stable blanket in cool weather or if altitude is changed, the trail rider should have a waterproof blanket, for shelter is rarely available on a trail ride. If there is a likelihood of cold rain, two stable blankets should be taken along, one of them preferably very absorbent. There is the possibility that rain will set in on the trail, in which case, if the weather is cold, the absorbent blanket can be put on when the horse comes in off the trail. It should be immediately covered with the waterproof blanket. As soon as the underneath blanket absorbs the moisture, a matter usually of an hour or more, it should be removed and the dry blanket put on. This procedure must be followed with caution because if the horse has not been allowed to cool out properly before ending his ride, or if the weather is warm, the two blankets will create too much heat and damage will be done. If the weather is warm and the horse comes in cool, the rain will not hurt him even if he stands tied without shelter or blanket all night.

Some trail riders let their horses stand in their trailers on a wet night. This is good practice if the trailer is hitched to a car or truck with brake well set and the trailer well blocked up so it will not move when the horse shifts weight. Of course, this method is good only with quiet horses that will not fret in a trailer.

Picket lines are used on many trail rides. I do not like to put my horse on a picket line because of the danger of his being kicked by other horses. I prefer to tie him to a low limb or a tree, being careful that he cannot go around the tree until his rope is so tight he will hang himself. If no tree is available, I am perfectly content to tie the horse to the side of the trailer. In such a case it is imperative to see that there is nothing on the side of the trailer that the tie rope will catch under when the horse puts his head down; for, as stated earlier in this book, a solid down pull on a horse's head will make him panic.

Danger cannot always be foreseen and guarded against. On a recent trail ride in California I tied my horse to the rail of a large exercise ring. Some thirty horses were tied in this manner inside the ring. However, it was large enough so the horses could be spaced with no strangers within kicking distance of each other.

I slept in a covered pickup just outside the exercise ring. At daybreak I was awakened by a pounding of hoofs. A horse was tearing around inside the exercise ring with about six feet of rail swinging wildly from his halter shank. Fearing my horse would have his leg broken by the flying rail, I quickly but quietly untied him, slipped on him bareback, and rode him out of the ring.

Fortunately, on this occasion, the loose horse was quickly caught and no harm was done to other horses, but the incident impressed on me the wisdom of sleeping near my horse and of tying to my own rig instead of to any communal rail or picket line.

After so much has been said in this book about danger of founder and the necessity of properly cooling out a horse, further caution here should not be necessary. However, even though knowledge of such matters is common among trail riders, on most large trail rides at least one rider is careless and has a sick horse because he let him drink out of a cold stream just before the ride ended; or he let his horse drink too much water from a bucket before completely cooling him out. Of course, there is always the idiot who not only fails to walk his horse the last mile into camp but, worst still, gallops the last quarter of a mile in a cloud of dust. By some irony of fate such riders are usually looked after by their betters and seldom come to grief; but the horse that gallops in must be walked until he is cooled before being watered or tied up.

Backs should be constantly watched for slight injuries. Over-medication of such things on a trail ride always causes trouble, for most medicines applied to a slight injury will remain for many hours. When a saddle blanket is put over them and the horse sweats, a large sore, scald, or blister results. Grease gathers dirt and adds to trouble. Any slight break in the skin may be washed with warm salt water. A bump or swelling, no matter how small, should be treated with an ice pack or a pack of the coldest water available. If the pack is applied long enough, tied on with an improvised surcingle, the horse will be perfectly fit for service in the morning.

It should be needless to say that saddle blankets should be kept clean and dried and that backs should also be kept clean. Warm salt water bathing of backs at the end of each ride is a good practice, though not necessary for every horse. Cinches should be kept clean and soft.

Part VI

EQUIPMENT

15

Saddles
and
bridles

Choosing the Saddle

The basic seat can be ridden in any of the saddles popular in America today. Such saddles can be generally grouped in two classes —stock saddles and flat saddles, the latter frequently called English saddles, though they are no more uniquely English than the stock saddle is Spanish or Mexican. The Whitman, a flat saddle, is a distinctly American manufacture and in many ways is an improvement over English flat saddles. It is an excellent flat saddle for riding the basic seat and frequently fits a horse's back better than many imported saddles.

Aside from stock saddles and flat saddles there are in use in America today a few other kinds of saddles, such as the Kentucky spring seat and the McClellans. They are, however, not sufficiently popular to warrant discussion here, though in passing it might be pointed out that it is very difficult to ride the forward or balanced seat in the Kentucky spring seat, the saddle originally used for the plantation horse, or Tennessee Walking Horse, as he is called today.

Just as there is no one best breed of horse, so there is no one best saddle. Whether you choose to ride a flat saddle or a stock saddle is a matter to be decided by your own personal preference, which will be influenced in large part by the kind of equipment most used by the horsemen in your community. If hunting, polo, and the English type of horse show classes are popular in your area, you may well choose to begin riding on a flat saddle, though if you prefer to start with a stock saddle you can ride the basic seat with it until you have acquired balance, rhythm, and the ability to relax and communicate with your horse. Then you can readily change to a forward seat flat saddle. Contrary to popular belief, I have observed that riders who change from stock saddles to flat saddles have much less difficulty than do those who change from flat saddles to stock saddles. I have known excellent horsemen and horsewomen who grew up in the East riding flat saddles, came west after maturity, and found it very difficult to learn to ride a stock saddle with comfort. I have never known a Western rider of any skill who experienced great difficulty learning to use the flat saddle, except for some difficulty in swallowing pride. Perhaps this is because the stock saddle is a little wider, or thicker, than the flat saddle. Also, the stirrups are hung farther forward on the flat saddle, and so it is a little easier to sit the basic or natural seat on it than on the stock saddle. Then, too, the stirrups on the stock saddle, or, more exactly, the stirrup leathers and fenders, are more nearly rigid than are those of the flat saddle; and until a rider uses a particular saddle long enough to "break in" the saddle to his own way of riding, it may not be entirely comfortable.

In choosing a saddle of any kind, there are three considerations that must come before all others: (1) Are the saddle and fittings (girth or cinches, stirrup leathers and stirrups) strong enough to be safe for the use to which the saddle is to be put? (2) Does the saddle fit the horse? (3) Does the saddle fit the rider?

Flat Saddles

If your choice of a first saddle is a flat saddle, you will probably do yourself and your horse a favor if you buy a good used saddle rather than a new one for a similar price. (See Fig. 22.) The most frequent cause of injury to the horse from a low-priced flat saddle is pressure on the horse's backbone. When new, the cheap saddle may clear the spine, but a weak tree (frequently used in cheaper saddles) will spread soon and let the saddle down onto the horse's backbone at either the front or the rear of the saddle, or both. As I have recommended for a first horse a sound animal with some age, it is necessary to emphasize here the importance of using a saddle that clears the backbone well. Many horses' withers become more prominent as they grow older. I have recently heard captains of polo teams say that they prefer using horses that are over nine

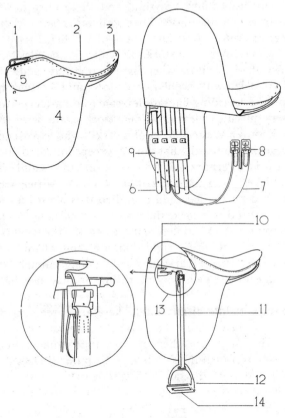

Fig. 22. Diagram of flat saddle: (1) pommel; (2) seat; (3) cantle; (4) saddle skirt; (5) stirrup bar flap; (6) billets; (7) girth; (8) girth buckles; (9) buckle guard; (10) safety stirrup bar; (11) stirrup strap; (12) stirrup; (13) detail of safety bar; (14) stirrup tread.

years old and that for that reason they are very careful about the fit of their saddles over their horses' withers.

Another reason why the used saddle is a better buy for the beginner than the new saddle is that a dealer is much more apt to allow the prospective purchaser to take a second-hand saddle home and try it out before buying than he is to take the risk of scars on a new saddle.

For a first flat saddle avoid extremes. The extreme forward seat has very definite use, but only after a rider has learned to relax and go with the rhythm of his horse and is ready for hunting in a fast field or for competitive riding of certain kinds. The flat saddle with the very long seat and stirrups hung far forward is comfortable and useful for certain special kinds of riding only. For learning the basic seat, on a flat saddle, such a tree as the old English Somerset or the Whitman (American) tree is satisfactory. Almost any of the older park seat flat saddles made by reputable American or English saddlers is good for a first flat saddle.

For safety's sake no flat saddle should be used without at least two girths or a good, strong double girth made either of mohair or folded leather, strong, soft, and pliable. Canvas girths are dangerous unless extremely well cared for and discarded as soon as they begin to deteriorate. Special attention should be paid to the leather tabs to which the girth is buckled. The leather in them should be live and pliable. Perhaps even more imperative for the safety of the rider is the open stirrup leather bar. This is the metal device that secures the stirrup leather to the saddle tree. On very cheap flat saddles it is sometimes just a metal loop, but on a properly made flat saddle it is shaped more or less like the letter L, so that when the stirrup leather is pulled backward, as is the case when a rider falls and hangs a foot in the stirrup, it comes loose from the saddle. Some flat saddles, especially those designed for hunting, are equipped with stirrup leather bars that have a locking device that opens with a spring much like a knife blade. This keeps the rider of the forward seat from pushing his stirrup leathers off his saddle when he gets his feet a little too far back. However, with such a device it is very important for the beginning rider to be sure that he rides at all times with the lock open, so that the leathers will come loose easily from the tree. (See Fig. 22.)

Before buying any saddle, always inspect the tree. Pressure exerted on the saddle just above where a rider's knees would come will usually reveal a break in the fork. To find if the tree is solid elsewhere, place a hand on the front of the saddle and another on the back. Exert as much pressure as possible with both hands to see if there is any give in the tree. When trying a saddle on a horse, place it properly, as I have described in directions on saddling, and then be sure there is at least an inch between the horse's backbone and the saddle at both the extreme front and rear of the saddle when you are sitting in the saddle. Another place where a flat saddle makes trouble at times is the back end of the padding on either side of the backbone, right over a horse's kidneys. If it is possible to ride a saddle for a few minutes before purchase, place a folded bed sheet or other smooth, clean cloth over the horse's back to keep the saddle from being marked with sweat. Then ride for a few minutes. A very little ride will make enough sweat mark on the sheet to tell if there is pressure at the extreme rear end of the saddle padding. This of course is very easy to remedy in some saddles. A little felt or folded gunny sack pushed in between the pad and the tree at the proper place by an experienced hand may eliminate the trouble, but the inexperienced horseman should be sure the trouble is not in the tree. This painful pressure at the rear end of the pad is found not infrequently in poorly made extended bar saddles, which when properly made are excellent saddles for the beginning rider if they fit the horse. Such saddles are sometimes called "officers' saddles." The bars of the tree that rest on the horse's ribs extend farther back than does the seat of such saddles. Thus they prevent the rider using the basic seat from sitting directly over his horse's loins.

PADS AND BLANKETS

If a flat saddle fits the horse properly and the part of the saddle that comes in contact with the horse is leather, the only reason for using a pad or blanket under the saddle is to lessen the work required to keep the saddle clean and the leather facing well soaped or oiled. If the saddle fits perfectly, the less blanket or padding there is between it and the horse the better. However, the perfect fit is rare. The best pad for such a rarity is a very light felt, seamless if possible, or one of leather perforated with small holes. Such pads should be shaped like the saddle and be a trifle longer than the saddle to give full protection if they shift an inch or so under the saddle. The pad must be provided with straps looped at the end so they may be held in place by the billets that the girth is buckled to.

For most flat saddles, the ones that approximate a fit, the best pad is one of heavy felt or clipped sheephide, wool side toward the horse. The best pad I ever used was one of very heavy graduated felt. These pads were made in Europe and were not available during the war. Since then I have not seen one, but a good importer might locate one. Any pad used must be kept clean and discarded if it becomes hard. Square blankets under a flat saddle are improper and unnecessarily heating. Sponge rubber is the newest thing in pads, both for flat saddles and for stock saddles. Reports from horsemen using them are conflicting, but the adverse criticism of them is probably due in part to a fixed notion that rubber is heating. Certainly any pad that is heavy enough to be a protection is heating. There is a very good chance that the sponge rubber lets more air in under the saddle than does wool or felt, but it is too early to be certain, though it deserves a trial. The biggest objection to sponge rubber for a stock saddle is that on a windy day it is difficult to keep the pad on a horse's back until the saddle is put on. Some horsemen are solving this by putting a Navajo blanket over the rubber. Certainly sponge rubber is easier to keep clean than other pads.

Eastern Bridles and Bits

BRIDLES

The term *English* is still used exclusively to designate the kind of bridle used conventionally with flat saddles, though we in America have certainly changed our "English" bridles so much that they would shock or amuse the audience if they appeared on Rotten Row or in an English show. When I was a lad, the first thing I learned about show ring equipment was that it must never be gaudy. My mentor, a charming gentleman from England, an excellent horseman and manager of the saddlery department of a large wholesale jobbing house, told me, "Good taste dictates that a bridle should be made entirely of good English stock not doubled or stitched and should have no rosettes or color on the browband, noseband or cavesson."

How shocked he would be today to see the gaudy "fronts" on most of the "English" show bridles. Polo and hunting bridles are still close to the English tradition, but I should not be at all surprised to see the hunting field or the polo team blossom out in color any day.

For a first bridle of the English type, the beginner should get one made as simply as possible. Double and stitched leather is always difficult to repair and not as easy to care for as plain leather. A patent leather browband of some bright color is attractive and can be kept clean easily. The first bridle may well be purchased with a cavesson or noseband for future use, but until the novice has learned to bridle his horse easily, the noseband had better be put away carefully in the tack room.

If the beginning horseman thinks he will want to learn to jump or do any kind of competitive riding, he will do well to choose a double bridle for his first English bridle. (See Figs. 23–27.) Until

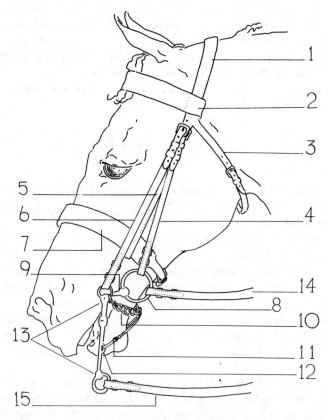

FIG. 23. Bit of bridoon or full bridle with cavesson: (1) crown; (2) brow band; (3) throatlatch; (4) snaffle cheek piece; (5) cavesson headstall; (6) curb cheek piece; (7) cavesson; (8) snaffle ring (bridoon); (9) snaffle mouthpiece; (10) curb chain; (11) lip strap; (12) lip strap loop; (13) curb shank; (14) snaffle rein; (15) curb rein.

he has progressed to the point where he can use a full bridle to balance his horse perfectly, he can put snaffle bit, headstall, and rein away in the tack room (after carefully soaping the leather). He had best note carefully before removing the snaffle headstall that it goes under the main crown piece of the bridle, that the noseband

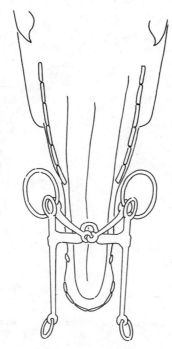

FIG. 24. Curb and snaffle inside horse's mouth.

goes inside the snaffle cheek pieces, and that the snaffle bit rides on top of the curb, with curb chain outside the snaffle bit.

BITS

The bits for the full, English bridle should be of a good non-corrosive alloy. The snaffle bit should have medium-sized rings. The mouthpiece should be not too fine. The larger the metal of the mouthpiece the easier the bit is on the horse's mouth. Good solid hunters that have to carry inept and careless riders who hang on by their horses' mouths are usually equipped only with big snaffles (bridoons) that have mouthpieces made of half-inch or larger metal. This enables the loutish riders to hang on without doing great damage to their horses' mouths. I must hasten to add, however, that the above is not the only use of the big bridoon. It is a very useful bit on some colts; and some hunters go better all their lives on this bit than on any other.

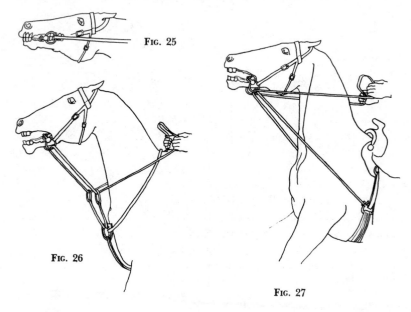

FIG. 25

FIG. 26

FIG. 27

FIG. 25. Snaffle bit. Gets nose out and balance forward because of pull on corners of mouth toward the horse's ears; not on bars.

FIG. 26. Snaffle with running martingale puts pressure on bars and decreases extremity of forward balance.

FIG. 27. Snaffle with draw rein—a harsh device preferred by some horse breakers.

To return to our first bridle, we have decided that the snaffle should be of medium weight, with medium-sized rings. The curb should of course have lip-strap rings. The best English-type curb for most purposes that I have ever found is one designed by and named after a great Missouri trainer, a gifted Negro long respected by intelligent American horsemen, Tom Bass. The Tom Bass bit has a medium shank. The mouthpiece is larger than that of the conventional English curb and can usually be obtained in five- and five-and-a-half-inch widths. The five-inch width is best for all but horses with exceptionally wide jaws. A narrower bit will pinch the corner of the mouth with the chain. At two points in particular the Tom Bass bit is superior to all other English-type curbs I have seen. One is where the mouthpiece joins the shank and the other is the part of the port that touches the tongue, the part

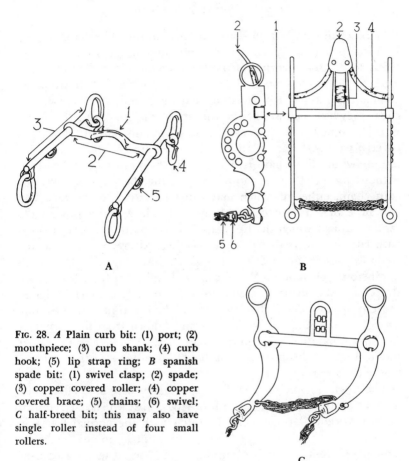

FIG. 28. *A* Plain curb bit: (1) port; (2) mouthpiece; (3) curb shank; (4) curb hook; (5) lip strap ring; *B* spanish spade bit: (1) swivel clasp; (2) spade; (3) copper covered roller; (4) copper covered brace; (5) chains; (6) swivel; *C* half-breed bit; this may also have single roller instead of four small rollers.

that touches the bar of a horse's mouth if the bit is jerked sideways. At these points in the Tom Bass bit there are no sharp angles. The joining of mouthpiece and shank is rounded and smooth. The bottom of the port has no definite angle, but turns up in a smooth curve. While the Tom Bass bit is now available with either a solid or open port, I recommend the latter strongly. If the horse does not have room to get his tongue under the bit, he may start putting it over the bit; and a tongue loller is a nuisance.

Curb Chains and Straps

Curb chains are far superior to curb straps. The latter always have some stretch. When a curb strap stretches a little, it is very likely to pinch the corner of the horse's mouth. Many head tossers were made to develop their vice by a pinching curb strap. So common is this fault of bridling that many old livery horses and cowponies have calluses at the corners of their mouths. If a horse is thin-skinned and the chain causes him discomfort, it can be covered with soft leather, rubber, or sheepskin. Another reason for my preference of a chain is that the lip strap can be attached to it without the need for a loop or for crossing the lip strap over the chin chain, either of which may cause irritation to the jaw. You will note that a curb chain always has a little extra link in the center through which the lip strap can be passed. Use a curb chain with large flat links that fit close together. Always be sure that the chain is twisted so that it is flat and smooth against the horse's jaw before you mount. Never use an English curb without a lip strap, or a shoestring as a substitute for one. It is much easier to prevent lipping the bit than to cure it. The lip strap should be long enough so that the bit can hang straight down from the corner of the horse's mouth but no longer than that. (The best and quickest way to break a lip strap, and probably a bridle, is to tie the horse by the curb rein.)

The English name for a curb is a *pelham*. There are pelham bits without ports, pelham bits with four rings, with which one rein can be used without leverage and the other with the normal leverage. There are roller-mouthed pelhams (Hanoverians), jointed pelhams, loose-jawed pelhams, and so on. There are special uses for each of them, but unless you are a professional trainer or have a horse that has been ridden satisfactorily for years with some trick bit, use either a single Tom Bass bit or the double bridle; that is, the curb and snaffle, or, as the British say, the bit and bridoon, Weymouth bridle, or full bridle. For most ordinary riding on a reasonably well-trained horse, a Tom Bass curb is all the bit needed. For more advanced riding, where shift in the balance of the horse is quite important, the double bridle may be very necessary; for, speaking very generally, the snaffle tends to get the horse's nose out (see Fig. 25) and balance forward and the curb tends to get his chin in, his hocks under him, and his balance back.

One last caution: see that the reins of the bridle you buy are full length. Some cut-rate bridles are skimpy on rein length. Also, such bridles are sometimes skimpy on length of throatlatch and noseband. It is possible to discard a noseband, but a throatlatch must be used on an English-type bridle; and if it is not plenty loose, loose enough so that you can insert at least four fingers under it easily, it will choke your horse when he pulls his chin in. The fact that even some experienced riders use a throatlatch so tight that it causes discomfort to their horses is no reason you should.

Stock Saddles

For a first stock saddle, a good second-hand one is a very good choice, unless cost is not of great concern or you have a dealer who will let you try a new saddle on your horse before you make up your mind about a purchase. Be sure of the fit of the saddle on your horse. Try it out with a clean light-colored cloth next to your horse. Ride with it until his hair begins to turn, but not until he sweats freely. If your horse is in good health there will be enough oil in his skin so that when he just begins to perspire the light cloth will bear the marks of greatest pressure. This is not a 100 percent sure test but is the best way I have ever found of predicting what a saddle is going to do to a horse's back. If the saddle seems to press either at the extreme front or extreme rear of the bars of the saddle—the part of the saddle that rests on the ribs just below the backbone—have no more to do with it. Be sure that with a pad no thicker than a single Navajo blanket, and after a ride of some duration, the saddle is at least an inch above the horse's backbone at the center of the front and rear of the saddle.

The soundness of the tree of any second-hand saddle should be tested by putting the saddle on its side on the ground and applying pressure to see if the tree is solid at all points. The saddle should also be placed on end and pressed by hand or knee to see if the tree is solid. The leather should not be hard and stiff at any place on the saddle and the latigo straps should be sound and pliable.

Scars or worn spots will not harm the riding quality of the saddle. The sheepskin lining, however, should be sound and smooth. If the fleece is worn so that it is less than one-quarter-inch thick, the saddle should not cost over half the price of a new one; but if the

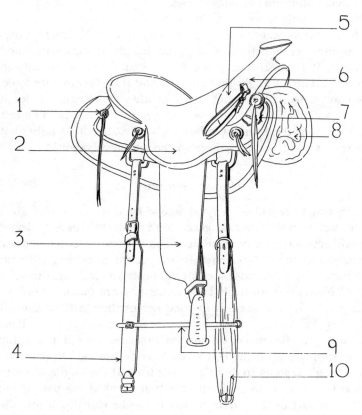

Fig. 29. Stock saddle—offside: (1) leather buttons or metal conchas; (2) seat jockey; (3) fenders or rosaderos; (4) hind cinch; (5) rope strap; (6) swell, fork, or front; (7) latigo carrier; (8) sheepskin lining; (9) cinch spacer; (10) front cinch.

worn sheepskin is smooth, the shortness of the fleece can be compensated for by the use of an extra Navajo double-weave or mohair blanket or other similar padding.

As there is one important matter concerning equipment that cannot be emphasized too often, it is appropriate to mention it here. No horse will have a back free from sores or blemishes very long unless his owner keeps the saddle blanket, pad, or whatever rests directly on his horse's back clean at all times. It is always wise to have a change of blanket, for many times you will want to ride when the blanket you last rode or last washed is not yet dry.

To return to the purchase of a first saddle, if it is a used saddle examine the saddle strings. One of the joys of the good American

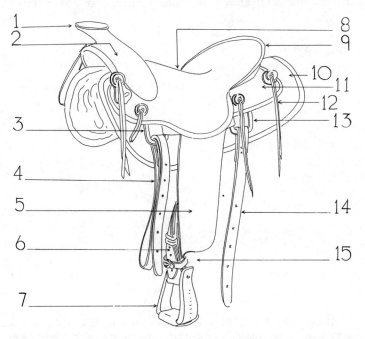

FIG. 30. Stock saddle—near side: (1) horn; (2) fork; (3) front rigging ring; (4) latigo; (5) fenders or rosaderos (these are made in one piece with stirrup leathers on this saddle); (6) stirrup leather; (7) stirrup; (8) seat; (9) cantle; (10) skirt; (11) upper flank skirt; (12) strings; (13) hind cinch ring; (14) hind cinch; (15) stirrup leather buckle strap.

stock saddle is that a slicker, jacket, lunch, or what-not can always be tied onto the saddle. It is hard on the religion to start to tie on a slicker and have a stiff saddle string break. After you buy a saddle and are taking care of it by properly soaping it and wiping it with an oily rag on occasion (use neatsfoot oil only), don't forget to keep the saddle strings well soaped (not oiled) and pliable.

The best rigging on a stock saddle for a beginner is a three-quarter; that is, one equipped with a single cinch that is hung a little farther to the rear than is the front cinch of a full or double-rigged saddle. Certainly the latigo straps that hold the cinch should be sound and the latigo keeper should be sound, strong, and securely fastened to the tree. The cinch should be of mohair and the wider and thicker the better. It should be long enough so that the rings come well above the horse's elbows at either side. Of

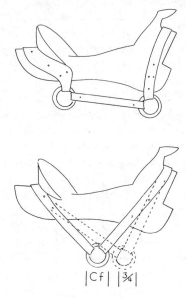

FIG. 31. Double rigged tree: (1) stock saddle tree with full rigging; (2) stock saddle tree, center fire rigging (three-quarter rigging shown in dotted line).

course if the used saddle you are looking at does not have such a girth and is very reasonable in price and otherwise satisfactory, you may discard the cinch it has and replace it with a new one. In any event, use no cinch but a wide, thick mohair.

After you have determined that the stock saddle you are considering will not injure your horse's back and that it is in reasonably good condition, make sure it is so constructed that you can ride the basic seat in it without discomfort to you or your horse. Be sure that the stirrups are hung a little farther forward than the deepest place in the seat and hung so that they will move back and forth freely.

Be sure that the saddle tree extends well behind the cantle of the saddle. If it does not, either you will be sitting over your horse's loins or the tree is so short that it will gouge your horse's back.

Unless the saddle you are considering is very old or has been specially made for a horseman who spends more time training or theorizing than he does in riding on range or countryside, the seat of the saddle will be built up so that the part just behind the fork is higher than that just in front of the cantle. Sometimes in achieving this build-up the saddlemaker gets his saddle so wide that it is uncomfortable for most riders, especially those that have learned to ride on a flat saddle. For your own comfort's sake pay especial attention to this. Also, if your saddle is unduly thick and wide beneath the upper part of your thighs, you will tend to use the back of your thighs and get your knees away from your horse, or at least to use the back instead of the inside of your knees. All of this means that you will not be riding the basic seat.

Of course if the seat of the built-up saddle is too long, it puts the rider too far back on his horse to ride the basic seat and makes it impossible to use a balanced seat; however, such saddles are fortunately not common.

Height of cantle and width of fork of the first saddle are not important as long as extremes are avoided. It is not likely that the beginning rider today will be tempted to buy a saddle with an extremely high, straight cantle or a saddle with a wide, form-fitting swell on the fork. The extremely low-down ropers so popular today are satisfactory as long as the beginner does not buy one made for wide-shouldered Quarter Horses and then ride it on a horse with shoulders that are not loaded and withers that are good. This error will be avoided, of course, if the beginner follows the advice given earlier in this chapter about observing the room at the front of the saddle between the horse's backbone and the saddle.

Stirrups that are round on the bottom are very uncomfortable to ride if the ball of the foot is used. Tapaderos are good protection in the brush, and in winter they can be stuffed loosely with straw for an effective prevention of cold feet; however, for the beginning rider they are a bit cumbersome and may interfere some with proper use of feet, ankles, and legs.

The lighter weight a saddle is if it has a tree guaranteed by a reputable maker, the better. I do not at this time recommend the new featherweight (seventeen to nineteen pounds) saddles now being recommended and said to be satisfactory for every use but roping. However, if use proves these saddles to have trees that do not spread, they may be the perfect saddle for the nonroper.

One last and most important caution to the beginner buying a stock saddle—if for some special reason you buy a saddle with a full rigging, that is, two cinches, be sure that the cinch spacer (the strap that goes between the front and hind cinch right under the middle of the horse's belly) is properly fastened to both front and hind cinch and is securely buckled. This may seem to old horsemen like superfluous advice; but a few months before this book was started a neighbor of mine paid a high price for a saddle. He was putting it on a quite frisky horse, well mannered but quite a handful for a rider with no more experience than his owner had had. My attention was called to the new saddle, and I admired it. Luckily I happened to notice that the saddle, a full-rigged one, had absolutely no tie between front and rear cinch. When I mentioned the fact, the new owner asked what I was talking about. As any old horseman knows, if that saddle had been put on the frisky horse and mounted by my friend, who is a rider of little experience, a serious accident would have resulted. Almost any horse will buck if the hind cinch slides back far enough. Almost all bucking horses (the *almost* is for the one in ten thousand) in rodeos are made to buck by the use of a cinch around the flank.

If a full rigging is used, much care must be taken to see that the front cinch is soft and clean and does not make the horse sore right behind the elbow. The front cinch of a double rigging comes so far forward that it is more apt to make trouble than a three-quarter rig (one with a single cinch).

The inexperienced horseman had best confine his choice of any kind of a saddle to those made by reputable saddlemakers of wide reputation and generations of experience. Saddles made in Mexico are often very tempting, especially when one takes a holiday across the border. Some really excellent saddles are made there; however, poor leather, poor trees, and other defects are difficult for the inexperienced to detect. I have known some experienced horsemen to be quite disappointed with saddles bought across the line at what seemed a bargain price, so I strongly recommend that the beginning rider confine his saddle buying to saddles made by reputable American firms of long-standing reputation.

16

Western bits, bridles, ~~~~~~~~~~~~~~~~~~~~~~~

and ~~~~~~~~~~~~~~~~~~~~~~~~~~~~~~~~~~~

other accessories ~~~~~~~~~~~~~~~~~~~~~~~

The breast strap is a very useful piece of equipment. It enables the mountain rider to keep his saddle in position without pulling his horse in two with the cinch; however, the beginning rider will do well to wait for the use of the breast strap (called breast collar by some) until he has need of it. He will do well to keep his horse properly fitted with a minimum of equipment and keep it in good condition.

With a very few horses a flat saddle will not stay in place without a breast strap (or breastplate, as the English variety is called). If one is used, the neck strap should not be so tight that it pulls the breast strap up tight against the neck. The breast strap should hang at the chest just where the neck joins the shoulder and the strap itself should be just tight enough to keep the saddle from slipping back more than three fingers' width behind the shoulder blades.

Martingales are devices that enable some calf ropers to bring home the jackpot. They are required equipment on the polo field, although the author is old enough to remember one eccentric polo captain who ordered a player off the field when the player presented himself for practice on a pony equipped with a tiedown (martingale). The caustic old captain's comment was, "If your hand isn't good enough to keep that pony's head out of your face without a tiedown, it isn't good enough to play on this team!"

Since that time, the rules of polo have changed and the type of pony used has changed radically. Polo ponies and roping horses are means to ends. If tying their heads down makes a split second of difference in their stopping or a slight difference in convenience to their riders, it is worth doing. However, the rider who rides to enjoy his horse will do well to see as little of martingales as possible, though I must admit that in my own stable there is a little roan gelding that was broken with a tiedown. Without one he shakes his head every time he checks speed. I use a tiedown on him and take the ribbing I get from friends, because he is a delightfully responsive, quick, and tireless little horse, with the sweetest disposition one could ask for. He is, however, one of the few horses I have ever kept that required a tiedown. Had that little roan been broken as I like to have one broken, he would not need a tiedown.

A martingale should be just tight enough to keep the horse from tossing his nose in the air but not tight enough to interfere with any other head movement. The strap from breastplate to girth or cinch should be loose enough not to chafe. The standing martingale (or tiedown) should be attached to a noseband or bozal, never to a bit.

Halters

Some horsemen find it quite a convenience to leave a halter on a horse when he is in corral or stall. In the Southwest, where a fly mask is a necessity in the summer, it is quite necessary to leave the halter on. A fly mask will not stay in place unless it is anchored to a halter. The halter that is left on all the time should not be too heavy. A Johnson rope halter is satisfactory if it is loose enough so that when it is wet and shrinks it does not rub the bottom of the cheekbone. Any halter should come below the bottom of the cheekbone and should not be so large and loose that it rubs the soft part of the nose. It should be loose enough not to interfere with breathing when the horse tucks in his chin but should be snug enough to keep from coming off over his ears when he rolls or shakes his head.

When going on any kind of an outing where I expect to need to tie up my horse, I use a Johnson halter under a split-ear bridle and use a piece of shoestring to tie the halter to the bridle at the poll to keep it from sliding back when my horse carries his head up and moves right along. For those who wish a smart appearance, the Johnson halter can easily be tied on the saddle. (The Johnson halter is ubiquitous in the West, is made of cotton and quite strong.) If a leather halter is used, even if very heavy, it had best be made of single-ply leather. A double- or triple-ply halter is hard to keep in repair and very difficult to keep pliable and clean. The leather halter that is worn in the corral should not be too heavy and should be kept very soft by soaping.

Bits, Hackamores, and Bridles

While the bit and bridoon bridle of the East is being used more and more in Western training establishments, the headgear of the West is still the curb and at times the hackamore. Many Western horsemen have long used a single snaffle bit to start a colt with, but it is considered generally only a colt bit. Not over a week before these lines were written I stopped to talk to a horseman friend. I was riding with a curb with a jointed mouthpiece (mouthpiece like a snaffle but with curb shank leverage). My friend asked, "How come you're riding that old gelding with a colt bit?" Such is the fixed idea in the West that a jointed or snaffle bit is for colts only.

A double rein usually means that a colt is being ridden with a hackamore and curb. One of the reins is quite likely a rope, possibly of soft mane hair. Perhaps the entire hackamore is of hair, though this very useful and once popular hackamore is now largely superseded by the rawhide bozal and the patented hackamore bit. The great difference in use of bits East and West suggests many differences in riding. The Westerner never hangs on to his reins; the Easterner rarely rides with a slack rein. Much more riding is done in the East with the horse's balance forward than in the West—fox hunting, steeplechasing, and other fast work on smooth sod. The Western horse must have his hocks under him much of the time cutting cattle, dodging ground squirrel holes, rocks, and what-not. Much of the competitive riding in the West demands extreme collection—barrel racing, calf roping, and other rodeo and horse-show work.

The idea that there are severe and mild bits is a trifle misleading.

The severity depends on the hand at the end of the rein. A horseman of my acquaintance has horses that show no evidence of any sort of discomfort. He rides only a loose-jawed spade bit, the kind that is thought by many to be an inhumane bit. However, he never allows anyone else to mount one of his horses while it has a spade in its mouth. This horseman has the lightest of hands and his horses seem to enjoy talking to him with spade bit. At least one four-year-old stallion he has tosses its head and frets when it has a stiff bit in its mouth but is perfectly steady and continually plays with the roller when wearing the spade.

Perhaps it might be going too far to say that the bits popular in the West indicate lighter hands than one ordinarily sees in the East, but it is a great temptation to say so.

In choosing a bit, the rider not the horse is the important factor. An expert horseman can get practically any performance from his mount that the horse is capable of with almost any kind of a bit. It is true that he can do so more easily with some bits than others. However, a good trainer or horseman who owns a simple curb with a five-and-a-half-inch mouthpiece and a seven-inch shank, and a good snaffle bit (with a good bozal thrown in), has all the bits that are a vital necessity to his trade. The heavy-handed rider should have a very short-shanked curb with a big mouthpiece, if he insists on using a curb. Better still, let him use a very mild hackamore bit or a snaffle with a runing martingale. (See Fig. 26, p. 174.) Of course, if his hand is heavy enough, the only solution is to get him interested in motorcycles.

As I have already said elsewhere, the effect of the snaffle and similar bits (this would also include the chain bit and the leather bit) is to get the horse's weight forward and nose out or skyward or both. This is because the pressure of the nonleverage bits (those just listed) comes on the corners of the mouth rather than on the bars; and just as soon as the horse puts his nose out, which he usually does to pull on the snaffle, the pull is toward his ears entirely and not downward or backward on the bars. (The bars are the lower jaws or gums, which seem to be made for a bit because there is a space of several inches without teeth between the front teeth and the molars, as you discovered the first time you put a bridle on a horse.)

This "stargazing," as it is called, is counteracted sometimes by the use of a running martingale. The English sometimes use two reins with a snaffle bit; one free and one run through a running martingale. Americans generally, and I suspect horses, too, prefer something more definite than the loose, jointed bit and flopping martingale. The curb bit, *properly handled,* is a definite and comfortable signal. If the rider is gifted and experienced, his horse can "talk" to him on a curb bit and can do so even more easily on a spade, though the spade in any but very exceptional hands is the cause of agony to a horse and frustration and tragedy to the rider.

Eastern bits are straight of shank (with the exception of the Walking Horse bit) and therefore need a lip strap to obviate the temptation to the horse to take the shank in the side of his mouth (called lipping the bit). The Western bit is curved and needs no lip strap. The old United States Cavalry bit of Indian war days was not only curved in the conventional S at the shanks but also had a large ring where the mouthpiece was attached, so large that it alone would have kept most horses from lipping the bit. That old bit was very useful with light-handed riders, though a trifle long in the shank for less-skilled hands. It is difficult to find now, though one bit maker makes a rather expensive copy of it with a copper mouthpiece. The copper suggests an interesting notion still sometimes encountered in the West. It is an idea, inherited from the Spanish, that copper in a horse's mouth makes him more docile. Perhaps the copper mouthpiece can be said to be the grandparent of Promazine (a proprietary equine tranquilizer now being advertised widely).

All but the cheapest of Western bits are curved out at the top of the shank, the part that is attached to the cheekpiece of the bridle. This helps prevent pinching the corners of the horse's mouth, though if the mouthpiece is too narrow or the curb strap or chain is too long, *any* curb will pinch. A shank should be, for average purposes, seven inches long, at least one-fifth of the shank above the mouthpiece; one-fourth is better. If the shank is flat and wide, as on some old Baja California bits, the curve of the shank is not too important, for the large, flat shank cannot be lipped. However, if the shank is of round metal, it must have a large S curve or be provided with lip strap rings (tiny rings on the shank midway between mouthpiece and lower end of shank). The lip "strap" can be a bit of whang leather or shoestring attached to the lip strap rings and run over the curb strap, if curb strap is used, or run through the center ring of the curb chain, if chain is used.

The lip strap should be just tight enough to prevent the horse from taking the shank in the side of his mouth but not tight enough to pull on the shank of the bit. Of course another function of the lip strap is to prevent the head tosser from throwing the bit upside down, a feat which the curved shank of the Western bit helps prevent. A mouthpiece that is too small around is not desirable, nor is one that is square at the bottom of the upcurve of the port or that has a corner where mouthpiece joins shank. All junctures and curves inside the mouth should be smooth and curved or rounded, as should be all parts of the bit that touch the outside of the horse. The mouthpiece of the bit should be at least five inches wide; five and a half inches is not too wide for most horses— better too wide than too narrow. The port should be large enough so that the horse can work his tongue comfortably under it. A curb with no port is a temptation to put a tongue over a bit. Some horses are so schooled that they work better with a curb having a mouthpiece that is jointed like a snaffle. With such a bit it is necessary to use great care in adjusting the length of the curb chain so that when rein is pulled the bit does not pinch the corners of the mouth against the chain. The chain should be short enough so that no amount of pull will bring the shank of the bit farther back than a forty-five degree angle with the mouth, if the shank is straight. If the shank is curved, evaluate the angle of the shank by imagining a line which is the continuation downward of the part of the shank that is above the mouth. (See Fig. 32).

HACKAMORES

The hackamore (Spanish *jaquima*) is neither a halter used for breaking horses nor a rope passed through a horse's mouth—the definitions given in *Webster's Collegiate* and in the *American College Dictionary*. It is a band of braided rawhide, rope, or other material which goes around a horse's nose at the lowest part of the bony structure of the head. The term *hackamore* is sometimes used to include the headstall which holds the nosepiece in place, as well as the reins attached to it. There is a very conventional kind of braided rawhide hackamore, specifically called a *bozal,* which is braided thick across the nose, has small braided balls to keep the headstall in place, and a larger ball to give weight enough to the back of the bozal to cause it to fall free from the horse's jaw the moment rein pressure is released. The hackamore is the

most valuable contribution made by the Spanish to American
horse training; it is used not only in training but also in Western
and Central and South American horsemanship for many purposes
that have nothing at all to do with training. Most of the pictures
of the old Spanish dons of Mexico show them on horses equipped
with bosals. Modern Argentine and Brazilian pictures frequently
show riders mounted on anything but colts and using hackamores
and various other devices that seem strange to North American
eyes.

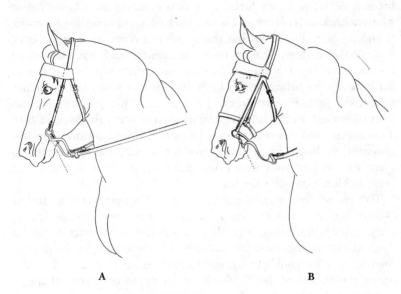

A   B

FIG. 32. Angle of bit. *A* Proper adjustment of curb strap to prevent pinching
corner of mouth (strap must be short enough to prevent bit shank from coming
back farther than a forty-five degree angle with mouth). *B* With slightly different
shape of bit shank.

Proper use of the hackamore is an art, one that cannot be covered
briefly. There are several reliable books in print on the art of the
hackamore. No good horseman ever pulls or hangs on to the
hackamore. It is used with deft, short pressure, sometimes very
sharply. The use of the hackamore takes skill somewhat like that
of handling a fly rod. It is an art worth special study but one to
be avoided without proper guidance or study. Much of the harm
done by improper use of the hackamore results from hanging it too

far down on the end of a horse's nose so that pressure comes on the soft cartilage and not on the bone. This may cut off much of a horse's air supply at times and cause him to fight back, if he is a horse of any breeding.

HACKAMORE BITS

The hackamore bit is a godsend to many horses. It is a device that makes it possible for a rider with poor or indifferent hands to ride a sensitive horse without coming to grief. The hackamore bit is a device made of metal that puts pressure on a horse's nose where a hackamore does and uses a curb chain or strap for leverage. It should be adjusted so that the shank can come only as far back as a forty-five degree angle with the mouth—as I have described for the curb bit. Hackamore bits are of many varieties. One is so made that a mouthpiece can be bolted into it when the rider has progressed to the point where he can use a bit (or the colt has learned enough in the rider's estimation to warrant the use of a bit). This is supposed to make an easy transition from hackamore to bit. However, it should be used with some caution because the mouthpiece has no port and may cause the horse to form the habit of keeping his tongue over the bit.

The oldest type of hackamore bit was T-shaped with a ring at each of the three extremities of the T. There was of course a T at each side of the horse's mouth. A noseband, sometimes of metal covered with leather (sometimes covered with nothing in the days of the old treat-'em-rough boys), was secured to the rings at one of the upper extremities of the T. To the other upper extremity of the T was attached a chin chain. The reins were of course attached to the rings at the bottom of the T. When chin chain was properly adjusted and pull exerted on the reins, very painful constriction of the nose could be achieved. However, in good hands that kind of hackamore bit is very useful. It is a definite and quick bit and I have seen excellent results from its use. More recently devised hackamore bits are less capable of being used for causing pain; but, by the same token, they are not as definite or as quick. Probably in skilled hands the old-timer is by far the best of the lot.

Sometimes the hackamore is successful in preventing the jigging or jogging of the horse that does not like to walk when in company or when going toward home, though the percentage of success is not high.

THE TACK COLLAR

The percentage of success in stopping jigging is somewhat higher with the use of the tack collar than with the hackamore in the hands of the nonprofessional horseman. The tack collar for ordinary use does not of course contain any tacks. It is a collar of rather wide (one- to two-inch) leather in which ordinary soft copper repair rivets have been closely spaced. The rivets are allowed to protrude through the leather a half inch or so on the side that is next to the horse. At the top of the collar is a handle of leather. The collar should not be heavy and should lie easily on the horse's shoulder, to be pressed against it by pulling on the handle whenever the horse is to be corrected or signaled not to jog. It is, obviously, a device for using a restraint different from the bit. Many trick teams that work in exhibitions without bridles are trained with tack collars (frequently with those that are more literally *tack* collars than the ones I have described). Certainly tack collars of any kind should be used with caution and with a deft, light, quick hand.

WESTERN BRIDLES

Styles in Western bridles change with ever-increasing rapidity. The simplest is the split-ear bridle. It undoubtedly stems from the days when money was scarce on the range and saddle shops were far away from work. A split-ear bridle could be made out of almost any piece of leather. The oldest fashion was to make them without buckles, the bit being held in place by a concha secured by a thong. Evidently conchas were easier to come by than buckles.

The split-ear is a satisfactory bridle if it is made of soft and pliable leather and the split is long enough and placed so that it does not chafe the ear. It is conventional to have the right ear go through the split. The crown of the bridle goes behind the left ear. As some riders of the modern age found that their horses were prone to rub a split-ear bridle off, saddlemakers began to offer split-ear bridles with throatlatches. It would seem that if one were going in for that much bridle one might as well go far enough to have the conventional bridle with browband. Another very popular bridle in the West is the one with cheeks and crown consisting of one long strap doubled through the bit at either side and buckled at the poll. This of course calls for a separate strap for throatlatch and rosettes to keep throatlatch and crown-and-cheek strap separated and smooth where they go through the browband. Variations of the types of bridles I have mentioned are almost numberless in the West. A good serviceable bridle should be one that can be adjusted easily for length at the cheek, should not be too heavy or skimpy at browband or elsewhere so that it chafes the horse, especially at the base of the ears. Throatlatch and nose-band should buckle on the left side with the tab of the throatlatch pointing downward and that of the noseband pointing back. The beginner will do well to dispense with the noseband until he has learned to bridle his horse easily. For ordinary riding on a well-mannered horse there is no functional value to a noseband, though in some competitive riding a noseband is a necessity.

Reins

Reins of the West are often unique. Some calf ropers use a short, endless rein, often equipped with a romel—a single strap with a loop through which the rein passes. Ropers' reins are often of braided rawhide. Longer braided rawhide reins are quite useful where horses are customarily broken to ground-tie; that is, trained to stand relatively still when the reins are dropped. This was a very necessary matter on grass range where there was rarely anything to tie a horse to if a rider had to stop to attend to an injured animal or just to rest. A relative of the writer's likes to use a horse that will ground-tie because the relative enjoys lion (cougar) and bear hunting. It is often necessary for him to dismount and leave a horse quickly to shoot or track without taking time to tie the horse. In such instances the braided rawhide rein is a great advantage because it will take a great deal of trampling. For this purpose of ground-tying Westerners use reins that are not fastened at the ends—a very dangerous practice for the beginner but a practice that has saved many a mile of walking if not life for cowboys of the old West. If a cowboy "dismounted unexpectedly" far out on the range and had long open bridle reins, he had some chance of recovering his horse, because stepping on the reins would slow down any horse; and if the horse was broken to ground-tie, he would stop when the reins hit the ground.

For comfort's sake bridle reins should not be heavy or stiff. Half-inch or seven-eighth-inch leather is plenty heavy. Rawhide, braided, makes excellent reins if the braiding is skillfully done and the reins have been properly softened; however, masters of the craft that makes such reins are getting to be very scarce.

There is one variety of headgear that is almost a museum piece today except in some remote areas of range country. It is the fiador. It is made of rope and is so knotted that it needs no buckles. The fiador is used only with the hackamore and usually only for broncos or partly broken horses. The fasteners used in place of buckles are identical with those used on hair bridles. They are of course reminiscent of frontier days when hardware was scarce and skill was not as rare as today.

Whips and Spurs

The idea that spurs and whips are devices for correction and punishment is ubiquitous but not quite in accordance with fact, especially if we are considering intelligent horsemanship. They are very useful to experienced horsemen when riding many kinds of horses, but neither whip nor spur should be used by the inexperienced without instruction.

A horse, like a person, likes signals that are definite and is confused and irritated by commands that are vague. The movement of a heel against a horse's side is easy to mistake for a casual matter of balance when it is meant for a signal, but the definite but light touch of a dull spur is unmistakable. A whip can be used to signal very definitely without causing the slightest pain or resentment.

WHIPS

Whips should be light enough to be carried easily, stout enough to resist breakage, and long enough to reach any part of the horse without the necessity of the rider's stooping or leaning. Whalebone used to be the ideal material for whips but is being superseded by spun glass. Rawhide is second best because rawhide whips are heavier and they are difficult to keep straight. A riding crop is sufficient for most whip signals, though not as versatile as a good whip. The crop, however, does have the advantage of the horn handle that will hook a gate and assist in closing it in fenced country. Also, of course, the crop has a loop to which a leash can be attached for use if the owner goes in for fox hunting in a very devoted way—and if he is a real horseman and lives in hunting country he surely will!

The old quirt of frontier days was useful when half-tamed men rode half-wild horses. It is of little use as a signal and has today little to recommend it other than that it can be hung on the saddle horn when not used. The loaded variety is of course some comfort when riding at night alone. A rap over the head with the loaded end of a quirt has discouraged more than one would-be hold-up man.

SPURS

English spurs with sharp rowels are very difficult to use as signaling devices, although there are riders who can and do so use them. The English spur without rowel is useful for more riders. If the beginner's horse is sluggish and is ridden with a flat saddle, English spurs without rowels may be very useful. The kind that has square ends is helpful on sluggish horses.

Western spurs are of great variety. Medium-length shanks are best for a first pair. Rowels should be dull, with points close enough together so that there is no danger of one doing damage in case of a fall. The length of shank may be increased or decreased as the rider gains experience. The long-legged rider on the small horse will find that a fairly long shank on a spur enables him to touch his horse without turning his toes out and down extremely. The short rider on the large horse will find that it is easier to keep from touching his horse accidentally with spurs if he uses very short shanks.

In no event should any rider wear spurs until he has learned balance and rhythm and can use restraint and impulsion reasonably well.

To the tyro it may be well to give the instruction that English spurs buckle on the outside and Western spurs buckle on the inside. The latter, of course, is for two reasons; first, the buckles might catch in the brush; and, second, the conchas and decorations are all on the outside and leave no place for a buckle! The English seem to feel that the smoother the rider can keep the part of his equipment that is next to his horse, the better.

Care of Equipment

No chapter on equipment would be in any way complete without a word about care of equipment. For the horseman who is busy at school or work, care of equipment may be kept at a minimum by the use of neatsfoot oil on all leather after thorough washing and drying. Washing may be done most effectively with English Crown soap if leather is extremely dirty from sweat. Ordinarily almost any good saddle soap or pure castile soap will do very well. Dry leather thoroughly but not in the bright sun of the Southwest or exposed to artificial heat. Then apply neatsfoot oil. If you apply repeated coats of neatsfoot oil until the leather has taken up all the oil it can, your equipment will be safe from deterioration for many months, especially if you have been careful to unbuckle all the buckles and to get oil in all the places that were hard from wear before you soaped them. However, oiled leather will not shine. Furthermore, if you put oil on the parts of the saddle that you will touch with your clothing, you will ruin any good riding clothes that are not readily washable in very hot water. If you use the labor-saving method of caring for equipment I have just described, ride your saddle in hot weather for several times with Levis, or until the oil stops coming out on your clothes. Of course it is very easy to use oil only on the parts of the saddle that do not touch your clothes and use plenty of saddle soap on the other parts frequently. In any event, always wipe off all excess oil with a dry cloth before using leather after cleaning and oiling. Care must be taken with Western saddles to see that oil does not get on the fleece of the lining. The only way to care for the fleece is to be sure that you always use a clean saddle blanket under it. The best are Navajo mohair. Next best are Navajo double-weave wool. However, I have seen horses that had such tender skin that a Navajo blanket was irritating. With them I used a folded Pendleton blanket with success. Many a good horseman uses only hair pads, and others use felt kept very clean. Watch your horse's back carefully. If it shows the slightest irritation from a clean blanket or pad, change the variety of pad to one of softer texture and keep it clean and smooth. "The eye of the master fatteneth his cattle." It also keepeth his horse's back sound and comfortable.

Part VII

ATTAINING

PROFICIENCY

17

A brief
word
on hands

The good horseman, "the man on horseback," caballero, cavalier, was long considered almost a breed apart from others. Perhaps there is some basis in fact for this. I have known officers who claimed they could tell a horseman by his walk, just as sailors can be told. Whether or not all horsemen have a distinctive walk, the horseman identifies himself the moment he approaches a horse. No one of his movements is more significant than others. They are mutually dependent. He and his horse are in communication, are aware of each other constantly. If you ask a good dancer what he does to make his partner move her left foot forward, or to the side, or to the rear, he probably will not be able to give you a very definite answer. All movements of the dancer flow into one another. Two dancers are continuously aware of each other. The same sort of constant rapport exists between horse and rider and no one part of the rider, no one movement is more important than another in maintaining the rapport. (See Plate 19.)

However, the rider's hands are a very obvious checkpoint and easily mark him as a horseman. A horseman's hands are rarely if ever entirely rigid and they are never fidgety. Even the driver of harness horse or pulling team when he uses his hands to steady his horse or horses does not use a rigid hand. He may be exerting what to the onlooker seems a very strong and steady pull, but close inspection would reveal that hands follow mouth and then, even with the hard, steady pull, there is a vestige of rhythm. In the horse-and-buggy days, one of the frequent faults of driving horses was the hard mouth that pulled on the reins. It was the result of the rigid hand. No good horseman ever made a puller.

To avoid the rigid or "dead" hand, keep the wrist slightly bent, with knuckles down or in toward the body, not out or up as in Plate 8. The bent wrist is more flexible than the straight one. It gives the horse a chance to "talk" to the rider on the reins. It is correct form for all riding except riding that is done with the forward seat. In jumping, the line of the arm from elbow to reins is straight. The entire arm goes with the horse's mouth. The beginning rider (and some older ones, too) at the top of the jump has his hands pressed against the sides of his horse's neck. However, with the exception of this very specialized kind of riding, good riding means flexed wrists. Whether the flexing is done with the knuckles turned down or (if reins are held in two hands) facing each other, is immaterial except for appearance. The accepted or "correct" way to hold the hands in three- and five-gaited classes, for example, is with the knuckles facing each other as in Plate 1. Of course the skilled rider does not sit on his horse with wrists permanently curled. The wrists are flexible and may momentarily straighten or even bend backward. The excellent horseman riding the five-gaited mare in Plate 17, has momentarily turned his right knuckles out, though the left wrist maintains the conventional bend with the knuckles facing toward the right.

The height of the hand varies with the purpose and kind of riding done. Very generally speaking, the rider of the gaited show horse or the parade horse and some Western riders carry the hands high. For most purposes, the experienced rider carries his hands just high enough to clear the saddle well. This puts the neckrein where it is used best and keeps the rider from upsetting the horse's gait by raising his head unintentionally. Many times the amateur rider who is having trouble keeping a gaited horse in a trot can solve his problem by lowering his hand.

The so-called light hand is certainly not a hand that never exerts a hard pull on a mouth. It is the hand that never exerts a "dead" pull on a mouth. It may momentarily put more pressure on the

Plate 19A

reins than any heavy hand ever exerts, but the timing of the pull is perfect and it is momentary. The light hand is deft, quick, sensitive, responsive, and strong; light as a feather most of the time. *It never exerts more pressure on the rein than is necessary to convey to the horse what the rider intends to convey.*

Communication with horses is a matter of movement almost entirely, supplemented slightly sometimes by the voice. The movement may be very slight and subtle, however. To ask whether movement of hands, legs, or body is most important is like asking which leg of a three-legged stool is most important. However, hand movements are possibly the most obvious or at least the first ones

Plate 19B

Plate 19. Two examples of perfect rapport between horse and rider. Note slack reins and relaxed seat in each case. *Courtesy Don Carlson, Tempe, Arizona; Ed Ryan, Tempe, Arizona*

learned, if we accept the awkward kick of the child beginning to ride on the sluggish horse.

The horseman, like the musician, is never finished with the perfection of his hands.

18

Saddling and bridling — eastern style

As I described in the first part of this book, the horse to be saddled is most conveniently handled if he is put on a cross-tie. His back should always be inspected carefully for abrasions or other signs of irritation before the saddle is put on. If the horse was properly unsaddled, the stirrups were run up on the stirrup leathers and the girth unbuckled and laid across the saddle or hung up. Before attaching the girth, set the saddle on the horse's back so that the front is just even with the back of the shoulder blades and the pad is centered under the saddle. Then with a hand firmly pressing down on the center of the seat, wiggle the saddle until it settles to a place one or two fingers' width behind the shoulder blades. Now with the hand still pressing down firmly on the seat, pull the stirrups down on the leathers, for it is easier to attach the girth if the right stirrup is put up over the seat of the saddle so the saddle flat can be raised high. Now attach the girth to the right side, but be sure that in doing so you have not moved the saddle farther back on the horse's back. Now pull the right stirrup back in place and go around to the left side and put the left stirrup over the saddle. Pull up the girth by tightening one buckle a little, then tightening another, then back to the first, and so on until you have the girth tight. As you tighten it be sure that you pass your hand under the girth a few times right behind the horse's elbow to see that there are no wrinkles. Pull the left stirrup back down in place.

If the horse is being saddled for a three- or five-gaited class in a horse show, the saddle should be put back at least four inches farther than described for normal saddling, farther back if the horse is large or has a long back. Then the girth, which should be a rubber-faced canvas girth in excellent condition (canvas girths are dangerous when not in excellent condition), should be pulled as tight as possible to keep the saddle from slipping forward. Of course no pad or blanket is used under the saddle. The show girth is made with the buckles attached to straps which are doubled and run through rings at the ends of the canvas. This gives a little extra leverage as the buckles are alternately tightened on each side. It is best to take up the show girth a little at a time, alternating sides of the horse so that when the job is finished the white canvas is centered and the buckles are about of equal height on either side of the horse. This also helps prevent wrinkling the skin on the left side.

If the horse is a hunter and equipped with martingale, the martingale is snapped to the ring at the center of the girth. If the ring is not centered, the girth must be let out on one side and taken up on the other until the ring is centered. If there is no ring and the girth slides through the martingale, the sliding must be done before the girth is buckled. If the martingale is attached to the breastplate, the breastplate must of course be slipped over the horse's head before the martingale is attached. The upper end of the martingale should fasten into a noseband or ring at the end of a bozal now popular in the East) and be just tight enough to keep the horse from tossing his head into his rider's face but not tight enough to prevent his putting his nose out for balance over a fence. If a running martingale is used, the rings should be just the height of the rings in the snaffle when the horse is holding his head normally at a standing position. The breastplate should be adjusted so it is not loose enough to flop around but does not pull down on the horse's neck at any time. The breastplate should be provided with wither straps that go from the rings on each side of the breastplate near the top to the d's in the front of the saddle. These little straps should not be tight enough to exert any pull on the breastplate but should prevent it from sliding forward on the horse's neck when he puts his head down.

If a breast collar or breast strap is used, it should be attached to the quarter rings on the saddle on either side just tight enough to keep from flopping but not so tight as to pull when the saddle is in place. If a strap across the withers to hold up the breast strap is used (which I recommend and which is always used on a Western outfit), it should be just tight enough to hold the breast strap at the bottom of the neck, so that it presses against the chest if the saddle slips back but does not pull up against the neck.

Pads used under flat saddles should always be shaped to the saddle and attached to the girth tabs or billets. They may be of felt, wool, sheepskin, or foam rubber, but they must be kept scrupulously clean.

When you are ready to bridle your horse, unsnap one side of the crosstie. Then slip the reins of the double bridle over his head. Hold the crownpiece of the bridle with your left hand. Never raise the bridle by pushing up with your right hand. Always use the left hand, holding the crown, to do the raising. Now with the back of your right hand toward the ground with fingers pointing from the back of the bridle toward the front, place your fingers under the bits, with the snaffle riding on top of the curb. At about this point, the beginning horseman wishes for a third hand to hold his horse's head with. Fortunately most horses are cooperative. However, it may be necessary for you to take the reins firmly under your horse's throttle, pull his head toward you, and quickly but not jerkily get the check straps of the bridle on either side of his nose to prevent his turning away from you. With your right hand guide the bits but do not push up on them. Use your left hand to raise the bridle. When the bits are against the meeting place of the horse's teeth, if he does not readily open his mouth, use your right thumb or even thumbnail to reach inside his lips behind the front teeth and press against the bar of his mouth (the place on the gum between the front teeth and molars where there are no teeth in the horse's mouth—the place where the bits rest). Almost invariably a horse will open his mouth when a thumbnail presses against his bar and you can raise the bridle with your left hand and guide the bits in over the tongue with your right hand. Then slide the crownpiece over the ears and pull the foretop out straight. Buckle the throatlatch, leaving it loose enough to allow the insertion of at least four fingers under it when the horse is standing at ease. (See Fig. 2 p. 16.) The curb chain should be adjusted so that when pressure is applied to the curb rein the shank of the bit will come back to an angle of forty-five degrees and no more. The lip strap should be just tight enough to keep the bit shank from flopping forward but not tight enough to exert any pull on the shank. (See Fig. 32.)

The first few times you put on a double bridle, remove the cavesson noseband before you start. You can ride without it a few times. If not, you can leave it off until you have your horse bridled and put it on the bridle after it is on your horse. Of course the best way to fail at bridling a horse is to lose your temper. Remember you are doing something as common and as easy as buttoning a child's shirt. If you find it difficult the first few times, laugh or weep; but don't become angry at the horse. It isn't his fault you want to put a bridle on him.

The snaffle bit should fit just snugly in the corners of the horse's mouth. For most purposes, the curb should hang just below it. However, some horses, especially those required to have high action induced by extreme collection, long toes, and heavy shoes, work best with the curb let down in the mouth until it just clears the bridle teeth, which are the first teeth it will touch if you let it down until it touches teeth, if the horse is a mature male. Most mares have no bridle teeth, but the bit should not hang lower on them than on geldings or stallions just because Nature has shorted them on teeth.

If the curb is let down in the mouth, it must be handled with extreme care for it is very severe so hung. It is even more severe if the noseband or cavesson is tightened. Ordinarily a noseband or cavesson is a mere decoration or something to pass a neckrope through when tying up a horse, but with some show horses it is a very useful piece of equipment. Ordinarily the cavesson or noseband should be loose enough to allow the horse to open his mouth or even to yawn, but some show horses for top performance need it very tight.

As explained and illustrated in Part I of this book, the beginner should use a curb strap or chain prefastened by an experienced horseman. For this reason bridling is illustrated in Part I with curb chain fastened. However, the more advanced horseman should always undo the curb chain, especially with a full bridle (see Fig. 28), before he starts to unbridle a horse; and he should be sure the chain is unfastened before he starts to bridle.

To unbridle, undo curb chain and throatlatch. Slip the crown piece over the ears, but be sure to keep holding it high and close to the horse's head, letting it slide down gradually in front of the horse's face as he lets the bits slip out of his mouth. If you pull the bridle off quickly and give a downward pull on the bits before they are out of the horse's mouth, you will hurt him; and he may throw you and the bridle across the stable.

All good curb chains have flat links and lie smooth against the jaw if properly put on. If not, they are very painful. After lip strap and curb chain have been properly adjusted, as I have described above, the right side of the curb chain should never be unfastened except for cleaning. This makes proper fastening and smoothing very easy. Do it this way: After the horse is bridled, take hold of the left (loose) side of the chain and twist it clockwise as many times as it will twist easily. You will see that the flat links have now all fitted smoothly against each other and the chain can be fastened at the length I have described above.

Eastern Cross Country Riding

Many Eastern horses are not taught to rein but are guided plow-line fashion, and reins must be held in two hands. (See Fig. 33.) This

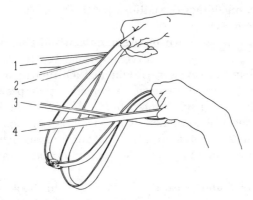

FIG. 33. Correct position of curb and snaffle reins in two hands: (1) off curb reins; (2) off snaffle rein; (3) near curb rein; (4) near snaffle rein.

is especially true in some hunting countries. The horse so trained will turn right, for instance, if the pressure on the right rein is slightly greater than on the left, and vice versa. If the horse is re-sponsive to the leg aids, this lack of response to neckrein is no handicap for any work an Eastern horse is asked to do ordinarily, though to a Western rider it seems extremely awkward, for he is used to plowlining his horse when he races or has his horse fully extended; but he is also used to having his horse "under him" at all other times and responsive to the neckrein.

It is always wise to get acquainted with any horse by riding it quietly in ring or corral before attempting to take it out across country, especially in company. By so doing you can find out how it reins and how much restraint and impulsion will probably be needed or tolerated.

For riding cross country in the East, if the ride is to be long and leisurely, with no difficult jumps, the suitable seat to ride is that which I have described as the Eastern pleasure or hack seat. If the ride is to be over stiff country at a fast pace and jumps of some magnitude are to be taken, the forward seat is the one to use.

Let us consider first the leisurely ride. If you are alone or are in company but have some share in the setting of the pace and the direction of the ride, do not ride for hours at the same rate of speed, for it is quite tiring on both man and beast. On the other hand a ride that alternates between wild, uncollected gallops and slow walks is an irritation to all old horsemen. Suit the pace to the terrain and choose terrain if possible that will call forth the entire repertoire of your horse, such as some good, firm footing for his fast, collected flatfoot walk, sod for a little good galloping, a bit of good dirt road for a smart trot, a little heavy going for an extended walk (a little goes a long way), and a modest jump or two for excitement. For a modest jump, you will not need a forward seat; but get up in the middle of your saddle; lean forward enough to be in line with the thrust of your horse as he takes off. Have him on the snaffle bit, with curb reins loose. Cross the snaffle ends in front of your horse's withers so you will have support upon landing if you are a bit too far forward.

If you cannot readily shift from curb to snaffle, some practice at home with your bridle over a door knob is in order. When you are using all reins in one hand and want to shift from one rein to the other or from equal pressure on both curb and snaffle to pressure on one bit only, let your bridle hand slide back on the reins without loosing your hold. Then with the right hand *behind* the bridle hand, take hold of the rein to be shortened. Hold it firmly with the right hand while you slide the left hand forward on it. (Figs. 34, 35.)

If you are riding a horse that must be guided by plowline with two hands and wish to take him on the snaffle, shorten the snaffle this way. Let both hands slide back several inches on the reins. Then with the right thumb and forefinger take a firm hold of the left snaffle *behind* the left hand. Hold the left snaffle firmly with the right thumb and forefinger while you slide the left hand forward

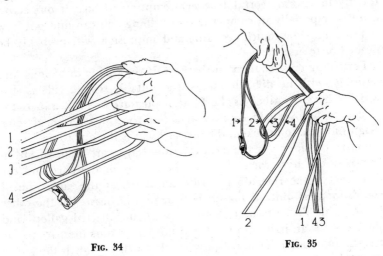

Fig. 34   Fig. 35

Fig. 34. Correct position of double reins in one hand: (1) off snaffle rein; (2) off curb rein; (3) near curb rein; (4) near snaffle rein.

Fig. 35. Shortening the snaffle rein: (1) near snaffle rein; (2) off snaffle rein; (3) near curb rein; (4) off curb rain.

on the reins. Now shorten the right snaffle by taking firm hold of it with the left hand *behind* the right hand, hold it firmly while you slide the right hand forward.

Jumping with Forward Seat

Before riding stiff country in the East, you should be at home in the forward seat (described in detail in an earlier chapter of this book) and have practiced enough with the full bridle so that you can shorten or shift reins while carrying them in one or both hands. The forward seat is useful because it enables you at all times to have your torso and lower legs in perfect alignment with the horse's line of thrust. Also it allows the maximum spring or movement of your body in going with the rhythm of your horse. The good jumping horse, especially the hunter, in going over a fence never breaks the rhythm of the gallop. The jump is one magnified or prolonged measure in the rhythm of the gallop.

PLATE 20. Excellent child rider using forward seat in jumping. *Courtesy Arlene Goodheart, Scottsdale, Arizona*

The line of thrust is not difficult to comprehend for anyone who is sufficiently mechanically minded to drive an automobile. If you are in an elevator that starts up quickly, you are aware that the line of thrust is vertical (straight up, so if you are standing upright you do not fall because of the quick start). If by some miraculous reason that elevator, instead of starting up as all respectable elevators do, would start quickly in a horizontal direction, you would fall to your knees at least, because the line of thrust is horizontal and the lines of your body were vertical. When a horse takes a four-foot obstacle at a good gallop the force that accomplishes the feat is both forward and upward. His line of thrust varies from almost horizontal at the approach to about a forty-five-degree angle with the horizon as he rises for the obstacle. (See Plate 20.) This change in line of thrust of course varies with each horse and somewhat with each jump, for the speed, height, and width of a jump are never exactly the same. The distance the horse jumps depends of course entirely on speed and height. The perfectly trained hunter continues his forward thrust throughout the jump, even at landing, though the first step on the far side of the jump rarely has full impulsion forward. However, the perfectly trained hunter is very rare; and most jumpers land with quite a momentary shift in the line of thrust. This means that upon landing, when mounted on some jumpers, your thighs and arms are the only parts of your body aligned with the line of thrust (if it can now be called a line of *thrust*). For this reason, your ability to use thigh and inside-of-knee grip is important. Also, it is important to have the ends of your reins crossed and held tightly with your hands about ten inches apart, so that upon landing it is possible to press the reins down on the horse's neck in front of his withers and to press hands against the sides of his neck just below the crest.

Of course, at the approach, take-off, and clearance of the jump your torso and lower legs, as I have said, were in alignment with the line of thrust of your horse, which means that your torso varied from about a forty-five-degree angle to a complete crouch over your horse's withers. Your lower legs were back from the knees, your heels were down. And your toes were at about a forty-five-degree angle with your horse's sides. On your face was a smile, and you were looking straight between your horse's ears.

HANDS FOR JUMPING

We have been so intent on considering your balance over a jump that we have completely ignored the most important part of taking a jump—your handling of your horse's mouth. A stout horse can negotiate cleverly a very high jump in spite of faulty balance of his rider, but if his mouth is so punished that he cannot use his head properly for balance, if he hits solid resistance on the bit as he thrusts his head forward at the top of the jump so that he automatically drops his hind legs—which he surely will do if he gets the jerk at the top of the jump—he cannot negotiate any jump well. Ideally your hands should keep constantly moving with your horse's head. As he takes off, your rhythmically moving hands will be well back toward your waist, for your well-trained horse will be well collected in his gallop at the start. As he takes off, your hands go forward until at the height of the jump your arms are stretched forward, as is your horse's neck. As he lands, your hands come back toward your waist. In this ideal way of jumping, the same pressure, right to the fraction of an ounce, is maintained on the reins throughout the entire performance. In disagreement with this method are some horsemen who feel that the horse should be told when to take off by a slight lift of the reins or a signal such as is used for increased collection. My own experience with quite a variety of horses leads me to differ with them and to let my horse take off as he sees fit. However, if you are hunting a horse trained to take off at signal, by all means take some instruction from the man who trained the horse, or at least from the man who is used to riding him, before you jump that horse. About all the help most good hunters need from the rider is to have their noses pointed at the obstacle. For everything else, the rider's chief concern is to avoid interfering with his horse's mouth or balance.

Until you have had much experience in hunting, it will be impossible for you to handle your horse's mouth in the ideal way I have described above. Therefore, here is an alternate method that will suffice for moderate jumping in cross-country riding on a well-trained horse. Carry your reins with ends crossed and held firmly so that your hands can get only ten inches apart. Have your reins as long as you can and still collect your horse as you approach the jump. This will mean that your hands are almost touching your waist as you start your approach to the jump. As your horse's forefeet leave the ground for the take-off, your hands go forward and press the reins across the top of his neck. They should reach out far enough so that when the horse's neck is stretched to its limit for balance at the top of the jump your reins will still be slack. As your horse lands, you will support part of your own weight with your hands that grip the reins by pressing them down on your mount's neck. As I have said above, if you are riding the perfect jumper, this support with your hands will not be necessary, for his line of thrust will be forward, even as he lands; and all you will need to do is straighten your torso a bit and ride. However, until you are sure you are mounted on the perfect horse, you had better have those reins ready on the top of your horse's neck to support your weight at landing time. And you will resume normal use of the reins without jerking them as soon as your horse has landed.

Each jumper has his own little eccentricities. Some need a little impulsion over the jump to help them tuck up their hind legs. Some jump much better on one lead than on the other. Others have to be restrained from rushing, and some have to be urged a bit. Start your jumping with the steadiest and truest horse you can use. After you learn half as much about jumping as a good horse knows, you can study good texts on the subject, obtain instruction from good horsemen and practice on different horses until you can jump any well-disposed animal suitable for taking fences.

Remember on your first jump: if need be, hang on to the saddle or fall off; but whatever you do, do not pull or jerk your horse's mouth as he goes over a fence! It is less dangerous to tumble off your horse's back than it is to take a chance of making him fall on you.

19

The western horse— saddling and bridling

Saddling and the use and care of blankets for Western riding are explained in the first chapter of this book. Since that explanation was for beginners only, it contained little information about the variety of riggings on Western saddles and their appropriate uses. More information is needed by the advanced horseman to enable him to select equipment proper for his use.

Western saddles are held on to the horse by straps called rigging that go over the saddle tree at either end of the saddle and terminate in rings. To these rings the latigo straps are attached. The latigo straps of course fasten the cinch or cinches to the rigging rings.

Rigging varies from what is called the center fire, and the only rigging to be seen in California, to the full rig or double cinch.

The rigging straps on the center fire saddle terminate in one ring on each side of the saddle, the front and back rigging straps on either side terminating in the same ring midway between front and rear of the tree. This kind of rigging has the least tendency to create sores behind elbows and is the best to keep a saddle in place when climbing a hill. However, it does not find favor with the roper who ties his rope fast to the horn; it has a tendency to let the saddle slide forward when the rider is going down a steep hill; and on some horses it makes the saddle bruise the shoulder blades.

The full rigging terminates in four rings, a front cinch being tied to the front or "quarter" rings by latigo straps. This kind of cinch is usually attached directly to the off (right) rear rigging ring and is fastened on the near side (left side) by a terminal buckle which buckles onto a billet attached to the near rear rigging ring. (See Fig. 30, p. 179.) Between the front and hind cinches under the middle of the horse's belly is a cinch spacer, a strap attached to the front and hind cinch. Its function is to keep the hind cinch from getting too far to the rear. It should never be farther to the rear at any point than are the back rigging rings. The hind cinch must never be pulled tight—just snug enough to keep out the daylight between it and the horse's belly, though a little daylight there after the saddle settles will do no harm.

The biggest advantage in the double or full-rigged saddle is in heavy roping or on steep mountain riding. On a horse with a very steep shoulder the elbows may be so close to the cinch that sores are unavoidable. On such a horse, even though the front cinch is put on far enough behind the elbows it will work forward if the saddle is double-rigged, and cause trouble.

The so-called three-quarter rig avoids the faults of both the center fire and the double-rigged saddle. In it the rigging terminates in two rings only but they are placed midway between the front rings of a double rigging and the rings of a center fire rigging. (Refer to Fig. 31, p. 180.)

There are many variations of these riggings. The riding to be done and the conformation of the horse being used should determine the choice of the rigging. The front cinch of a double rigging cannot be put back, or it will not stay back as far away from the elbow as will other cinches of other rigging. However, the saddle so rigged will stay put on an uphill pull and for heavy roping. Always remember to cinch up the hind cinch last and, *most important of all,* always unfasten the hind cinch before you untie the front cinch. Fasten the hind cinch only tight enough to keep the slack out of it. For all but very special kinds of riding, the three-quarter rigging is most satisfactory. If mountain riding is in prospect, a breast collar and a three-quarter rigging will be very satisfactory.

Breast Collars and Martingales

The terms *breast collar, breastplate, martingale,* and *tie-down* sometimes bewilder the beginning horsemen because they are often used interchangeably but, also, they are sometimes used to indicate specific pieces of equipment. *Breast collar* usually refers to a piece of harness very closely resembling one called by the same name used in a driving harness. Its use is to keep the saddle from sliding backward. *Breastplate* when used very specifically means a decorative strap, a sort of collar, sometimes held back to the saddle by strings or straps at the tip of the shoulder and usually terminating at the bottom in a strap that runs between the forelegs and fastens to a ring in the center of the cinch or front cinch. Sometimes a strap runs from a ring at the bottom of the breastplate to a ring on the noseband. This strap, then, is called a martingale, but so is the entire piece of equipment called, if the collar is not decorative or large! The term tie-down is a very loose one and refers to any device used to keep a horse from tossing his head.

Let us consider first the use of the breast collar.

The breast strap on the breast collar should be wide and smooth and not too stiff. A sheepskin covering is needed on some tender-skinned horses when they first wear a breast strap. It should be attached to the rigging rings of the saddle, never the cinch rings.

The front cinch of a full-rigged saddle is hung farther forward than is any other cinch. Any forward pull on it by a breast strap will make it chafe a horse behind the elbows. Western saddles with single cinches are not so prone to make trouble here, but attaching the breast strap to the cinch rings of a single cinch will tend to tighten the cinch rather than hold the saddle on an uphill trail. The breast strap should be loose enough so that there is no pressure on the horse's chest when the saddle is in its proper place and the horse is moving on level ground. It should be tight enough to prevent the saddle from sliding back when the horse is climbing a steep trail.

The neck strap should be just tight enough to keep the breast strap on the breast just below the neck but should not pull it up against the neck.

When the breast collar includes a tie-down, the strap from breast collar to cinch should be just short enough to keep any upward pull of the horse's from raising the breast strap. It should not be so tight that it touches the horse between the legs when the head is not pulling up on the tie-down.

Any martingale or tie-down should be loose enough to allow for normal movements of the head, especially for balancing when jumping a log or ditch. It should be just tight enough to prevent sticking the nose out for rearing or resisting a stop. On the parade horse, the martingale and breast collar or breastplate are merely decorative, and the tie-down should be very loose.

Any tie-down used for other than decorative purposes is indicative of one or more of three things: (1) a poor hand; (2) an improperly trained horse; (3) a horse used for very special competition, such as polo or calf roping, in which the winning is much more important than the horse or the perfection of the rider's hand.

The corona (decorative wool blanket outlining the saddle with a large roll, used principally in parade outfits), like any other decorative blanket, should be used over a protective blanket to keep it clean.

Bridling

The Western bridle should be adjusted so that the bit fits snugly up against the upper extremity of the mouth but does not pull or wrinkle it, as I have explained in discussing the Eastern bridle. Some Western bridles present more of a problem than Eastern bridles. The latter have adjustments on both sides of the cheeks so the crown of the bridle can be kept centered over the top of the horse's head, even if taken up a great deal for a very small head. Western bridles frequently have only one adjustment for length. On split-ear bridles this may cause trouble when adjusting an average-size bridle for a very small head, because the ear may be so high on the bridle on the side opposite the adjustment buckle that it will be irritated. The remedy of course is to discard the bridle or take it to a competent harness maker. Do not use a pocket knife on it, for the rough edges you will make will soon rub an ear raw.

Western bridles, especially those in which the throatlatches and head pieces are individual straps separated by a rosette where they pass through the browband, should be watched continually to see that the browband does not slide up on either side to irritate an ear or down enough to bother an eye.

If when oiling or soaping such a bridle one loses a rosette or if one is broken off by accident, always tie the browband securely in place with a stout string until the rosette is replaced.

In discussing Western equipment earlier I explained that a bozal, hackamore, or hackamore bit should never be used lower on the nose than the bottom of the hard bony structure. It is particularly important for the advanced Western rider to remember this, for he may become interested in calf roping, barrel racing, or some other competitive activity where he sees professionals make time by using a tie-down with a bozal or wire cable noseband. Any such device should be used only with good professional advice; and even then, regardless of the advice, if you have any regard for your horse you will keep the noseband, bosal, or what-not well above the cartilage of the nose.

Desert and Mountain Riding for the Novice

The most obvious difference between Eastern and Western riding is the difference in equipment, a difference that is less important than it seems as far as saddles are concerned; for almost any kind of a seat can be ridden in either Eastern or Western saddles. The most important difference is the use of reins and the difference in the response of horses. Many Eastern horses are used on snaffle bits alone. Even many of those ridden with a full bridle are ridden largely on the snaffle. Eastern riders are prone to keep a firm hold on the reins. Western riders do much with slack reins, and hold reins in one hand. (See Figs. 36 and 37.)

The Eastern rider who is in the habit of "riding his bridle" may move to the West, rent a horse, get on it, and in no time at all have the horse over on top of him or at least have it in a great dither. Most Western horses worth anything work well with a light hand. When the ride is long and the horseman is just going down the trail, his rein will have plenty of slack. Of course if the trail is quite smooth, the old pony may get careless and stumble. Then his rider will wake him up and pull him together, but just long enough to reprimand him.

When a Western rider takes hold of his reins, he wants action; so when our Eastern bridle rider gets on old Paint, he gets action. The more action he gets, the more he pulls. The more he pulls, the more collected and active old Paint becomes. It is difficult for the Eastern rider to realize that it is possible to maintain communication with a horse on a slack rein, yet such is the case, the rule, in the West. (See Plate 19.)

This loose rein riding poses one problem and perhaps creates one danger for the newcomer. How is he to be prepared to check a sudden burst of speed if his horse is startled? This is no problem to the Western rider because, casual as he seems about his reins, he is quite deft at shortening them or at picking up a slack rein. The newcomer had best at first slack his reins by keeping his bridle hand well forward. This will enable him to keep his rein short enough when slack to give him room to exert pressure on the bit quickly if needed.

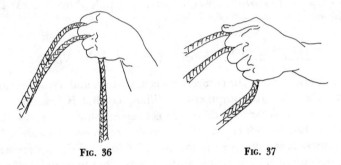

FIG. 36   FIG. 37

FIG. 36. Single rein in one hand for neck reining. Sometimes called the roper's hold.

FIG. 37. Single rein in one hand for neck reining—Western.

If you are a rider of some experience, you will wish to enjoy desert and mountains of the West from the back of a good horse. If you are a newcomer to the desert and have brought your horse with you, give him time to get used to the new terrain before you ask him to move faster than a walk. Much of the desert is populated by rodents that have peculiar habits of residence, making footing unsafe for strange horses, and some native ones as well. Almost every horse ridden on the desert has to learn about cholla cactus. An unclipped fetlock is pretty sure to pick up a bur. If cholla is picked up on the trail, unless the horse is very steady, the best thing to do is to ride to the nearest ranch and get help before trying to remove it. If the horse is too nervous, you may have to lead him. The cholla will do no permanent harm unless psychologically. When moistened sufficiently, the burs drop off or can be easily removed.

Rivers in the West (defined by some newcomers as "dry washes") are frequently very dangerous to cross when they have water in them. Quicksand is more common in the West than in the East; at least I have encountered much more of it here than in my youth in Kentucky and Ohio. A good rule is, "Let the other rider go first."

Mountain trails present few hazards if the rider is willing to trust to the judgment of his horse. Never get in a hurry on a mountain. If a horse is not pushed and is ridden over ordinary mountain trails or desert, there is little danger of founder by giving him water when he comes to it. However, on a group trail ride in California in the wintertime I witnessed a bad case of founder. The end of a long ride by a group of some seventy riders consisted of several miles of dry river bed. It was sandy and the going was difficult. The day was cold and windy. Horses did not show sweat. Most of the horsemen withheld water from their horses for some time after they reached camp. However, one rider gave his horse a good big drink as soon as he reached camp. The horse foundered very quickly and a veterinarian was called immediately.

Inexperienced riders may unwittingly cause suffering and sometimes injury to their horses on a long trail ride because of their lack of awareness of their animals' "gestures," as we might call them. Some horses are quite loathe to urinate when mounted, but if a horse's bladder, especially a gelding's or stallion's is so full that he is uncomfortable he will, almost always, give some sign of distress or of interest in stopping when he walks over sand, fallen leaves or other material that would prevent his splashing his legs if he relieved himself. If a ride is long, it is a good idea to stop a horse briefly in such a spot after an hour or so of riding. If at the first stop the mount does not relieve himself, the stopping should be repeated at intervals until he does. Mares do not suffer quite so much from this ignorance of the rider. They are able to go longer without distress and, also, they are a little less loathe to stop and relieve themselves than are geldings and stallions.

Certainly mock modesty should not deter a rider from stopping to relieve his or her horse when riding in a group. Horsemen who go on trail rides are generally quite civilized and intrinsically decent folk. They are much more concerned about and respectful of consideration of horse comfort than about observation of some obscure amenity.

Organized Trail Rides

Riding on group trail rides is one of the most enjoyable kinds of riding for many horsemen; and such rides are being organized and well-conducted with increasing frequency throughout the South-

PLATE. 21 Twain Harte Ride, one of the finest organized trail rides in the West. It is conducted in the High Sierras. *Used by permission of Andre Photo-News*

west. Traditional Western hospitality prevails among most trail ride groups and the newcomer is welcome if he is a reasonably competent horseman, pays whatever the prorated cost of food and transportation of camp gear is, and observes the rules of common courtesy. Some of the important rules are:

1. Don't allow your horse to do anything that will disturb or interfere with others.

2. When you are on a tricky part of the trail, don't stop and make others stand in a difficult position; if you want to hesitate, drop out to one side and let others pass.

3. Keep at least one horse's length between you and the horse ahead; if the man behind you rides too close, don't criticize him; just drop out and choose another part of the line to ride in.

4. If you are the last man through a gate, be sure it is left the way the first rider found it, either open or closed.

5. Never tie your horse where there is any chance the horse nearest him may reach him with his heels.

6. Never hold on to a branch you pass under; it may swing back and hit the next rider.

7. Never play with your rope or indulge in horseplay on the trail.

8. Never be among the idiots who gallop or trot the last quarter mile or so into camp—there always is at least one on every trail ride.

20

Endurance ◆◆◆◆◆◆◆◆◆◆◆◆◆◆◆◆◆◆◆◆

rides ◆◆◆◆◆◆◆◆◆◆◆◆◆◆◆◆◆◆◆◆◆

Competitive trail rides are the most newly popular form of Western competitive riding. Not more than a year before this book was started, a young lady of slight build and mild, charming manner won a one-hundred-mile ride with an Arab mount and then did the remarkable feat of entering a competitive ride of almost eighty miles within a fortnight after the one-hundred-mile triumph. As far as available records go, this is without precedent. A horse that takes a one-hundred-mile ride, traveling the distance within a twenty-four-hour time span, as the Arab did, is usually out of competition for the rest of the season, if not for life. While the owners attribute the feat to the superiority of the Arabian breed and to the pluck of one horse in particular, I suspect that a great deal of the credit should go to the skill of the people who put the great little horse in condition. Certainly the knowledge of how to do so is something of an innovation in the horse world. I feel, too, that there is a feeling toward horses today that enables us to do things with them that were never before possible, though the attitude was hinted in a Book about twenty centuries ago.

Preparation for such feats is not a mere matter of rigid routine exercise and scientific feed formulas. Both feed and preparatory work must be constantly related to the needs and condition of the horse. This relating can only be done by a gifted, intelligent, and devoted person.

Competitive trail rides today are not simply races. Horses are judged on their condition as well as on their accomplishment. Competent licensed veterinarians are in attendance and animals are inspected before, during, and after the ride. Such competitions are probably less cursed with chicanery, gimmicks, and artificial cover-ups than any other form of equine competition today. Certainly there is no substitute for the excellence of health and conditioning that a horse must have to compete successfully. On the trail, the rider must use a seat that enables the horse to carry him with least effort. The gaits used are the trot, never more than moderate in speed, and the walk; for these are the gaits that get over the ground in a given time with the least effort to the horse. (If there are admirers of the natural pacer who read these words, I bow to their criticism.)

There is not room in a book of this kind to do more than hint at this new competitive art of horsemanship; but it is important that the beginning rider should know of this field of competition, that it is a wide-open and growing field in which some horsemen find much pleasure and sometimes profit.

The horseman interested in competitive trail riding should make a study of feeds and feeding by reading the standard text by Frank B. Morrison, one used for generations in most colleges of agriculture (*Feeds and Feeding*, 22nd ed. Clinton, Iowa: Morrison Publishing Co., 1956). He can also get much valuable information from U.S. Department of Agriculture bulletins (about which any Congressman will be very happy to assist if he expects to remain in office). Also most county agricultural agents are knowledgeable about such matters and have bulletins from local colleges and universities. These are usually moderately reliable sources of information though frequently written under compulsion by those who are stronger in theory than experience.

In addition to proper feeding practices, exercise is an important matter of course in fitting a horse for a competitive trail ride or endurance ride. Study about this factor is a much more complicated and broader task, even, than study of feeds. A good veterinarian is an excellent source of advice. The most recently successful competitors I have talked with about this matter have some very new ideas about exercise, though certainly aware of and carefully following old and proven principles. One endurance rider who has been very successful was shocked when a horseman asked her if she gave her horses a certain amount of exercise daily. She launched forth on a little lecture to the effect that a horse that could win a tough endurance ride today is more than a mere machine. He is a creature of temperament and would become bored to death if he were required to do the same thing every day. This rider is strongly of the opinion that there is an important temperamental, or even psychological, factor in the fitting of a great endurance horse.

Certainly no one breed of horse has a monopoly on endurance, though the proponents of at least three recognized breeds frequently make such a claim. In the last years of the existence of the United States Cavalry Remount Service a six-hundred-mile endurance ride was held annually by the Service. While those tests did not attract top animals of all breeds, some interesting facts came out of them. One was that the only matter of conformation that seemed to have any correlation with endurance is heart girth; this of course excepts marked anatomical defects. The horse with the large room for heart and lungs seemed to have a great advantage. Such highly touted indicators of endurance as extremely short backs, exceptional muscles of one kind or another, etc., did not seem to matter a great deal. Not enough of the animals from those rides were kept track of until death and given post-mortem examinations to learn much concerning internal structure, but a fairly reliable study of race horses was made a good many years ago which seemed to indicate that in the great race horse the adrenal glands were unusually large, as well as the heart and lungs, of course.

In gait, the horse that wings or paddles has little chance of winning a stiff competitive trail ride, according to students of those old six-hundred-mile rides. The horse of true action, round and not too high, had the best chance if all other factors were equal. Again, as in most equine competition, the good big horse seems to have a slight edge over the good little horse, but the small horse frequently came out at the top of the list of winners. In many groups of contenders in various fields there is not a big horse that is equal in quality to some of the smaller ones.

21

Show ring competition

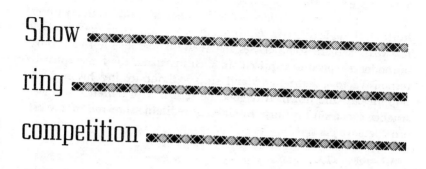

Western Pleasure Class

The beginning horseman who wants to compete in Western classes in horse shows will do well to get a Quarter Horse of the conformation I have described earlier as the ideal for the breed. He should pay particular attention to the trueness of action of the animal, for a horse that paddles or dishes is difficult to win with. The horse should not have a stride so long as to be uncomfortable in a stock saddle at the trot nor should the gait be short and choppy.

The simplest class to compete in is the Western Pleasure class for amateurs; and it is a good place to start a show career, if one is modest.

While I have recommended the Quarter Horse, because he is the most popular breed in the West at the time of writing this book, a horse of any breed can win a Western Pleasure class so long as he does not have a set tail—a grotesque mutilation not in favor with Western riders outside very limited classes. I have seen representatives of every recognized breed among the ribbon winners in Western Pleasure classes.

Aside from conformation that will measure up well by general standards, the Western Pleasure horse must have true action, round and free but not excessively high. The chief requirement is that he be responsible to a slack rein at all times and on all gaits. He must walk, jog, trot, gallop, and slow lope, or in some instances do a real canter on a slack rein, and do the last-named three on either lead as requested by the judge. He is required to back quietly at command and to stop with his feet well under him and stand without fretting, though this last requirement is less universal than it was a few years ago. In some classes for Western pleasure horses a burst of moderate speed is required. In such instances, the horse must be responsive to a light hand and stop without tossing his head or hopping up and down. Any good horseman with patience and persistence can train his horse to make a creditable showing in a Western Pleasure class.

TRAIL HORSE CLASS

In Trail Horse classes, the horse is required to do all that the good Western pleasure horse can do. In addition, he is required to do a number of stunts which are supposed to simulate things necessary in loading in a trailer and in different situations on trail. These stunts change from year to year, but they usually include something that tests the ability of both horse and rider (though only the horse is judged unless the program specifies otherwise) to back up with promptness and as much control of direction as when walking forward. This of course means that the horse must be responsive to the aids, for the legs do most of the guiding when a horse is backing through a maze, though deft hands are also required.

To back the well-trained horse through a maze, he is turned to the right, for example, by using the left leg pressed against his side behind the hind cinch or several inches behind a center-fire or three-quarter-rigged cinch. He is kept backing by a pressure on his mouth that is light and almost imperceptibly rhythmic. When turning his hind quarters to the right, as in the situation I am describing, the horse may require that the rider use slightly more pressure on the left rein than on the right and use neckrein to keep the forequarters in the maze. Some mazes are constructed of car stakes (pieces of wood roughly some six inches square and ten or twelve feet long) laid lengthwise on the ground in a pattern that outlines a path just wide enough for a horse to walk in and with one or more right-angle turns.

The horse must also be handy at gates, so the rider while mounted can unfasten a gate, open it, ride through, and close it without letting go of it or having to swear at his horse. This, of course, is another test of a horse's responsiveness to leg aids and reins. Frequently the gate is so made that it is necessary for the rider to drop his reins and the horse to stand still while the gate is being unfastened and/or fastened.

Very low but tricky jumps, two or three of them, are usually required. For instance, two low jumps, say eighteen inches or two feet in height, are set close enough together so that there are not more than two or three strides between them. The rider is required to jump the first while mounted, stop his horse between the jumps, dismount and lead his horse over the second jump. The first year such a stunt was tried there were some bitter contestants, for some very good horses are quite startled when the rider tries to lead them over a jump. It is a very good idea to teach your horse to lead up beside you at all times so that you can walk or run at his shoulder while he keeps pace with you, either on the level or hopping over a jump. This also is a very necessary feat when showing a horse in hand (led by halter or bridle and without saddle).

Another variety of stunt is a sort of teeter-totter bridge. It is supposed to test a horse's willingness to go where he is asked and to go up a trailer ramp. As the bridge starts down, many horses are frightened and jump instead of walk down the last half of the bridge.

Automobile tires are sometimes laid on the ground and the horse is required to step in them with forefeet or to stop with hind feet in them. One judge, considered unreasonable by some, required that the horse make a half circle around the tire with the feet that were outside it, while not removing the feet inside the tire. It should, of course, be possible to hold the forequarters of a horse in relatively one spot with the neckrein while the legs guide his hindquarters in a complete circle. Also, it should be possible to hold the hind feet (by use of leg aids) in one place and turn the forequarters around it.

Each year some ingenious soul thinks up a new stunt or two for the trail horse. If possible the competitor should find out the nature of the stunts he will have to perform and practice them at home before the show. However, the horse that has complete confidence in his rider (or leader, as the case may be), is responsive to the aids, has a good mouth and excellent rein, will stand with a slack rein,

and can do all that a Western pleasure horse is required to do—
such a horse will do well almost any stunt that can be devised for a
trail horse.

An exception is that of walking through a trap made of large
round posts some eight or ten feet long. Two of the posts of ten-
inch diameter or larger are laid parallel on the ground. Then four
or five posts are laid crosswise on them at equal intervals. The horse
is supposed to put one foot at a time between the cross posts and
travel between the parallel ones. This is a dangerous stunt for
horses, and I hope it quickly loses its popularity. Certainly by starting with a couple of cross posts laid flat on the ground and progressing gradually a horse can be taught to negotiate such a contraption,
but to ask a horse to walk through it without previous training
leading up to the stunt by gradual degrees is quite apt to lead to
bruised pasterns or worse injury. The wise horseman will withdraw
his horse from any competition such as this if the stunt is a surprise
to him and re-enter, if he must, at a later date after he has shown
his horse how to solve the puzzle. If your horse is not worth swallowing a bit of pride for, either he is a very poor horse or you are
no horseman.

Competition in horse show classes for stock horses, for cutting
horses, and classes labeled Reining Horse class are included in many
Western shows. Such classes when open to professional trainers pose
a problem for the owner who keeps a horse primarily for the pleasure of riding him. To win such events necessitates one detail of
training that detracts considerably from a horse's ability to give a
highly enjoyable ride to many horsemen, especially those who like
the follow-through movement of the horse that has a good neck
and the ability to use it naturally. Professional trainers of stock
horses and reining horses now train them to work with unnaturally
low heads. This is done by working them, in some instances only
when the owner is not present, with chains over their heads where
the crown piece of the bridle should go or where a browband should
go or both. The chains, of course, are secured to a tie-down and
cause the horse considerable discomfort, to say the least, until he
learns to avoid pain by keeping his head low at all times.

The use of head chains is not an extremely difficult trick to learn.
The chains are worn under the bridle. The trainer starts in, usually,
with moderation. Finally he has the tie-down short enough so that
the horse performs with his head never higher than the saddle horn,

or whatever height is currently fashionable. Most horses respond very quickly after the head becomes a little sore from the chain.

I was shocked by one use of chains I witnessed during the winter of 1962. At the Arabian show in Scottsdale, Arizona, a sweet little gray mare won a cutting class, without chains, of course. Immediately after the show, hardly waiting for the photographer to get a picture, the trainer took the little mare out behind the arena, put chains on her head, and gave her a little workout just to remind her where her head must be. Had this happened at a Quarter Horse show, I would not have been so shocked, for I am accustomed to seeing the Quarter Horse used purely as a means to an end; but of all special breed enthusiasts, the Arabian fancier talks most about how "natural" the use of Arabian horses is; and the Arabian fancier more frequently than fanciers of other breeds seem to regard his horse as a personality and a friend, not something to work with a sore head and in chains.

If you have an ambition to show in stock horse, reining, or cutting classes, make a study of a few shows in the area in which you expect to show. Requirements of performance change at least in some details from year to year. Some details of equipment that were quite proper and essential last year may be out of place this year, or some new ones may have been added. Notice the proper length and thickness of tails and the way the foretop and mane are prepared for the ring. Note whether it is currently fashionable to leave some hair at the withers, if clipped manes seem to be in fashion. Such magazines as *Horse Lover's Magazine* and *Western Horseman* are useful aids in this study. Now, start collecting gear and grooming your horse for competition; and *practice*.

If you expect to enter stock horse classes you will need practice on uses of the aids of course, but in particular you will need to develop to the utmost your skill in "picking your horse up" from a standstill and "lifting" his forehand a quarter of a turn to right or left, or more. There is no secret to this. You simply hold the horse's hindquarters in place with your legs, put pressure enough on the reins to keep him from going forward, while at the same time you lift up and sideways on the reins. The problem for the beginner is to learn how much to pull back, how much to pull up, how much and how quickly to rein to the side, and how hard to squeeze with the legs. Experience is the only solution. The well-trained and seasoned horse, one that knows much more than you do, will not be upset by any mistakes you make at first. Learning how much impulsion to balance against how much restraint to get a good walk, jog, gallop, and slow lope is no more difficult for your present purpose than for your first riding. You have studied the shows to determine what is wanted in the class you are preparing for. Now practice producing it at home before you appear before the judge.

Leads were discussed at length earlier in this book. It is important for both stock horse and reining classes that you know what the leads are and what to do about them. In both stock horse and reining classes you must always give enough lift to your horse when you turn him to get him to lead with the inside foot on each turn. If you do not give him enough leg aid, he may not shift leads behind and will do the "disunited" or "crossfire" gallop I mentioned earlier in this book. You will find that the turns taken at a fast gallop are easiest to change leads on, but the slow ones take a lot of lifting, impulsion, and other leg work.

If you are going into the show ring for blood, learn how to get your horse to do all the required kinds of performance before you start working his head down. If and when you do start on the head lowering, do it very gradually and work your horse very slowly at simple performance—walk, trot, jog, and gallop—before you start asking him to swap leads while his head is tied down.

For all fast and competitive work with the stock saddle, use a seat that keeps your body always in constant alignment with the horse's line of thrust (see Plate 8), described in detail in connection with the use of the flat saddle. This seat in the stock saddle is coming to be called the "balanced" seat, though it differs little from the forward seat of the flat saddle rider. You sit in the middle of the seat of your saddle if the seat is long and flat. If the seat is built up you should be sure that it is not too long and that the seat of the saddle is near the center of the bars, not over the rear end of the bars of the tree. Your weight should be carried, as in the discussion of the balanced seat in an earlier chapter, on the bones of the pelvis (not the fleshy part of the buttocks) and on the stirrups. Your feet, like those of your horse, should be under you at all times and your waist should be so flexible that your body is constantly aligned with the ever-changing line of thrust of your horse.

On turns, especially fast ones, do not lean too far to the inside of the turn. Better be a little on the too-upright than the too-leaning side. Many a pony has been pulled off his lead behind by the heavy rider who leans too much, especially if he rides a trifle behind the center of balance.

In stopping the fast-working Western horse, lift him just enough to bring his hocks under him as he stops, and hold his quarters steady with heels as well as reins. If you lift and squeeze him too much as he stops, the forequarters will come up in the air too high and bounce. What goes up must come down, I have heard. This is painfully true of the front end of a stopping horse. On the fast stop, your body should be aligned with the horse's forefeet, not his hind ones. If you align your body with his hind feet, as some do, you will be leaning back in an almost horizontal position with your weight punishing your horse's loins and interfering mightily with his use of his haunches. When your horse stops quickly his hind legs are not thrusting back; they are sliding. All the thrusting is being done with the front legs, the ones your body should be in alignment with.

The only way to practice cutting is with calves and, if possible, with an assistant. This art can be treated in nothing shorter than an entire volume. However, in general it is wise to go only as fast as you can go and at the same time be sure your horse is working the cattle. Some trainers are now using cues to aid their horses, but the only way to learn about this is from the man who trained the horse you are using. Do your early cutting work, if at all possible, under the guidance of an experienced cutting horse man. It should not be necessary to emphasize the fact that cutting cattle is done on a loose rein at all times. The thing to hold on to is the horn of the saddle.

Showing in Halter Classes

Showing a horse in halter classes is more of an art than many beginning horsemen realize. These classes are also much more important than most spectators realize. Among the most coveted of awards in all the shows in Kentucky, where fine horse competition is as keen as anywhere in the world, are the Futurity awards. These are won by yearlings shown "in hand" (handled by a man on foot) in some of the largest classes seen in major shows.

The objective of the good showman in a halter class is to keep his animal always alert, always appearing at its best. When he is asked to display his animal's movement, it should always step out of line *with* him, never after him in response to a tug on the halter shank. When it trots or walks, the handler should be at its shoulder, never out in front. In some Western shows, the animal shown in halter is asked to go only one way of the ring. This should be to the left, for the proper side to lead from is the left side, and whenever possible it is polite for the handler to be between his animal and the judge, who is, theoretically at least, in the center of the ring. When turning the animal shown in hand always be careful that it does not swing its hindquarters in the judge's face. A judge is supposed to be fair and objective and to judge the horse, not the handler; but he is certainly not adversely affected by the deference or courtesy of a showman.

When an animal shown in hand is asked to stand or line up it does not need to stand forever like a statue, but it should be well mannered enough to stand still a few moments at a time and trained so that it will pose properly if the breed is one that conventionally poses; if not, it should stand up squarely on all four legs, with head and ears alert. If the animal is a Saddlebred or a Morgan from some sections of the country, or of any other breed that conventionally poses, it should be trained to stand with front legs vertical, not poked forward like a street-sore delivery horse, and with hind legs appearing to push backward a trifle. Never stretch any animal. It is a horse, not a cantilever bridge, you are showing. It is the mark of an amateur or a circus performer to stretch a horse out. The object of the pose, of course, is to show off a good shoulder, to let the judge see that the horse is short in the back, level in the hips, and long in the belly; but the stance of a horse that is sore in the front feet is that of the amateur's animal that is stretched, and you don't want the judge to wonder how you stove up that nice colt.

Some of the most amusing, interesting, crowd-drawing, and intensely competitive classes in the horse show world are the little colt classes in Kentucky shows. When the babies are lined up, the handlers are all sweating blood and a trainer often in a derby hat and formal attire—and cigar—is out in front of each colt frantically operating a toy parasol, jumping jack, or anything else that he hopes will intrigue the baby, make it put its ears up, and pose prettily for the judge. Awards in such classes mean much to the trainer of the colt, owner, and farm that bred the little hero or heroine. It is only in horse-breeding areas that rivalry is so intense and artistry so great in colt classes, but any horseman has much to learn from watching them.

Parade Riding

The parade horse of today is a far cry from the parade horse of a few decades ago. About the only thing in parade riding that has remained constant is the seat used. (See Fig. 17.) The long-legged, forked-radish parade seat, described in an earlier chapter of this book, is the seat used. The Spanish dons who built the first fine haciendas in California rode that seat. It has been and still is the standard parade seat both in parades and in parade horse classes in horse shows. However, the most elaborate saddles and bridles of twenty years ago would look very modest today. The horse of color and considerable cold blood that was generally the parade horse of the early part of this century could not make a showing in a present-day parade class nor could he win the prize in the parade. The horse that would make the perfect parade horse today nobody seems to have thought of training for a parade—the hackney. His extreme action and animation with a level head would make him ideal if out-crossed to get a little flash of color, although I have seen hackneys of golden sorrel with plenty of white.

Artificially high action induced with long feet, weighted shoes, and extreme collection are the chief requirements in performance of the parade horse. He needs but one gait, the slow trot. In some parade horse classes in horse shows a little more speed is permitted, but the real parade horse should when asked be able to trot in place; that is, trot without moving forward. The one exception to the trot being the universal gait of the good parade horse was a gray horse seen for several years in Arizona parades. He did a very slow rack until years of shoeing with long feet and no frog pressure made his feet uncomfortable. Then he did a high pace. From the sparkles on the feet to the silver-mounted bridle, the parade horse must display all the elegance that man has devised for horse. He is ridden constantly in a high degree of collection while in the ring or on parade. Rules in most areas now forbid weaving the horse back and forth on the line of march in order to give him opportunity to show himself off. Generally he is required to stay in place in the parade and to travel in a straight line in the show ring. Collecting the parade horse requires the same technique as has been described in this book for collection of riding horses. A well-trained parade horse presents no problem for a rider of ordinary experience and a little intelligence.

Generally speaking, it is the rider who can induce the highest state of collection in his horse that gets the high score for performance in parade classes.

Showing the Gaited Horse and the Walker

Unless a Saddlebred horse has had its tail succesfully set before it was purchased, the owner must have it set before the animal enters a three- or five-gaited ring. If the owner lives in any one of many areas of the West and enjoys riding in company, he will put considerable strain on the self-restraint of his friends if he has his horse's tail set and then continues to ride in group rides. Nothing seems more grotesque and wryly amusing to horsemen in many parts of the West than the mutilated tail of the Saddlebred, especially the three-gaiter. The ignorant frequently refer to setting a tail as breaking the tail. This is so far from the truth that if by any accident a tail is broken the horse is no longer fit for showing.

Setting the tail is a muscle-cutting, stretching, and healing operation that should be performed only by a competent, licensed veterinarian experienced in the art of tail setting. Get full instructions from him about care of the tail after the operation (as important as the operation itself) and follow them to the letter. If you do all this and keep the tail in a proper set, your horse will suffer a minimum of discomfort and the chances are good that he will have what Saddlebred show horse fanciers call a beautiful tail.

Your next problem is to grow luxuriant hair on that tail if the horse is five-gaited, for a natural tail is a great advantage in the show ring—and in the stable. Besides that, wigs are expensive. Daily care is the secret. Use a brush until the tail begins to get long. Then use only your fingers to separate the hairs, for a brush will pull and break. In most climates a favorite practice is to keep a little bottle of rainwater and kerosene—equal parts. Always shake it well before using. Take a little swab of cotton, moisten it with the emulsion and rub it on the roots of the hair lightly, taking up one little strand of hair to expose the roots and then another. In the drier parts of the Southwest this will not work. Successful beauty parlor methods of stimulating human hair growth will frequently work on horses' tails. The hair of the mane, of course, should have as much care as the tail, and the same kind of care.

While you are preparing your horse's tail for the show season (even if the tail was set when you bought your horse, you will have to start putting it up in a set several weeks before the first show), you will get his feet in condition for showing. As soon as you decide you will show your Saddlebred, consult your farrier. If there is time enough to grow a foot on the horse, fine. If not, the farrier will have to shim up the feet with pads. In any event, keep rubber pads on your horse as soon as his feet begin to get long. They are vital to keeping frog pressure. When the shoes are reset, turn the old pads over and put the new ones over them. Keep your stable clean; keep proper packing under the pads; and your horse will never have thrush, a fungus that is the curse of keepers of dirty stalls and un-clean, unprotected feet.

The seat you must learn to ride, ride easily and well, before at-tempting to learn to handle a gaited horse in the ring is called the show seat. It is so called because at least to most of us old-timers the gaited horse is the *real* show horse. Other kinds may be better or more costly, perhaps; but the prima donna, and dramatic star of the tanbark, is the dazzler that can respond when "Rack on!" stirs the pulses of spectators and riders alike. He is Mr. Show Horse in person and the seat used on him we call the show seat.

The show seat is the most difficult of all seats to learn to ride well. Once learned, it is not as tiring as the extreme forward seat, but more so than the park seat and what I have called the basic seat, of course.

The show seat, as I have described earlier, is ridden with a show saddle which is made to be used well back on the horse, though it is also very comfortable when put up where a saddle normally goes and ridden with a basic or a park seat. The rider sits well back in the saddle, with weight on his crotch rather than on the buttocks. His back is straight and erect, leaning neither forward nor back. His legs are as nearly straight down as it is possible to get them without sticking his toes straight out. (Here's where bowlegs are a great ad-vantage!) His feet are directly under the weight in the saddle, and they are level and carried at about a forty-five-degree angle with the horse's body.

In posting the fast trot, the movement is forward and back rather than up and down; and it is very slight. The most skillful riders simply sit it. The rack is ridden sitting well back on the saddle, with feet slightly forward, ankles working a little in rhythm with the beat of the forefeet. The canter is also ridden sitting well back in the saddle and using the ankles. The latter are used a little more at the canter than at the rack. The rhythm of the foot pressure is that of the nodding head of the cantering horse.

When you are lined up in the ring and have your horse pose, sit up straight in the saddle with your legs as straight down as possible, even if your toes are out a bit. Shove your heels down so you can straighten your legs a little more than when moving. It is at the lineup that the judge usually pays a little extra attention to conformation. Show off your horse's front by sitting well back with legs straight down. This will also tend to level out the top hip line. A slight rhythmic jiggling on the reins with hands held high may be needed to remind your mount to keep his head set and to maintain his pose.

While you are learning by plenty of slow daily riding to use the show seat, you can well be getting your horse in condition to show. Never take any horse to a show until you have the last ounce of hard meat on him that the best feeding practices and regular, intelligent exercise can produce. It is all very well to admire the trimness of a greyhound or a race horse, but it is the pound of flesh, especially the last pound, that often wins the horse show. Don't say, "I just can't get meat on my horse." Call the veterinarian, consult your county agricultural agent or do something else to find out what you are doing wrong. Walk down the center of any good show horse barn and you will see horses covered with hard fat on either side of you. It is only the rank amateur who brings the thin horse into the ring.

When you enter the show ring on that sleek and shining masterpiece of nature perfected by your own hands, ride as if you were on Pegasus. Choose your horse's best gait, preferably trot or rack, for your entry and use that gait or alternate it with the second-best one until the steward begins to call for specific gaits. It is always expected that riders will work at will while the contestants are entering or until the steward begins to give out the judge's requests. Sam Haines, one of the best and most popular judges I ever rode in front of, once told me, "You can often pick a winner as he comes into the ring." After you enter the ring remember you are on display every moment. At the walk, never take an uncollected step. When the steward says, "Trot, please," and tips his hat (in these degenerate days it may be just a loud-speaker), don't *ease* into a trot, *snap* into it! Use as much speed as possible with full collection. Never override your horse at the trot—or any other gait, for that matter. To override means to ride your horse faster than he can go in good form, to ride so that he looks as if he were desperately struggling for speed and is all sprawled out to catch it. In the big stakes in Kentucky and Missouri, five-gaiters develop as much speed at the trot as is seen in some harness races; but the hocks are always under, the action is always round—as high as it is long—and heads are always beautifully set, never stretched out like a runner's.

The slow gait, according to the specifications of the American Saddle Horse Breeders Association formulated at the beginning of this century, may be a stepping pace, a fox trot, an amble, or a running walk; however, as the five-gaited horse is most valuable today as a show piece, with spectator appeal being his greatest commercial asset, the only slow gait seen in our shows is the stepping pace. This is the flashiest of the slow gaits. Once in a while we see a horse who shows only a very slow rack for a slow gait. While this is not quite cricket, it is close enough to get by. The proper slow gait is a gait that is just faster than a flat-footed walk and has all the action, the elegance, that is possible for a horse to display at the speed demanded. The gait must be even and smooth as well as elegant.

The rack, when "Rack on!" thrills the crowd and the contestants, is a race; but speed alone is not enough. The rack must be true, a four-beat gait with the same interval after every hoofbeat. A syncopated rhythm means a pace, not a rack. If at the trot or the rack a rider looms up ahead of you, don't pull up; pull out; hunt a hole and go around. Don't crowd the judge and don't hug the rail if a ringful of horses is between you and the judge. Steady your horse on the turns so that he won't break. However, if he does, don't faint; the world is not lost. Settle him to his gait as quickly as possible and squeeze him on into speed again.

When the canter is called for, continue your walk until you reach the turn. You will be walking when the canter is called for if the show is properly judged; but if not, don't criticize. Nobody twisted your arm to make you enter the show. If you are doing some gait other than the walk when the canter is called for, pull your horse quickly to a collected walk—watch the fellow behind you so he won't step on your heels—and continue at a collected walk until you reach the turn. Now, get your horse's nose into the rail and be sure he takes the proper lead and settles into a collected canter immediately. Hold him as slow as possible without losing that good three-beat rhythm. If he begins to slop a bit, lift him with your reins a trifle each time his head comes up, and keep him squeezed up onto the bit. Of course if I am not talking about your kind of a horse, your problem may be one of quieting him down and letting him use quite a little speed to keep from dropping into a lateral gait. If so, you've been through all this many times while working him out at home. Don't forget what you learned then. Keep him going enough to keep up a good nod until "Walk, and reverse!" is called. Then come quickly to a collected walk, cut across the ring in a figure eight; and when you get to the turn again, get his nose into the rail and squeeze him into the right lead on a canter. (Left lead is always called for first.)

When the class is lined up, your horse may be hot; if so, line him up as directed and pose him properly (as I described when discussing halter classes); but if the lineup continues for over one minute and your horse is hot, take him out of the lineup on the side away from the one on which the judge is working—behind it if he is at one end of the ring—and walk your horse in a small circle. Of course you should be alert to see that you do not pull out just as the judge is coming to your horse to examine him for conformation. However, it is very dangerous to let a hot horse stand, especially on a hot afternoon in the Southwest, where the high evaporation has foundered more than one horse. Watch the judge and get your horse back in line for inspection by the time the judge reaches your place in the lineup.

When you are asked to back your horse, back straight. Do not get in a hurry. Speed is not required, though if your horse is extremely prompt in his response, so much the better. After backing, bring your horse immediately up into line and remain there until the judge has passed on to inspect another horse. Then you may walk your horse again if he is still hot.

After the class loosen the girth and get a good New Zealand or Australian wool cooler on your horse immediately. Walk him quietly until he is cool before removing the saddle. Then walk him until he is almost dry. If you have an assistant, he may reach up under the cooler with a linen rub rag (salt sack variety, if you can get one) or a good terry-cloth towel and rub shoulders and loins. A swallow or two of water now and then as your horse is cooling will not hurt him, but he should not get all the water he wants until he is cool.

THE THREE-GAITED HORSE

The three-gaited class for the Saddlebred (or any other breed that can perform adequately) requires less speed at the trot than does the five-gaited class. The canter must not be too fast and it must be stylish, with good, round action. A five-gaited horse can sometimes win with a canter that is little more than a slow gallop, but not a three-gaited horse. The walk must also be snappy and true. Many successful five-gaited horses never show a real flat-footed walk. However, the three-gaited horse must do a four-beat walk, though it may be a little on the prancy side.

Instructions just given for the five-gaited class will apply to the three-gaited class except for the fact that only three gaits are requested. The three-gaited class seldom creates the heat that the five-gaited class does, though I have seen some lather worked up in Kentucky and Ohio three-gaited classes.

The beginner will do well to keep in mind that it is perfectly correct to pull a horse to a walk for a few steps when changing from one gait to another.

THE TENNESSEE WALKER

The Tennessee Walking Horse has changed his role so greatly in recent years that as definite instructions for showing him cannot be given as they can for the Saddler. The set tail is now seen on the Walker. Most Walkers today that are trained for show are trained to work on the Walking Horse bit, a bit with a long S-shaped shank that is bent at the juncture of the mouthpiece in such an angle that, by using a fairly loose curb chain or strap, the horse can be allowed to lean heavily into the bit and get no leverage on it unless he tosses his head up, or sticks his nose out. As the balance of the Walker is rather forward, he leans heavily into the bit (in show ring performance but not among his home folks) and throws his feet on high. The original Tennessee walk was a smooth, graceful four-beat gait in which the horse always had one foot in contact with the ground. He slid easily from the running walk into a low, easy, graceful canter. Mr. Burt Hunter, whose valiant efforts put the Walker on the map of the horse world, kept artificialities to a minimum in showing the breed. He kept it as a breed of fine horses that affluent men could buy and *use* with comfort and pleasure. However, Mr.

Hunter had not long been in his grave before the emphasis of the breeders centered on the horse's appeal to spectators rather than riders. Today the Walker is shown with very long feet, heavy shoes (and perhaps bruised coronets), and anything else that will induce excessive action. In many shows the walk resembles a rack more than the old original running walk of plantation days. The canter is a high, rocking affair that suggests the possibility of seasickness. The remarkable thing about all this is that a good Walker in spite of all the trainers do to him, unless the use of chains around the coronet have inflicted permanent injury, is the most pleasant of animals to ride after he gets away from his show ring training.

If you have a Walker to show, study the performance in shows in your area. Then practice at home at the gaits used. The flat-footed walk should be fast but not as collected as that of the five-gaiter. The running walk, or whatever passes for one in your area, should be done with the horse leaning heavily into the bit. Impulsion, if needed, can better be given the Walker with the whip than the heel, for the heel tends to shorten stride and make his walk choppy rather than loose and flowing as it should be. If your horse has been properly trained and you are using a good Walking Horse bit, it should not take much whip to get him to lean into the bit. You may hold your reins in two hands, guiding your horse plowline fashion, for that is the way he is trained. (After you have finished showing him, it will be easy to teach him to rein.) As he is probably well trained, he guides very easily and you can, if you prefer, hold your reins in one hand, crossing them on your palm with the ends coming out of either side of your fist. (See Fig. 38.) Holding the reins

Fig. 38. Single rein in one hand for plow reining: (1) off rein; (2) near rein.

this way, you can turn your horse with just a slight twist of the hand. Your right hand will be free to use a whip for signal.

The Walker, unlike the Saddler, slides into his canter from a running walk, but it is wise to take advantage of the rail when easing into the canter so that you can be sure of getting the proper lead.

22

Prevention or correction of bad habits

The old term for the most common bad habits horses form as defense against human abuse is *vices*. The term is applied when a habit becomes firmly fixed and quite objectionable. Some vices are getting behind the bit, shying, pulling or cold-jawing, halter pulling, kicking, biting, rearing and whirling, cribbing and wind sucking, weaving, and stall pawing or kicking. The last three are the result of confinement combined with nervous tension. The others result from specific abuse by rider or handler. The congenital disposition of a horse may make him more susceptible to abuse than others, but I have never seen a "naturally" vicious horse—though I have seen killers and other very dangerous horses.

Getting Behind the Bit

The peculiar, and often dangerous, vice called *getting behind the bit* is not as common as the vice of pulling on the bit, often called *getting ahead of the bit*. It is caused by a heavy hand, by pain from a chin chain or strap that pinches, by a crudely made bit having sharp points or corners that hurt, or by constant overcollection to get high action or appearance of animation. When a horse has suffered from any one of these causes sufficiently he will bow his neck quickly to remove all hold on the bit. He will even tuck his chin back against his neck or chest. If the rider immediately takes up the slack, the horse will attempt to rear. If thwarted in this attempt by a clout over the head or a drastic lowering of the hands, he will fly back, often running backward at considerable speed for several rods.

The cure of course is to remove the cause. The first thing to do is to throw away the bit and ride the horse with a hackamore or bozal. No bit should be put in his mouth until all fear of his rider's hands is dispelled. Then a bit should be hung in his mouth but no reins attached, and he should be ridden on the bozal or hackamore with a bit hanging useless for several days. When the bit is equipped with reins, the reins should be used very lightly and only as a supplement to the bozal. The variety of bit used is not as important as the quality of the hands on the other end of the reins. However, a snaffle with a big mouthpiece and the reins run through a running martingale is about as nearly fool-proof as a bit can be. If a curb is used, the shorter the shank and the bigger the mouthpiece the less damage it can do. Of course the chin chain or strap must be properly adjusted.

If the horse still flies back at any touch on the rein, after several weeks of unfailing care in the use of the method I have described, a competent professional should be employed. He may decide that with expert timing a cut with the whip as the horse tenses to fly backward may be indicated. If the professional is really competent, this may help. However, most use of the whip or spur on the horse that is getting behind the bit is like pouring kerosene on a blaze.

Uncompromising kindness and patience are the best remedy for most horsemen to use in curing this vice.

Shying

Shying is frequently caused by the inept or sadistic trainer who forces the colt under whip and spur to go up close to objects that terrify him. It may also be caused by the timid rider who begins to tighten up on the reins and use leg grip whenever he approaches anything he thinks his horse may be afraid of.

Horses, like people, are afraid of what they cannot understand and of the unfamiliar. Any force to make them come close to the feared object increases the terror and makes them fear the one who uses the force. When the horse encounters a fearful object he should be allowed to go out of the trail around it, but not in panic. How far he should go from it is a matter to be determined for each situation. Certainly he should be firmly held to some discipline, but forcing him up to the object just for the sake of discipline is making a bad matter worse. He should be kept going and not allowed to turn around and head toward home. If the horse is very young and a bit on the green side, he will want to stop a moment and stare. This is allowable if the colt is not allowed to jump to the side or turn. It is also understandable, for a horse normally has binocular vision and a monocular focus for staring takes a conscious effort on his part, as conscious an effort as it does for you to hold your breath. He has to stand still and concentrate.

The old offender who is constantly and unexpectedly jumping sideways at real or imaginary objects just enough to unbalance his rider is a different problem. He has been spoiled by experts. A skillful rider with expert timing and a deft heel for the spur and a quick, light hand can catch the horse *every* time he shies and catch him *as he shies,* with heel to drive him on and with rein to keep him in the straight and narrow path. Regular riding by such a rider for thirty days will usually have a very salutary effect on the confirmed shyer. If that will not cure him, he is not worth working with further.

The Puller or Cold-Jawed Horse

It is the pulling rider, not the pulling horse, that makes the cold jaw. When a horse becomes hard-mouthed and habitually pulls on the bit, most riders start looking for more severe bits. This is unfortunate, for under the sustained torture of a severe bit the nerves become insensitive and the trouble is increased.

On television I once watched Pablo Casals giving a lesson. The pupil played a passage. The master stopped her and said, "No, crescendo, crescendo, diminuendo, diminuendo! Not all on one level!" So it is with the reins. It is the dead level pull with no crescendo or diminuendo that makes the cold jaw. A good hand cannot be described. It is learned largely by trial and error and by a sort of sixth sense, an ultra-sensitive response to the horse. It also requires as keen a sense of timing as does the dance or the drama. The best way to prevent a bad mouth on a horse is to develop a good pair of hands on the rider.

If the puller with the bad mouth can be cured, the first thing to do is change riders or change bits. If he has been ridden on a curb, change to a snaffle with a draw rein or a gag rein. If he has been ridden with a snaffle, change to a short-shanked, rubber-mouthed curb or a leather-mouthed bar bit with reins through running martingales. The horse should be worked alone for a while and set down hard and quickly each time he takes a hard hold of the bit. This can be done by holding one rein very firmly and steadily and with the other giving a hard, quick pull that swings the horse's head to the side. This is very similar to the quick snatch on the reins used to throw a running horse for the movies. It requires considerable skill to snatch a horse back properly, so professional help should be employed for the job if at all possible. However, it should be skilled professional help, not just a would-be bronc buster.

For the puller that has been ridden with a bit, sometimes a change to a hackamore bit is helpful. But here again we merely aggravate our trouble if the rider has dead hands on the reins. Any sort of hackamore or hackamore bit requires a deft, quick hand, not unlike that needed in trout fishing. With the hackamore rein, the letting go is just as important and requires just as much skill as the pull. There are good books in print on the use of the hackamore. They are advertised in *Horse Lover's Magazine* and in *Western Horseman*. Before attempting the first use of the hackamore or hackamore bit, one of such books should be studied carefully. The biggest harm done with hackamores and hackamore bits by the ignorant is done by improper adjustment. The nosepiece should come just where the bone and cartilage join on the nose, never down on the soft part of the nose where the wind will be cut off. There is a widespread notion among amateurs and new arrivals in the West that the hackamore, bozal, or hackamore bit is used to cut off a horse's wind. It may be so used, but if it is, unless the horse is utterly fool-proof, trouble will result. The hackamore and similar devices work by pressure on the nose and, even more, by pressure on the jaw. It is largely the jaw pressure that does the work in many instances, but the pressure is always momentary only.

Halter Pulling

A horse is sometimes tied too low, too short, or so long that he gets a foot over the tie rope, or he may be tied to a pole or tree at proper height but so loosely that the rope slides down on the tree or pole. He is sometimes tied with a halter or rope too flimsy, or is tied too close to something terrifying, like a steam exhaust or automatic pump, so that he flies back and breaks a halter or rope. If a horse is tied and breaks loose he is a potential halter puller. The number of times required to make him a confirmed halter puller depends upon the intensity of his fright when he pulls loose and upon the temperament of the horse. One bad experience may make a halter puller that is hard to break.

There are many time-honored gimmicks to break halter pullers. Each old-timer thinks his is the best. All of them are successful in the majority of cases if used by an experienced hand. The most common gimmick is the use of a rope, which must be of cotton and five-eighth inch or larger. The rope is doubled and the middle is placed under the horse's tail or under the middle of his belly, where a flank cinch goes (the kind used in rodeos to make horses buck). Each end of the rope is then passed through a large ring just in front of the croup. Then the ends are passed through the halter ring and tied to a very stout tree, tall post, or solid ring in the side of the barn. When the horse flies back and gets the pull under his tail or belly, he will lunge violently up and forward, so he must not be tied to an ordinary post or rail on which he could easily injure himself. A variant of this gimmick is to tie a cotton rope around a front pastern. The rope is then passed through the halter ring and, finally, tied to a tree or ring in the side of the barn.

There is some danger of injury to the horse in each of these gimmicks, but I have seen each of them used many times, sometimes with the horse being flogged over the head with a sack or blanket to make him fly back; and I have never seen an injury result, with the exception of a slight rope burn under the tail, which was easily cured by application of Corona Wool Fat, a useful patented product.

Laurence Richardson, an old friend and one of the best horsemen of my acquaintance, uses a gimmick I have never seen anyone-else use. He has better success with it than I've seen from any other. The horse stays broken; you can tie him with a shoestring and he leads up promptly when led from another horse or on foot. Richardson also uses the same system to break a horse that rebels at going into a trailer.

His gimmick is very simple. He replaces the crownpiece of a stout halter with a piece of number nine smooth fence wire. I would not have the temerity to use such a contraption myself, but I have seen him use it many times, including once on a spoiled mare we bought in partnership; and he has never had an injury result from it.

I have used the rope under the tail and the rope around the belly, and was always successful with both. I quit use of the tail method because I disliked having to cure rope burns.

One grandson of Bourbon King I bought in Kentucky as a five-year-old was a bad halter puller; but in his early show training I knew he had suffered so much that I did not have the heart to subject him to any more misery in which he could see no sense. I started tying him with a three-quarter-inch cotton neck rope, tied with a bowline knot, passed through the halter ring and tied to a stout limb of a tree at the height he normally carried his head. I made sure the limb was stout enough to hold the entire weight and pull of the horse but had just a little give, so when he went back on it he would not hit a solid pull.

For many months I tied the horse no other way. When I finally tied him to a ring bolted solidly to the heavy timber of the stable, he went back on the rope a time or two, but did not become hysterical as had been his habit before I started to work with him. Eventually I could tie him anywhere.

The method I have just described obviously takes more time and requires much more sustained care and attention than the use of the tail or belly rope, all of which illustrates a very important point. The point is that any gimmick, from longe line or bitting rig to tail rope for a halter puller, is a short-cut substitute for time and the patient skill of a competent horseman. Sometimes the result of use of the gimmick is as good for the end in view as the longer method, though usually not as safe for the horse.

Kicking

The timid horse is most apt to become a kicker. The mule is a much more timid animal than the horse and is subjected to even worse abuse than horses outside show stables. He is quite usually a kicker.

The way to prevent the vice of kicking is to be ever watchful that you do not frighten a horse by stepping up behind him suddenly when he does not know you are around. Always speak to him before you approach from the rear. Never, never approach him with arms extended and torso leaning forward. You would not slip up on a friend from the rear and poke a hand out at him to see if he would kick. To keep a horse from becoming a kicker in company, be ever watchful for the idiot or the ignorant who rides up on the heels of other horses.

There is no one method that will help cure all kickers. A trace chain from a work harness (or chain of similar weight or length) buckled around the hind pastern with a soft, heavy strap, such as a strap off a pair of hobbles, will help in some cases. The chain or chains, if one is used on each hind leg, can be left on while the horse is in a stall or corral. If there is a competent reinsman still alive in the neighborhood, he can drive the horse in a breaking cart with stout hickory thills. With a deft snatch of the rein and flick of the whip as the horse starts to kick, the reinsman can throw him and an assistant who rides on the step of the breaking cart can get to the horse's head and hold him down for a few minutes of thoughtful repentance.

This method was standard practice in horse-and-buggy days and was usually effective, though some horses had to be thrown several times. Throwing should always be done on sod, sand, or some other soft surface free from stones, though in the horse-and-buggy era it was often done on a gravel road with considerable loss of hide and sometimes broken knees. The method of throwing in harness is of course the same as that used in Hollywood by stunt riders.

The horse that kicks at other horses in company is especially dangerous and should never be taken on a trail ride. In the hunting field such a horse should wear a red ribbon on his tail, and the rider must be constantly vigilant to keep out of the vicinity of other horses, especially while hounds are drawing cover or the field is waiting for anything else.

I do not like the job, but I have broken horses from kicking in company by the use of two methods, usually using both on the same horse. The kicker, which I ride with a full bridle, is tempted by a skilled mounted assistant, to kick, the assistant being careful to ride just close enough to tempt a kick but not close enough for his horse to receive it. The instant the kicker's heels left the ground, I would collect him and use a whalebone or rawhide whip around his belly. The more definite the mark made the better. Even a little blood was not bad. However, one cut with the whip and one only was the iron-clad rule. More horses have been ruined by repeated cuts than have ever been helped by any kind of use of the whip. Continuous pain never makes the horse do what is wanted; it usually merely aggravates a bad action. The puller on the reins is usually made worse by the rider's use of a severe bit and constant pull.

The more a balking horse is clubbed, the stiller he stands. It is the sharp, well-timed cut with the whip, touch with the spur, or pull on the bit that gets results, when results can be obtained by a whip, spur, or bit.

When riding a colt or horse of unknown disposition the rule is always to keep the animal well collected and his head up as other riders approach. A horse cannot do much damage with his heels while he is extremely collected and has his head well up. Of course a skilled and careful rider can ride any horse and keep him from kicking in company. However, the spoiled confirmed kicker will watch his chance and may catch even the best of riders off guard, so don't ride a kicker in company.

Biting

Many good colts raised in back yards are spoiled and made into biters. I do not subscribe to the notion that pet colts necessarily make mean horses. It all depends on what kind of pets they are. A colt can be taught to lead a few days after he is foaled—just as soon as his legs quit wobbling. He can be taught to cooperate with and not to fear human beings, but at the same time he must be taught to mind. Never caress a colt by putting a hand out toward the front of his head nor stroke the front of his face or nose. A colt's automatic reaction to such gestures is to nip. Watch colts at play; they illustrate what I am talking about—a reach for the head and a nip in return.

It should be unnecessary to say that the owner who allows a small colt to be teased and made to nip should never be permitted to own an animal of any kind.

There is a wide assortment of favorite "cures" for biting. An old favorite was a small paddle stuck full of nails and hidden in a sock or glove which the horse was encouraged to bite. Variations of this are easy to imagine. A farrier uses a sharp-pointed punch or divider. A cowboy uses a hot shot electric prod. The expert horseman, if the horse is young, frequently puts his faith in time, removes the cause (ignorant handling), and waits for the youngster to grow out of the nippy stage. If no time is available, the expert will use a whip. If the colt tends to nip when groomed or when held, the horseman will keep a firm hold on halter or bit and put one welt on shoulder or ribs each time the horse nips, restraining him from lunging forward by the hold on bit or halter. Rarely is it possible to punish the horse about the head without making him head-shy. Any horseman is ashamed to have a horse in his stable that jerks up its head whenever a hand is moved in front of it. The horse that gives evidence of fear of being struck about the head is a disgrace to his owner.

Very rarely is a horse a biter in company, but such a horse should wear a muzzle.

Rearing and Wheeling

Almost any young horse may overcollect and get his forefeet off the ground once in a while. This will only become the habit of rearing if he is mishandled.

When a horse comes up off the ground with his forefeet, the rider should instantly release pressure on the reins and lean forward over the horse's neck, being careful to put his head down *beside* the horse's neck, not on top of it, where he may well have his nose broken. The instant the horse is on all fours again, the rider must push him forward by whatever impulsion is required, using only enough restraint to keep contact on the reins. This is to prevent the horse from coming up a second time.

The rearing horse is usually the product of the heavy-handed rider. Almost any horse can be made to rear if he is kicked or whipped and jerked at the same time. The extremely sensitive horse with plenty of heart will rear if given almost any signal of impulsion (a light squeeze with the legs, a slight backward movement of the heels, or a clicking noise made by the rider's tongue) and is restrained by the bit from going forward. If he is made to rear this way a few times, rearing will become a habit. The first thing to do for a cure is to remove the rider by any legal means. Then a martingale can be used and the horse ridden by a more experienced rider. If a standing martingale is used, it should be attached to a noseband or bozal, never to a bit. It should be just long enough to allow the horse to carry his head comfortably in his normal or natural way, but short enough to prevent his putting his head up to rear.

If a running martingale is used, only snaffle reins should go through the martingale ring. It should be so adjusted that there is no downward pull on the reins unless the horse puts his head higher than he usually carries it.

Some horses become so confirmed in this habit that they can rear in spite of martingales. They often combine rearing with whirling, refusing to leave the stable or a group of riders in the field. Such a horse is called stable-bound or herd-bound.

Gimmicks for curing such cases range all the way from a paper sack filled with water and broken over the horse's head as he rears to a hot shot applied by an assistant as the horse whirls. If the rearing horse is pulled on over backward and the rider steps off and holds the horse prostrate for a few minutes, the animal loses its enthusiasm for two-legged walking. Once will usually break the horse of the vice, but if not he should be pulled over and held down each time he comes up. Three times is the limit I have ever known a horse to rear when so handled. This trick is of course useful only to skilled riders and should be done on sod or other soft footing. It is dangerous and should never be attempted by any but expert riders of long experience and by them only after all other methods of cure have failed.

Cribbing and Wind Sucking

In some parts of America *cribbing* is used to designate the chewing of wood corral fences, mangers, and stalls.

The term *cribbing* in other parts of the country is used to designate only the act of hooking the upper teeth over a post, stump, or other solid object, pulling back and swallowing air.

The mere chewing of wood often leads to the more harmful vice just described, called *wind sucking* or *stump sucking*. Theories about causes and cures of cribbing and stump sucking are numerous. Certainly the horse suffering from a nutritional deficiency is more prone to eat wood than is a healthy horse. However, I am not the only horseman who has tried all the vitamin and mineral supplements known and has found nothing that will stop wood chewing. In a few cases a bale of straw (opened and wire removed, of course) kept available to the horse helped some, but it was not a complete cure. Some horses chew wood all their lives, regardless of condition. Others chew only at times. Some never touch the stuff.

There is no sure prevention of this vice except to keep the horse where there is no exposed wood. There is a creosote base white paint that helps. Painting all exposed wood with creosote is as near an effective prevention, or cure, as I have found where it is impossible to keep wood away from the horse, or the horse away from wood; but this method is not very sightly. Stripping boards with metal is sometimes effective but dangerous, especially in the arid parts of the country, because the roofing nails tend to drop out or are easily pulled out when the wood shrinks from the heat of the sun. As every old horseman knows, roofing nails are the worst kind of hardware for getting in a horse's foot.

In my own corrals I use an electric wire to keep horses from wood. Once in a while a smart animal will find a place I have not protected. Then I put in some insulators and string more wire. Any electric fence unit adequately underwritten is probably safe, but I use only the battery-operated variety, powered by a six-volt hot shot battery.

Fortunately few horses become wind suckers or stump suckers. This vice is even more baffling in regard to cause and cure than wood chewing. It occurs more frequently among horses that are constantly confined in small quarters than among others. It is very rare, so rare that I have never seen it, among horses that work regularly. The only "cure," which is merely a deterrent, is a fairly wide leather strap buckled tightly around the throttle. The best of these is made with an extra bit of leather that serves as a pad under the throttle. These are called cribbing straps and can be bought at most saddlery stores. The strap is tight enough to prevent distention of throttle muscles, but not so tight as to interfere with eating. Some wind suckers do not take in enough air to damage their general health. With such mild offenders nothing need be done except remove from their corrals all objects that will tempt them to hook their teeth on something solid, pull back, and swallow air. Other horses seem almost frantic to suck in air and will use almost any solid object to crib on. They often lose weight and vigor. A strap should be used on them.

Weaving

Weaving is a vice seen usually in young horses in poor condition kept in tie stalls or very small box stalls, though a horse of any age or condition may be a weaver. The weaver will stand in relatively the same spot for hours but will continuously shift weight from one front foot to the other as do some carnivores in cages in the zoo. Both the prevention and cure are to keep animals where they have ample room for exercise and are free from fear and tension. One very competent horseman recommends putting the horse in a stall where he can look out of a window at traffic.

Stall Pawing and Kicking

The horse that pawed or kicked in the stall used to be very common in horse-and-buggy days in city stables where horses had to stand in tie stalls, sometimes for weeks in winter without being out. This leads me to suspect that the cause is largely confinement. If so, prevention is simply a matter of giving the horse room to exercise. A cure is a leg chain such as I have described for kicking. A more humane and possibly more effective cure is advocated by another horseman. It is a rubber ball attached to a rubber band

PLATE 22. Two Arizona-bred horses discussing scent at start of lion hunt. *Photo by Rosemary D. Taylor*

which, in turn, is fastened to the horse's leg by a strap. Whenever the horse strikes or kicks, the ball bounces on his leg. Though I have never seen this tried, it should be effective, for it is the timing of punishment, not the severity, that makes it effective.

Glossary

AMBLE—This is a broken or syncopated slow pace.

BARREL—The body of the horse between hips and shoulders.

BARS—(1) Part of the mouth on which the bit rests. It is between the incisors and molars. (2) A metal device to hold stirrup leathers to the saddle tree.

BOW—To bow a tendon is to tear the lateral ligaments of the cannon.

BOWLINE KNOT—A special kind of square knot that will not slip or slide and that can usually be untied easily.

BOSAL—Noseband.

CANTER—A slow, stylized gallop in which the center of balance is farther to the rear than in the gallop, and the action is higher. The sequence of hoof impacts on the ground is the same as in the gallop.

CANNON BONE—A bone that supports the leg from the knee or the hock joint to the fetlock; the enlarged metacarpal or metatarsal of the third digit in the horse.

CANTLE—Rear of a saddle.

COLLECTION—Use of impulsion and restraint to bring in the horse's chin, his hind legs well under him, and his center of balance farther toward the rear than natural.

CORONA—A decorative wool saddle blanket usually used in Western parade riding.

COW-HOCKED—Hocks closer together than stifles or pasterns.

CROUP—Top of the hips of a horse.

CROWN—The part of the bridle that lies on top of a horse's head behind his ears.

DISHING—Turning the forefeet inward as they are raised for each forward step.

ELBOW—Joint of the foreleg where it joins the body.

EXTENDED BAR SADDLE—Sometimes called officers' saddle. The saddle tree extends several inches behind the cantle of the saddle, thus keeping the rider off the horse's loins.

FARRIER—A person who shoes horses as a profession.

FIRED—Pin-fired. White-hot needle is pushed into a horse's leg at close intervals on the theory that a "weak" or lame leg will be restored to usefulness.

FLAT SADDLE—An English-type saddle, including such distinctly American saddles as the gaited show saddle and the Whitman. The saddle jockeys use for racing is also a flat saddle.

FORK (of saddle)—Part of a Western saddle to which the horn is attached.

FORWARD RIDING—Use of the forward seat and the schooling and control that go with it.

FORWARD SEAT—Posture on horseback in which the rider uses short stirrups, inclines his body forward, and sits farther forward on the horse than other riders.

FOUL ROPE—A rope tied around the horse's neck. The lariat is passed through it to keep the horse facing the calf when it is roped and the horseman is hog-tying it.

FROG (of hoof)—The triangular-shaped, rubbery pad that is the back part of the bottom of a horse's hoof.

GAIT—(1) The relationship and sequence of hoofbeats; e.g., the trot, in which a diagonal pair of feet hit the ground together, and the pace, in which the two feet on the same side hit the ground together. (2) The way a horse moves his legs; e.g., a horse with proper or "true" gait does not swing his feet out to the side but moves them straight back and forth.

GALLOP—A gait in which the sequence of hoof impacts on the ground is as follows: one hind foot; then the front foot on the same side simultaneously with the other hind foot; then the remaining front foot, which last is said to be the leading foot.

GALLOWAYS—One of the earliest known strains of English horses. They were small and very easy-gaited.

HACKAMORE—A nosepiece, or a headstall, usually of braided rawhide, sometimes used in place of a bridle.

HALTER—A device of leather or rope to put on a horse's head for the purpose of leading him or tying him to manger, hitch rack, etc.

HALTER RING—Large ring on a halter lying below the jaw and used to attach halter rope or shank for leading or tying.

HAMMER-HEADED—Having a Roman nose and eyes set too high in the head.

HAUTE ÉCOLE—Literally, high school, but usually a term used to indicate a set of movements or tricks the horse performs while mounted, movements said to be stylized versions of those he executes when playing in the pasture.

HAZER—A mounted assistant in a rodeo arena. Among his many jobs is that of taking the rider off a bucking animal after he has ridden for the time required.

HEADSTALL—Bridle minus bits. May be either half of a double bridle.

HEART—(1) Extremely courageous, ambitious, and fearless temperament. (2) The girth just behind the forelegs.

HOBBIES—One of the earliest known strains of English riding horses. They were small and easy-gaited.

HOME—Riding with the feet *home* is riding with feet thrust through the stirrups so that the instep just in front of the heel of the boot is resting on the stirrup, as in polo, jumping, and some Western riding.

IMPULSION—Impetus to move forward. It may be intrinsic in the horse and is supplemented by the rider's use of leg, heel, spur, or whip.

JACKPOT ROPING—Usually calf roping for a prize consisting of a "pot" to which each contestant has contributed.

JOG TROT—A very slow trot.

JOHNSON HALTER—A patented rope halter widely used, especially throughout the Southwest.

LATIGO STRAP—The strap on a stock saddle that fastens the cinch to the rigging ring.

LONGE LINE—A rope or strong web or leather strap thirty or more feet in length with a swivel and snap at one end. It is used by some trainers for schooling young horses.

MARTINGALE—(1) Standing: a strap that is attached to the noseband at one end and to the cinch or girth at the other. (2) Running: a Y-shaped strap attached at one end to the girth; the other ending in two rings through which the reins pass.

NEAR SIDE (of horse or gear)—The left side of a horse.

NECKREIN—Use of pressure of rein on the side of a horse's neck to guide him.

NERVED—Having suffered a neurotomy, the severing or removal of a nerve in a horse's lame foot to eliminate pain.

OFFSET—A quarter turn, a rolling turn with weight on haunches, using hind feet as a pivot.

OFF SIDE (of horse or gear)—The right side of a horse.

PACE—A gait in which the two hooves on the same side strike the ground simultaneously. It is, except when very slow, suitable only for harness racing and is the fastest gait a horse has other than the gallop. In many old writings the word *pace* is used to include all gaits other than walk, trot, gallop, and canter. Many of the so-called Canadian pacers of colonial days probably racked or did a fast running walk rather than what we call a pace.

PADDLING—Turning the hoof outward as it is raised to take a forward step.

PARIANI SADDLE—A saddle especially designed for riding the forward seat. It is named after the designer.

PASTERN—The part of the horse's leg immediately above the hoof. (See Fig. 20, p. 86.)

PLOW-REIN—To guide a horse as a plow horse is guided; i.e., to pull back on the right rein for a right turn and back on the left for a left turn.

POLL—The top of a horse's head and the area just behind it.

POMMEL—The highest part of the front of a flat or English saddle.

PORT (of bit)—The upward curve in the center of the mouthpiece of a curb bit to give tongue room, or, if very high, to exert pressure on roof of mouth.

POST—Rising out of the saddle on alternate hoofbeats of the trot.

QUARTER RINGS—The front rigging rings of a Western saddle.

RACK—A four-beat gait which may be said to be exactly midway between a trot and a pace. Each hoof has a separate impact and is followed by exactly the same interval during which no foot is touching the ground. To the eye the gait looks more like a pace than a trot, but the ear can instantly detect the syncopated rhythm that is counterfeit— a broken pace or a fast fox-trot, not a rack.

RO's—A very fine strain of Quarter Horse developed at the RO Ranch of the Green Cattle Company of Arizona and Mexico.

ROPER, LOW-DOWN—Western saddle with low cantle, very popular among professional calf ropers.

RUNNING HORSE—Thoroughbred, race horse for racing under saddle.

RUNNING WALK—A four-beat gait now made famous by the Tennessee Walker. It differs from the true or flat-footed walk in that there are intervals when no foot is in contact with the ground. The currently fashionable manner of executing this gait is for the hind foot to greatly overstep the track of the front foot, the front feet stepping high as if on hot coals.

SCOUR—To have diarrhea.

SEAT—Posture of the rider of a horse.

SHANK—(1) Part of the curb bit at the side of the mouth. (2) A rope, strap, or chain, or combination of the latter two, attached to a halter to lead a horse.

SLICKER—Raincoat made especially for riding.

SLOW-GAIT—One of the requirements for a five-gaited horse. It may be a fox-trot, amble, running walk, or slow pace. The fox-trot is just faster than a walk. In the fox-trot, the diagonal forefoot strikes the ground just before the alternate hind foot, making a syncopated rhythm.

SPANISH BIT—Usually a decorated bit more severe than others.

STIRRUP LEATHERS—Straps that hold stirrups to the saddle.

TANBARK—The show ring.

TAPADEROS—Leather hoods over stirrups to protect feet from brush, also useful to keep feet from hanging in stirrups when rider falls from horse. They are frequently highly decorated.

THILL—The shaft of a buggy or cart.

THROATLATCH—Strap passing under a horse's throat to keep the bridle from being rubbed or tossed off over his ears.

THROTTLE—The throat of a horse.

TIE-DOWN—Any device connecting a nosepiece to a girth or cinch to keep a horse from raising his head extremely.

TROT—Diagonal, two-beat gait in which off fore and near hind feet strike the ground at the same time and the near fore and off hind feet strike the ground at the same time.

TWITCH—A stout stick, such as a handle of a Boy Scout ax, with a loop of stout rope or light chain at one end. The loop may be put over a horse's upper lip and twisted tight to cause so much pain that the horse will be immobilized.

WALK—A four-beat gait with the same interval following each hoofbeat. In this gait there is no interval when all feet are off the ground.

WEAVING—The horse will stand in relatively the same spot for hours but will continuously shift weight from one front foot to the other as do some animals in cages.

WING—To swing the feet out to the side as they move forward.

WITHERS—Highest point of a horse's back just behind the juncture of neck and back.

Index

A PERSONAL WORD FROM MELVIN POWERS
PUBLISHER, WILSHIRE BOOK COMPANY

Dear Friend:

My goal is to publish interesting, informative, and inspirational books. You can help me accomplish this by answering the following questions, either by phone or by mail. Or, if convenient for you, I would welcome the opportunity to visit with you in my office and hear your comments in person.

Did you enjoy reading this book? Why?

Would you enjoy reading another similar book?

What idea in the book impressed you the most?

If applicable to your situation, have you incorporated this idea in your daily life?

Is there a chapter that could serve as a theme for an entire book? Please explain.

If you have an idea for a book, I would welcome discussing it with you. If you already have one in progress, write or call me concerning possible publication. I can be reached at (213) 875-1711 or (818) 983-1105.

Sincerely yours,

MELVIN POWERS

12015 Sherman Road
North Hollywood, California 91605

MELVIN POWERS SELF-IMPROVEMENT LIBRARY

ASTROLOGY
_____ ASTROLOGY: HOW TO CHART YOUR HOROSCOPE *Max Heindel*	5.00
_____ ASTROLOGY AND SEXUAL ANALYSIS *Morris C. Goodman*	5.00
_____ ASTROLOGY MADE EASY *Astarte*	3.00
_____ ASTROLOGY MADE PRACTICAL *Alexandra Kayhle*	3.00
_____ ASTROLOGY, ROMANCE, YOU AND THE STARS *Anthony Norvell*	4.00
_____ MY WORLD OF ASTROLOGY *Sydney Omarr*	7.00
_____ THOUGHT DIAL *Sydney Omarr*	4.00
_____ WHAT THE STARS REVEAL ABOUT THE MEN IN YOUR LIFE *Thelma White*	3.00

BRIDGE
_____ BRIDGE BIDDING MADE EASY *Edwin B. Kantar*	10.00
_____ BRIDGE CONVENTIONS *Edwin B. Kantar*	7.00
_____ BRIDGE HUMOR *Edwin B. Kantar*	5.00
_____ COMPETITIVE BIDDING IN MODERN BRIDGE *Edgar Kaplan*	7.00
_____ DEFENSIVE BRIDGE PLAY COMPLETE *Edwin B. Kantar*	15.00
_____ GAMESMAN BRIDGE—Play Better with Kantar *Edwin B. Kantar*	5.00
_____ HOW TO IMPROVE YOUR BRIDGE *Alfred Sheinwold*	5.00
_____ IMPROVING YOUR BIDDING SKILLS *Edwin B. Kantar*	4.00
_____ INTRODUCTION TO DECLARER'S PLAY *Edwin B. Kantar*	5.00
_____ INTRODUCTION TO DEFENDER'S PLAY *Edwin B. Kantar*	3.00
_____ KANTAR FOR THE DEFENSE *Edwin B. Kantar*	5.00
_____ KANTAR FOR THE DEFENSE VOLUME 2 *Edwin B. Kantar*	7.00
_____ SHORT CUT TO WINNING BRIDGE *Alfred Sheinwold*	3.00
_____ TEST YOUR BRIDGE PLAY *Edwin B. Kantar*	5.00
_____ VOLUME 2—TEST YOUR BRIDGE PLAY *Edwin B. Kantar*	5.00
_____ WINNING DECLARER PLAY *Dorothy Hayden Truscott*	5.00

BUSINESS, STUDY & REFERENCE
_____ CONVERSATION MADE EASY *Elliot Russell*	4.00
_____ EXAM SECRET *Dennis B. Jackson*	3.00
_____ FIX-IT BOOK *Arthur Symons*	2.00
_____ HOW TO DEVELOP A BETTER SPEAKING VOICE *M. Hellier*	4.00
_____ HOW TO SELF-PUBLISH YOUR BOOK & MAKE IT A BEST SELLER *Melvin Powers*	10.00
_____ INCREASE YOUR LEARNING POWER *Geoffrey A. Dudley*	3.00
_____ PRACTICAL GUIDE TO BETTER CONCENTRATION *Melvin Powers*	3.00
_____ PRACTICAL GUIDE TO PUBLIC SPEAKING *Maurice Forley*	5.00
_____ 7 DAYS TO FASTER READING *William S. Schaill*	3.00
_____ SONGWRITERS' RHYMING DICTIONARY *Jane Shaw Whitfield*	6.00
_____ SPELLING MADE EASY *Lester D. Basch & Dr. Milton Finkelstein*	3.00
_____ STUDENT'S GUIDE TO BETTER GRADES *J. A. Rickard*	3.00
_____ TEST YOURSELF—Find Your Hidden Talent *Jack Shafer*	3.00
_____ YOUR WILL & WHAT TO DO ABOUT IT *Attorney Samuel G. Kling*	4.00

CALLIGRAPHY
_____ ADVANCED CALLIGRAPHY *Katherine Jeffares*	7.00
_____ CALLIGRAPHER'S REFERENCE BOOK *Anne Leptich & Jacque Evans*	7.00
_____ CALLIGRAPHY—The Art of Beautiful Writing *Katherine Jeffares*	7.00
_____ CALLIGRAPHY FOR FUN & PROFIT *Anne Leptich & Jacque Evans*	7.00
_____ CALLIGRAPHY MADE EASY *Tina Serafini*	7.00

CHESS & CHECKERS
_____ BEGINNER'S GUIDE TO WINNING CHESS *Fred Reinfeld*	5.00
_____ CHESS IN TEN EASY LESSONS *Larry Evans*	5.00
_____ CHESS MADE EASY *Milton L. Hanauer*	3.00
_____ CHESS PROBLEMS FOR BEGINNERS *edited by Fred Reinfeld*	2.00
_____ CHESS SECRETS REVEALED *Fred Reinfeld*	2.00
_____ CHESS TACTICS FOR BEGINNERS *edited by Fred Reinfeld*	4.00
_____ CHESS THEORY & PRACTICE *Morry & Mitchell*	2.00
_____ HOW TO WIN AT CHECKERS *Fred Reinfeld*	3.00
_____ 1001 BRILLIANT WAYS TO CHECKMATE *Fred Reinfeld*	4.00
_____ 1001 WINNING CHESS SACRIFICES & COMBINATIONS *Fred Reinfeld*	4.00

_____ SOVIET CHESS *Edited by R. G. Wade* 3.00

COOKERY & HERBS

_____ CULPEPER'S HERBAL REMEDIES *Dr. Nicholas Culpeper* 3.00
_____ FAST GOURMET COOKBOOK *Poppy Cannon* 2.50
_____ GINSENG The Myth & The Truth *Joseph P. Hou* 3.00
_____ HEALING POWER OF HERBS *May Bethel* 4.00
_____ HEALING POWER OF NATURAL FOODS *May Bethel* 5.00
_____ HERB HANDBOOK *Dawn MacLeod* 3.00
_____ HERBS FOR HEALTH—How to Grow & Use Them *Louise Evans Doole* 4.00
_____ HOME GARDEN COOKBOOK—Delicious Natural Food Recipes *Ken Kraft* 3.00
_____ MEDICAL HERBALIST *edited by Dr. J. R. Yemm* 3.00
_____ VEGETABLE GARDENING FOR BEGINNERS *Hugh Wiberg* 2.00
_____ VEGETABLES FOR TODAY'S GARDENS *R. Milton Carleton* 2.00
_____ VEGETARIAN COOKERY *Janet Walker* 4.00
_____ VEGETARIAN COOKING MADE EASY & DELECTABLE *Veronica Vezza* 3.00
_____ VEGETARIAN DELIGHTS—A Happy Cookbook for Health *K. R. Mehta* 2.00
_____ VEGETARIAN GOURMET COOKBOOK *Joyce McKinnel* 3.00

GAMBLING & POKER

_____ ADVANCED POKER STRATEGY & WINNING PLAY *A. D. Livingston* 5.00
_____ HOW TO WIN AT DICE GAMES *Skip Frey* 3.00
_____ HOW TO WIN AT POKER *Terence Reese & Anthony T. Watkins* 5.00
_____ WINNING AT CRAPS *Dr. Lloyd T. Commins* 4.00
_____ WINNING AT GIN *Chester Wander & Cy Rice* 3.00
_____ WINNING AT POKER—An Expert's Guide *John Archer* 5.00
_____ WINNING AT 21—An Expert's Guide *John Archer* 5.00
_____ WINNING POKER SYSTEMS *Norman Zadeh* 3.00

HEALTH

_____ BEE POLLEN *Lynda Lyngheim & Jack Scagnetti* 3.00
_____ DR. LINDNER'S SPECIAL WEIGHT CONTROL METHOD *P. G. Lindner, M.D.* 2.00
_____ HELP YOURSELF TO BETTER SIGHT *Margaret Darst Corbett* 3.00
_____ HOW TO IMPROVE YOUR VISION *Dr. Robert A. Kraskin* 3.00
_____ HOW YOU CAN STOP SMOKING PERMANENTLY *Ernest Caldwell* 3.00
_____ MIND OVER PLATTER *Peter G. Lindner, M.D.* 3.00
_____ NATURE'S WAY TO NUTRITION & VIBRANT HEALTH *Robert J. Scrutton* 3.00
_____ NEW CARBOHYDRATE DIET COUNTER *Patti Lopez-Pereira* 2.00
_____ QUICK & EASY EXERCISES FOR FACIAL BEAUTY *Judy Smith-deal* 2.00
_____ QUICK & EASY EXERCISES FOR FIGURE BEAUTY *Judy Smith-deal* 2.00
_____ REFLEXOLOGY *Dr. Maybelle Segal* 4.00
_____ REFLEXOLOGY FOR GOOD HEALTH *Anna Kaye & Don C. Matchan* 5.00
_____ 30 DAYS TO BEAUTIFUL LEGS *Dr. Marc Selner* 3.00
_____ YOU CAN LEARN TO RELAX *Dr. Samuel Gutwirth* 3.00
_____ YOUR ALLERGY—What To Do About It *Allan Knight, M.D.* 3.00

HOBBIES

_____ BEACHCOMBING FOR BEGINNERS *Norman Hickin* 2.00
_____ BLACKSTONE'S MODERN CARD TRICKS *Harry Blackstone* 3.00
_____ BLACKSTONE'S SECRETS OF MAGIC *Harry Blackstone* 3.00
_____ COIN COLLECTING FOR BEGINNERS *Burton Hobson & Fred Reinfeld* 3.00
_____ ENTERTAINING WITH ESP *Tony 'Doc' Shiels* 2.00
_____ 400 FASCINATING MAGIC TRICKS YOU CAN DO *Howard Thurston* 4.00
_____ HOW I TURN JUNK INTO FUN AND PROFIT *Sari* 3.00
_____ HOW TO WRITE A HIT SONG & SELL IT *Tommy Boyce* 7.00
_____ JUGGLING MADE EASY *Rudolf Dittrich* 3.00
_____ MAGIC FOR ALL AGES *Walter Gibson* 4.00
_____ MAGIC MADE EASY *Byron Wels* 2.00
_____ STAMP COLLECTING FOR BEGINNERS *Burton Hobson* 3.00

HORSE PLAYERS' WINNING GUIDES

_____ BETTING HORSES TO WIN *Les Conklin* 5.00
_____ ELIMINATE THE LOSERS *Bob McKnight* 3.00
_____ HOW TO PICK WINNING HORSES *Bob McKnight* 5.00
_____ HOW TO WIN AT THE RACES *Sam (The Genius) Lewin* 5.00
_____ HOW YOU CAN BEAT THE RACES *Jack Kavanagh* 5.00

___ MAGIC POWER OF YOUR MIND *Walter M. Germain*		5.00
___ MENTAL POWER THROUGH SLEEP SUGGESTION *Melvin Powers*		3.00
___ NEW GUIDE TO RATIONAL LIVING *Albert Ellis, Ph.D. & R. Harper, Ph.D.*		3.00
___ PROJECT YOU *A Manual of Rational Assertiveness Training Paris & Casey*		6.00
___ PSYCHO-CYBERNETICS *Maxwell Maltz, M.D.*		5.00
___ SALES CYBERNETICS *Brian Adams*		7.00
___ SCIENCE OF MIND IN DAILY LIVING *Dr. Donald Curtis*		5.00
___ SECRET OF SECRETS *U. S. Andersen*		7.00
___ SECRET POWER OF THE PYRAMIDS *U. S. Andersen*		5.00
___ SELF-THERAPY FOR THE STUTTERER *Malcolm Fraser*		3.00
___ STUTTERING AND WHAT YOU CAN DO ABOUT IT *W. Johnson, Ph.D.*		2.50
___ SUCCESS-CYBERNETICS *U. S. Andersen*		6.00
___ 10 DAYS TO A GREAT NEW LIFE *William E. Edwards*		3.00
___ THINK AND GROW RICH *Napoleon Hill*		5.00
___ THINK YOUR WAY TO SUCCESS *Dr. Lew Losoncy*		5.00
___ THREE MAGIC WORDS *U. S. Andersen*		7.00
___ TREASURY OF COMFORT *edited by Rabbi Sidney Greenberg*		5.00
___ TREASURY OF THE ART OF LIVING *Sidney S. Greenberg*		5.00
___ YOU ARE NOT THE TARGET *Laura Huxley*		5.00
___ YOUR SUBCONSCIOUS POWER *Charles M. Simmons*		5.00
___ YOUR THOUGHTS CAN CHANGE YOUR LIFE *Dr. Donald Curtis*		5.00

SPORTS

___ BICYCLING FOR FUN AND GOOD HEALTH *Kenneth E. Luther*		2.00
___ BILLIARDS—Pocket • Carom • Three Cushion *Clive Cottingham, Jr.*		5.00
___ CAMPING-OUT 101 Ideas & Activities *Bruno Knobel*		2.00
___ COMPLETE GUIDE TO FISHING *Vlad Evanoff*		2.00
___ HOW TO IMPROVE YOUR RACQUETBALL *Lubarsky Kaufman & Scagnetti*		3.00
___ HOW TO WIN AT POCKET BILLIARDS *Edward D. Knuchell*		5.00
___ JOY OF WALKING *Jack Scagnetti*		3.00
___ LEARNING & TEACHING SOCCER SKILLS *Eric Worthington*		3.00
___ MOTORCYCLING FOR BEGINNERS *I. G. Edmonds*		3.00
___ RACQUETBALL FOR WOMEN *Toni Hudson, Jack Scagnetti & Vince Rondone*		3.00
___ RACQUETBALL MADE EASY *Steve Lubarsky, Rod Delson & Jack Scagnetti*		4.00
___ SECRET OF BOWLING STRIKES *Dawson Taylor*		3.00
___ SECRET OF PERFECT PUTTING *Horton Smith & Dawson Taylor*		5.00
___ SOCCER—The Game & How to Play It *Gary Rosenthal*		5.00
___ STARTING SOCCER *Edward F. Dolan, Jr.*		3.00

TENNIS LOVERS' LIBRARY

___ BEGINNER'S GUIDE TO WINNING TENNIS *Helen Hull Jacobs*		2.00
___ HOW TO BEAT BETTER TENNIS PLAYERS *Loring Fiske*		4.00
___ HOW TO IMPROVE YOUR TENNIS—Style, Strategy & Analysis *C. Wilson*		2.00
___ PLAY TENNIS WITH ROSEWALL *Ken Rosewall*		2.00
___ PSYCH YOURSELF TO BETTER TENNIS *Dr. Walter A. Luszki*		2.00
___ TENNIS FOR BEGINNERS, *Dr. H. A. Murray*		2.00
___ TENNIS MADE EASY *Joel Brecheen*		4.00
___ WEEKEND TENNIS—How to Have Fun & Win at the Same Time *Bill Talbert*		3.00
___ WINNING WITH PERCENTAGE TENNIS—Smart Strategy *Jack Lowe*		2.00

WILSHIRE PET LIBRARY

___ DOG OBEDIENCE TRAINING *Gust Kessopulos*		5.00
___ DOG TRAINING MADE EASY & FUN *John W. Kellogg*		4.00
___ HOW TO BRING UP YOUR PET DOG *Kurt Unkelbach*		2.00
___ HOW TO RAISE & TRAIN YOUR PUPPY *Jeff Griffen*		5.00
___ PIGEONS: HOW TO RAISE & TRAIN THEM *William H. Allen, Jr.*		2.00

The books listed above can be obtained from your book dealer or directly from Melvin Powers. When ordering, please remit $1.00 postage for the first book and 50¢ for each additional book.

Melvin Powers

12015 Sherman Road, No. Hollywood, California 91605